THE QUIET RADICAL

The Biography of Samuel Longfellow

JOSEPH C. ABDO

Tenth Island Editions

THE QUIET RADICAL
The Biography of Samuel Longfellow

Tenth Island Editions

Rua São João da Mata, 5-3.º
1200-846 Lisbon, Portugal
e-mail: joe@abdo.net

Produced by Maria Esther – Gab. Artes Gráficas, Lda

ISBN: 978-972-99858-2-9
Depósito legal: 283653/08

Table of Contents

INTRODUCTION

Samuel Longfellow is one of the least known protagonists of the 19th century. This is somewhat surprising considering that he knew a great number of the individuals who were having a great effect on poetry, literature, history, social movements and religion during the middle part of the century.

He did not just know them, but through speaking and writing, he was a respected contributor to their ideas and accomplishments. He was not in the spotlight, but was generally a step ahead of the direction the light was moving.

This book aims at showing Samuel Longfellow's life and activities among his friends and other persons he had contact with. Of course his family was involved in his life, but a large part of his social and theological contributions over the years were carried out together with his friends, organizations with which he participated and the places he worked.

The primary document about Samuel Longfellow is *Samuel Longfellow Memoir and Letters*, edited by Joseph May in 1894. It gives a basic view of Samuel, but does not go into much detail of his life and relationship with others. Other information is available in articles published in contemporary magazines, some summarizing his life, others mentioning him in articles that supported or opposed a specific issue or belief.

Unfortunately, Samuel did not write much about himself. He wrote a few articles and essays on religious topics. In addition, he published a number of his sermons. He also gave speeches at conferences, which presented his liberal, often radical, viewpoint on conference themes. However, his best known published material were the hymns he wrote for the hymnbooks he and Samuel Johnson produced, as well as some written on request for friends to use in their churches or organizations celebrating an important event.

Samuel was not a very diligent journal writer. At times, he would let a year lapse between entries, as he recognizes in an entry on January 28, 1838: "After the lapse of nearly a year, the whim has again taken me of Journalizing." Another problem Samuel created is in a letter he wrote to Rev. A. M. Haskell in 1882 where he mentions "having destroyed [his] Journals" of earlier times. In fact, there are no personal journals after 1847, but he did keep travel journals up to 1866. Furthermore, there is an indication in the journals that exist that he may have kept more than one set of journals at a time. A hint at this is a short journal entry on March 6, 1845: "A clever fresh March west-wind, drinking up the moisture from the ground, to send it down again in spring showers – In the morning walked and wrote Journal." If there were, indeed, more than one set of journals, they went the way of the others that he destroyed.

The main source of information about Samuel Longfellow is his letters. Regrettably, he did he did not keep much of his correspondence. Few letters other than those to Samuel's family came into the possession of the Longfellow National Historic Site. Among the Longfellow family, Samuel's main correspondent was his sister Anne. Samuel's main correspondent over the years was his best friend Samuel Johnson. Some letters entered other collections, such as the collection of the publisher Ticknor in the Library of Congress and the publisher Fields in the Huntington Gardens and Library in California.

Sources of information about his friends were obtained from books and articles about their lives and activities. Several of them also wrote articles about their social concerns, their lives in Cambridge or histories of the times, movements and people and included the involvement with Samuel. There were even a few articles by people who did not know Samuel, but were aware of his contribution to their topic.

Not everything about Samuel Longfellow could be included in this book. One of his greatest interests not addressed was gardening. It is mentioned in a few letters, however, there are entire letters to his sister Anne that discuss various types of plants and gardens, especially from the Azores from where he brought a number of cuttings and seeds. Another interest of Samuel's not mentioned was his enjoyment of drawing. He put drawings in some of his letters, and the Longfellow Site has drawing books from various periods of his life.

Acknowledgments

I greatly appreciate the moral and practical support provided by George Abdo, Audrey Un Silva, Nancy Keller and Jeff Childs. I would also like to recognize the assistance of the staff members at the Harvard Divinity School Library, the Houghton Library of Harvard University, the Library of Congress and The Huntington Library (Pasadena, CA). My very special appreciation goes to Anita Israel and Jim Shea of the Longfellow National Historical Site for their time, assistance and support.

CHAPTER 1 – THE LONGFELLOWS
AND THE WADSWORTHS

Over the centuries many explorers ranging from the Vikings to the Europeans of the Middle Ages landed on the jagged Maine coast that had been carved out by the Ice Age. Some of these visitors stayed and built settlements while others went on to what they thought might be greener pastures. Prior to the arrival of visitors from the east, Maine was home to tribes of hunter-gatherers living there since before 3000 BCE. Two of the Native American tribes that lived in the territory when the Europeans began to settle there were the Micmacs and the Abnakis.

Despite the establishment of more permanent settlements in Maine from the early 17th century on, most of the settlers were not able to endure the severe climate, deprivation and hostile tribes. By the 18th century only about a half dozen settlements still existed and the Colony of Massachusetts purchased most of the vacant, wilderness land claims.

France disputed the English ownership of Maine and supported the local tribes in their raids on the settlements. The Treaty of Paris in 1763 ended French claims on the territory of Maine. As a result of the more peaceful situation, the population of the area began to grow. When the American Revolutionary War began, the men of Maine actively joined in the fight for independence. After the war, the frontier settlers wanted their own independence and wanted to break free from Massachusetts. However, the coastal merchants held off any action until after the War of 1812, which demonstrated that Massachusetts could not, or would not, protect the people of the territory from British raids.[1]

Among the families taking up residence in Maine were Samuel Longfellow's ancestors, the Longfellow and Wadsworth families, who had previously lived in Byfield in the Massachusetts Bay Colony where they had arrived in the 17th century from England.

Samuel's father Stephen was not the first with this name in the family. The name Stephen had been used in the Longfellow family for the oldest son during several generations. The first Stephen Longfellow had been a craftsman and farmer who was destined for fame as the model for his great-great-grandson Henry's poem "The Village Blacksmith."

Taking advantage of the opportunities for higher education that were becoming available in the New England colonies, the second Stephen attended Harvard from which he graduated in 1742 and became a schoolmaster. He moved to Portland in 1745, which at that time was still an area subject to attacks from the French and Indians in Canada. He became a leading citizen in Portland and was clerk of the First Parish for 23 years and town clerk for 22 years, as well as being the Register of Probate and clerk of the Judicial Court for 16 years.

Stephen III followed his father's steps into the legal field and became Judge of the Court of Common Pleas in Portland. When the family's house was burned down during a British assault in 1775, he moved to his farm in Gorham where he spent the rest of his life.

Stephen IV, Samuel's father, was born in Gorham in 1776, but left to go to Harvard University in Cambridge, Massachusetts from which he graduated in 1798. He returned to Portland and became a highly respected lawyer and was elected as a Massachusetts Legislator in 1814. After Maine became a state in 1820, he served one term as a Federalist Congressman for Maine from 1822-24. The Federalist Party was created following Alexander Hamilton's views and favored a strong central government. Most of its supporters were New England merchants, businessmen, farmers and the wealthy. However, these groups were hurt by the War of 1812 and the American victory helped them in the election at the time. Nevertheless, the party was tied to this issue and began to lose influence and by the time Stephen Longfellow was elected it was on its last legs.

After Stephen's national political activities, in 1826 he represented Portland in the Maine Legislature, and in 1834 he became

President of the Maine Historical Society. He also served on Bowdoin University's Board for 19 years. Stephen IV retired from politics and dedicated himself to his law practice until his health deteriorated to the point that he was virtually an invalid for the rest of his life.

The Wadsworths trace their ancestry to the pilgrims who landed at Plymouth and had a more colorful history than the Longfellows who arrived in America in 1678. Samuel's mother was named Zilpah, a name taken from Genesis 29:21-24. These verses tell the story of Jacob who had agreed to work for Laban for seven years in order to marry Laban's younger daughter Rachel. However, when the seven years were up Jacob gave him his older daughter Leah instead, along with her handmaiden Zilpah. Laban said the custom was to give the older daughter before the younger and said he could marry Rachel after completing his wedding week with Leah. However, he told Jacob that he would have to continue to work seven more years for him, an offer and condition which Jacob accepted.

Samuel's grandfather on his mother's side, Peleg Wadsworth, was a person around whom legends arose and his story was surely repeated numerous times to his children and grandchildren. Peleg's name also derives from the Old Testament. As related in Genesis 10:25, "Two sons were born to Eber: one was named Peleg [*Peleg* means division], because in his time the earth was divided; his brother was named Joktan." There is disagreement whether the division of the earth refers to language (Babel), water, land or culture.

Peleg Wadsworth graduated from Harvard in 1769 at the age of 21 years. He taught in Plymouth, but early in the American Revolution entered the army as a Minute-Man Captain and became aide to General Artemas Ward. In 1777 he became a militia Brigadier General, and in 1779 he was second in command of the Penobscot expedition, one of the major events in his celebrated life.

The American colonial militia carried out a campaign to remove the British from their fortified location at the mouth of the Penobscot River in order to decrease the danger to Massachusetts from the east. Unfortunately, the attack failed and the American fleet was destroyed because of the incompetence of the American commander. Peleg demonstrated great courage and emerged from the debacle with his reputation improved while many other officers were dishonored, including Paul Revere who faced a pro forma court martial.

In 1780 Peleg Wadsworth was appointed military commander of the District of Maine, an area whose loyalties were split between pro-British and pro-Revolutionary residents. One of the Tory loyalists informed on Peleg and in February 1781, a group of 25 British regulars surrounded his house and shot their way in. During his determined defense he was wounded in the left arm and had to surrender and was imprisoned at Fort George.[2] Being a high-ranking prisoner he was treated well and his wound slowly healed. However, he was afraid he might be shipped back to Britain as some other prisoners had been. There he might be tried as a as a rebel and executed if America lost the war. As a result, he decided to escape along with a fellow prisoner.

Following careful planning, the two prisoners worked at night and gradually sawed a hole in the ceiling, at night, filling in the cut with chewed-up bread to hide it during the day. Finally ready, they took their chance during a driving thunderstorm and went up through the hole in the ceiling. They inched quietly along the rafters without disturbing either the guards below them or the chickens roosting in the attic. When they reached the end they dropped down and escaped through the door. They then went over the fortress walls and through the surrounding forest to finally arrive back home to everyone's surprise.

After the war, the Commonwealth sold Peleg 7,800 acres of land northwest of Portland in the hills between the Ossipee and Saco rivers at a rock-bottom price. He established the town of Hiram and built Wadsworth Hall as his residence. In order to support himself he became a successful merchant in a part of Portland that was still rural. In 1792 he entered the State Senate of Massachusetts and was then elected to Congress as a Federalist and remained in office from December 1793 to March 1807. Finally, he retired to a Country Squire's life at Wadsworth Hall, continuing to dress in the old pre-Revolutionary style.

In addition to having a father in the army, Zilpah had two brothers in the navy. One had a long, successful career, but her favorite brother, Henry, was killed off the shores of Tripoli. In 1894 he had gone to sea as a nineteen-year old midshipman on the *USS Constitution* under Commodore Preble. They traveled to the Mediterranean to overcome the Barbary Pirates who sailed from the port of Tripoli, in what is today Libya, and harassed American merchant vessels. In order to destroy the Barbary Pirate fleet Commander Preble sent the ketch *Intrepid* loaded with explosives with a ten-man crew under Lieutenant Wadsworth. They were to sail into the midst of the pirate fleet, set the *Intrepid* to explode and then flee in a small boat. However, some unidentified incident took place and the *Intrepid* exploded and killed the entire crew. Samuel says that his Uncle Henry died in service to America, "Preferring death to slavery."[3] [*Henry Wadsworth Longfellow, v. 1, p. 3*].

Zilpah had loved her brother greatly and she and Stephen named their second son Henry Wadsworth in his memory. Nevertheless,

> "Despite her military traditions, and her having in her girlhood presented a flag, with a speech, to a company of soldiers, she had in maturer years a horror of war, and was an untiring advocate of peace."[4]

Zilpah's advocacy of peace unquestionably influenced her family over the years and Samuel was a strong opponent of war throughout his life, including the Mexican campaign in the 1840s and the Civil War.

Stephen Longfellow and Zilpah Wadsworth were married on New Year's Day 1804. At first they lived with Stephen's sister at the corner of Fore and Hancock streets in Portland. Their first son, named Stephen of course, was born in 1805 and their second, Henry, was born in 1807. About a year after Henry was born, the Longfellows moved into the house Zilpah's father had built in the mid-1780s on Congress Street in Portland. It was the first brick house in Portland and Stephen and Zilpah lived there the rest of their lives. Stephen and Zilpah both became invalid through ill health, and their children, principally Anne, took the responsibility of caring for them.

The Longfellow family life that Samuel knew is described in his *Memoir.*

> "It was refined, orderly and religious; but easy and cheerful. Parents were respected, but loved still more, and not feared. Brothers and sisters lived together in a perfect mutual affection which the passage of years could not weaken."[5]

On the subject of his father he says,

> "In his family he was at once kind and strict, bringing up his children in habits of respect and obedience, of unselfishness, the dread of debt, and the faithful performance of duty."[6]

Samuel has more to say about his mother, for whom he "cherished a peculiar, tender devotion" and to whom Samuel was closer than his father.

> "She was fond of poetry and music, and in her youth, of dancing and social gayety. She was a lover of nature in all its aspects. She would sit by a window during a thunder-storm, enjoying the excitement of its splendors. Her disposition through all trials and sorrows, was always cheerful, – with a gentle and tranquil fortitude. Full of tender, simple, unquestioning piety, she was a lover of church and sermon and hymn; a devout and constant reader of the Bible, especially of its Psalms. She commended religion by its fairest fruits. It was the religion of the two great commandments. (...) She was a kind friend and neighbor, a helper of the poor, a devoted mother to her children, whose confidant she was, the sharer of their little secrets and their joys and the ready comforter of their troubles, the patient corrector of their faults."[7]

> "(f)rom her he may well have inherited his exceeding sensitiveness; his love of beauty in nature and in all the forms of art; his serene and cheerful disposition; his fortitude in suffering; and especially his clear, intuitive, spiritual faith and childlike piety."[8]

This special relationship with his mother is not surprising considering that his father spent much time in Washington as a Congressman when Samuel was 4-5 years old. In addition, when Stephen, Sr. returned to work in Portland, "he devoted himself assiduously to his profession in which he was absorbed."[9] The Longfellow home also had less male than female figures in it because his two oldest brothers had already entered Bowdoin College and resided there while Samuel was still an infant.

Cultural activities were an important part of life in the life of the Longfellows. Since Portland was a small town in a predominantly rural area, it attracted virtually no visiting theater groups or concerts, although the town did have a library. As a result, it was important for families to have their own resources if they were interested in ensuring that their children were introduced to some of the finer things in life.

> In the home, there were books and music. His father's library, not large, but well selected for the time, gave him, as he grew up, access to Shakespeare, Milton, Pope, Dryden, Thomson, Goldsmith; the Spectator, the Rambler, the Lives of the Poets, Rasselas, Plutarch's Lives; Hume's, Gibbon's, Gillie's and Robertson's Histories, and the like. For Sunday reading, which was scrupulously separated from that of "week-days," there were Hannah More's Works; for some reason, possibly theological, The Pilgrim's Progress seems not to have been on the shelves.[10]

> In the evenings, there were lessons to be learned; and the children opened their satchels, and gathered with their books and slates, round the table in the family sitting-room. (...) Studies over, there would be games till bed-time. (...) When bed-time came, it was hard to leave the warm fire to go up into the unwarmed bed-rooms; still harder next morning to get up out of the comfortable feather-beds and break the ice in the pitchers for washing. But hardship made hardihood.[11]

The girls played the piano, a talent that Samuel also had, and the family joined together in singing the familiar music of the period. Along with this, "the lessons of the dancing-class were repeated in the parlor."[12] This latter activity had the double attraction of being an enjoyable activity, as well as a way to keep warm during the frigid Maine winter.

The winter was also holiday time. The Longfellows celebrated holidays somewhat differently than in many other homes. When he was older, Samuel wrote a letter to a young friend describing them.

> I believe that to New Englanders Thanksgiving Day is more than to any other people; its associations running back to days before Christmas was observed in this part of the world. In my boyhood, even Christmas was not observed, except by the Episcopalians and Roman Catholics (who then were few), and our gifts were always exchanged on New Year's Day. On Thanksgiving Day, everybody went to "meeting," or church, in the morning, where was always a wonderful and elaborate anthem sung by the choir. And at dinner were gathered at the old home children and grandchildren, and all the boys and girls were allowed to have as much turkey and as many pieces of mince-pie and pumpkin-pie, and as many nuts and raisins as they could hold. In the evening they played blindman's buff.[13]

The proper religious education of the Longfellow children was probably of greater importance to the family than providing a suitable cultural background.

> "On Sundays, according to the habit of the time, all ordinary books and occupations were laid aside. There was church-going twice a day, – 'going to meeting,' it was always called, – never to be omitted by any of the family, save for reason of sickness."[14]

> "There were no Sunday-schools as yet; but on Sunday afternoons, after the meeting, the mother gathered her children around her, to read in turn from the great family Bible, and to look over, and talk over, its rude engravings of Scripture scenes and events; or to turn for the hundredth time, to the "family

record" of deaths and births which grew upon the pages between the Old and New Testaments. On Sunday evenings there was always the singing of hymns to the familiar psalmody of the old 'Bridgewater Collection,' – St. Martin's, and Dundee, and Brattle Street, with its favorite hymn by Helen Maria Williams."[15]

The earliest Longfellows and Wadsworths in America practiced the prevailing Calvinism of the period. As time passed, religion in America changed and the family's beliefs accompanied this movement from moderate Calvinism to early Unitarianism. A significant influence on the religious beliefs of Samuel's father Stephen came from his former classmate and close friend William Ellery Channing.

Although Samuel did not come into contact with Channing until he entered Harvard, Channing's influence through his speeches and writing was extensive. He had been a classmate of Samuel's father in the Harvard class of 1798 and then went on to study theology. After graduation, he was ordained at the Federal Street Church in Boston in 1803 where he remained as a minister until his death in 1842. He was on the Board of Harvard and worked for the founding of the Divinity School. In the clash between the viewpoints of the orthodox and liberal churches, Channing was recognized as the spokesperson for the liberal, or Unitarian, churches within the Massachusetts area. Nevertheless, he did not support a split that would break up the fellowship of Churches in New England, a fellowship that had existed from the beginning of the Colony. However, it happened anyway with churches on both sides of the issue refusing to share their pulpits with each other.

Channing's sermons argued against Calvinist doctrine and opened a path to Christian humanism in recognizing the moral nature of man. In 1819, his sermon "Unitarian Christianity" acknowledged the *de facto* split and clarified the establishment of a distinct Unitarian Church in the community of churches. His opinions were highly respected and he was considered a model of Christian piety and stood up for human rights and dignity, becoming incensed at every invasion of human rights.

Another minister who had an influence on Samuel's life was Dr. Nichols, the minister of the Portland church he grew up in. The First Parish Church in Portland had preached moderate Calvinism under Rev. Deane in the early 19th century, and in 1809 Dr. Ichabod Nichols was appointed associate pastor. Dr. Nichols was born in 1784 and graduated in Mathematics from Harvard in 1802, where he taught this subject while he studied Theology.

Dr. Nichols was a conservative Unitarian and his appointment caused a split in the church with some members leaving. In 1814 he became the church's only minister when Rev. Deane died and he became one of the best-liked pastors the First Parish ever had. The increase in the size of the congregation required the building of a new church that was dedicated in 1826.

In addition to his pulpit, Dr. Nichols was active in the temperance movement, a supporter of the Sunday School Movement and served as the second president of the American Unitarian Association, a trustee of Bowdoin University and vice-president of the American Academy of Arts and Sciences. In 1855 he resigned his pastorate after 46 years and moved to Cambridge where he was involved in scholarly pursuits until his death in 1859

Dr. Nichol's sermons and Sunday school along with the writings of Channing had a great influence on Samuel's life. As a matter of fact,

> "If the tradition repeated by his son [Samuel] is correct, that it was at his [Stephen Sr.'s] instance that the covenant of the First Parish of Portland was modified in the direction of progressive thought, we may have a hint of the source of his son's ever-forward look, and his strictness of fidelity to personal convictions, however finely distinguished."[16]

Notes:

[1] Brunelle, Jim. *Maine Almanac.* MHS.

[2] Longfellow, Samuel, Ed. *Henry Wadsworth Longfellow, Vol. I.*, 1886. p. 20-21.

[3] Ibid., p. 3.

[4] Ibid., p. 4.

[5] May, Joseph, Ed.. *Samuel Longfellow: Memoir and Letters.* Cambridge: The Riverside Press, 1894. p. 2.

[6] Longfellow, Samuel, *Longfellow, Vol. 1.* p. 5.

[7] Ibid., p. 4.

[8] May, Joseph, *Memoir.* p. 3.

[9] Longfellow, Samuel, *Longfellow, Vol. 1.* p. 5.

[10] Ibid., p. 11.

[11] Ibid., p. 14-15.

[12] Ibid., p. 14.

[13] May, Joseph. *Memoir.* p. 252.

[14] Longfellow, Samuel, *Longfellow, Vol. 1.* p. 12.

[15] Ibid., p. 13.

[16] May, Joseph, *Memoir.* p. 252.

CHAPTER 2 – THE LONGFELLOW SIBLINGS

Stephen and Zilpah Longfellow had a total of eight children between 1805 and 1819. The four boys and four girls were close knit and maintained contact with each other throughout their lives even though the paths they took were quite different.

As already mentioned the oldest of the siblings was born in 1805 and named Stephen in keeping with family tradition. The second oldest, Henry Wadsworth Longfellow, was born February 27, 1807, and named after his mother Zilpah's favorite brother who died in fighting the Barbary pirates at Tripoli. There are many books about Henry Wadsworth Longfellow's life and work, the first biography being written by his youngest brother Samuel, on whom he had a significant influence.

On the other hand, Samuel was not as close to his brother Stephen who was regarded as a difficult and exasperating child, although he was also considered charming and well meaning. While still a teenager he began to drink heavily and keep questionable company. His temperament troubled his parents a great deal, in contrast to the behavior of their second son, Henry. In a letter to Stephen, Sr., Zilpah stated, "our sons are different, very different. I think they are so naturally and it cannot, I think be imputed as a fault to one that he is not like the other."[1] In spite of Stephen's faults, it appears likely that Henry loved his brother, and was much closer to him than to his younger brothers, Alexander and Samuel.

In 1821, 16-year old Stephen and 14-year old Henry entered Bowdoin College, which was 28 miles north of Portland and where their father was a trustee. Although Harvard was Unitarian and would seem to be a more logical choice for his sons, Stephen Sr. most likely sent his sons to Bowdoin because of pride in the new state's college. The two boys lived at home during their first year, probably because their parents felt that

Henry was still too young. Another likely reason for keeping the boys at home the first year was that Stephen, Sr., felt that his son Stephen still needed supervision. The following year the two boys lived at school, and resided in the house of Rev. Titcomb. About 30 years later Prof. Calvin Stowe and his wife Harriet Beecher Stowe lived in this same house while he taught at Bowdoin and where she wrote *Uncle Tom's Cabin*.

In 1831 Stephen, Jr. married Marianne Preble, daughter of Judge William Pitt Preble. They had six children, the first, a boy, was named Stephen following family tradition, however, he lived only a year. Their second child was also a boy who became heir to the name Stephen, the sixth in the sequence. Unfortunately, the marriage had problems as the result of Stephen's alcoholism, and in 1849 he was sent to a hydrotherapy spa for an attempt to cure him. However, the treatment was unsuccessful and his marriage to Marianne ended in divorce in January 1850. Stephen then married Miss F. Fuller, but their marriage was destined to be very brief since Stephen succumbed to problems related to alcoholism and died in September 1850.

The Longfellow's third child was a daughter born in 1808 and given the name Elizabeth. She was Henry's favorite sister, but unfortunately she came down with tuberculosis. While Henry was on his first trip to Europe in the 1820s, her tuberculosis quickly became very grave and she died on May 5, 1829 at the age of 21. This was while Henry was still in Europe and Samuel was 10 years old. During the last part of her life the rest of her family was present and toward the end so was her fiancé William Pitt Fessenden (later Lincoln's Secretary of the Treasury and the Senator from Maine whose vote saved President Andrew Johnson from impeachment). She was the first of Samuel's generation to die and her death created a break in the close-knit household. Elizabeth's siblings were greatly distressed and her parents never completely overcame this first loss, although Zilpah wrote, "To see a timid feeble girl meeting without dread the messenger who so often appalls the stoutest heart was indeed a most consoling sight."[2]

Anne Longfellow was the fourth to be born and was the second daughter. Born in 1810, she died in 1901 and spent 87 of her 90 years living in the Wadsworth-Longfellow House in Portland. In 1832, she married George Washington Pierce, one of Henry Wadsworth Longfellow's good friends and his classmate in the Bowdoin class of 1825 along with Nathaniel Hawthorne and the future U.S. President Franklin Pierce. George died only three years after he and Anne were married and Anne moved back to her parent's home where she remained until her death. As a result, she became the focal point around which the family could gather. Of all the siblings, she was the one with whom Samuel shared the greatest number of interests and they exchanged correspondence with regularity.

After the death of Stephen and Zilpah in 1849 and 1851, respectively, Anne Longfellow Pierce remained in the house and kept it up until she died in 1901. She left it to the Maine Historical Society when she died, including the recent outhouse, which supposedly was the last one for which the city of Portland issued a permit. With Anne's death, approximately 115 years of Wadsworth-Longfellow presence in the Portland house ended.

Alexander Wadsworth Longfellow was the fifth child and third son in the Longfellow family. He became a civil engineer and lived in Portland most of his life, and his work involved wide-ranging coastal surveys by the U.S. Government. He and his wife, Elizabeth Clapp Porter, had five children. Their oldest daughter, Mary King Longfellow, was born in 1852 and became a well-known painter, and studied with artists Ross Sterling Turner and William Morris Hunt. Their oldest son, Alexander Wadsworth Longfellow, Jr., was born in 1854. He became an architect and one of his projects was the Maine Historical Society Library building.

Mary Longfellow was born in 1816 and married James Greenleaf in 1839. In 1850 the Greenleafs moved to New Orleans where he formed a partnership named Greenleaf and Hubbard, which arranged for the purchase and shipment of cotton to northern ports for use in the mills there. Every summer the Greenleafs traveled north to New England to visit their relatives and they finally built a house at 76 Brattle Street, not far from the Craigie House at 105 Brattle Street where Henry Wadsworth lived. Greenleaf was a strong supporter of the Union and in May 1860 the partnership was dissolved and the couple moved north just prior to the Civil War in order to avoid the conflict. The Greenleaf property in New Orleans was seized at the beginning of the war, but was returned after the hostilities ceased. However, James died in August 1865 and, since the couple had no children, and Mary decided to live in Cambridge where she maintained a close relationship with the Cambridge and Portland family members.[3]

The last daughter to be born was Ellen Longfellow, but her short 16-year life did not allow her time to develop a reputation beyond the family group.

The baby of the Longfellow family, and the subject of this biography, was Samuel. He was born on June 18, 1819, in the city of Portland, nine months before Maine was made a state and, fourteen years after his oldest brother, Stephen. During the time he was growing up, the family group was a little smaller than that experienced by his siblings.

His father spent much time in Washington, D.C. from 1822--1824 when he was a federalist congressman, and later was busy as a Maine state legislator. Aside from his political activities, Stephen Longfellow had his law practice, some of it in his home office, plus activities on the Board of Trustees of Bowdoin College in addition to his community and church activities. These all decreased the amount of time he could spend with his family.

Stephen, Jr. and Henry entered Bowdoin College in 1821, although they lived their first year at home. In the Fall of 1822, the two brothers began to live on Campus and continued to do so until they graduated in the class of 1825. Their move to campus was the same year that their father was busy in Washington, D.C. After Henry graduated he left to travel in Europe in 1826. As a result, Samuel did not see Henry very much for several years and a letter from 9-year old Samuel to Henry in 1828 shows that he missed his older brother.

> I now take the opportunity to write you a few lines. I am very well, and I hope you are the same. I hope you will come home soon for you have staid (sic) away a long time. I shall be

9 years old next June, and the folks say I have grown so much you will hardly know me when you come home.[4]

Samuel, being the youngest person in the household, grew up in a somewhat different atmosphere than his older siblings. Having so many older family members around, Samuel was able to absorb their opinions on the subjects they discussed, some of which shaped his ideas in the future.

Considering Samuel's situation, modern studies on families show the likelihood of different personality traits for children based on birth position. One therapist's report on the character of the youngest child states:

> Perhaps the truest and most consistent finding is that last born children tend to be slower at accepting responsible roles, since they have not experienced being older and more capable than someone else in the family. It is easy as a youngest to question your judgment and abilities, unless of course there are other mitigating factors that help you to gain confidence in your ability to handle responsibility and making decisions.[5]

Providing some support for the above idea, in his *Memoir* Joseph May describes Samuel's early life and what he enjoyed doing.

> There are signs that he was not only the youngest, but also the darling of the family. His traits may well have fitted him to be such. Of somewhat delicate organization, yet healthy and hearty, fond of fun, and peculiarly susceptible to the ludicrous, he was, as an early friend describes him, intelligent without precocity; by no means wanting in masculine qualities; and not unsocial, though fond of his own companionship, and rather the intimate friend of a select few than the hail-fellow of the many.
>
> In one of his youthful poems he describes himself as a 'dreamy child.' He was quiet, but happy; full of fancies of his own; early coming to love reading, writing and sketching; preferring these, and in summer botanizing and the cultivation of his garden, and long rambles in the woods and fields, to the

more usual sports of boys. Besides their own ample home, with its books, music, and evening games, the family was blest with a grandfather's home at Gorham, a few miles away, and, in earlier days, another, somewhat father, where the children always had a welcome from their venerable relatives, and could enjoy a taste of country life and the habits of the farm. In the youthful poem we have referred to, Samuel calls up the happy hours spent in these scenes, and it may be that he had them in mind when, late in life, he said: 'I always love to look upon a picture of a pine-tree; it reminds me of my boyhood.'[6]

Samuel believed that "In all New England there is no pleasanter town than Portland in the State of Maine."[7] Until he went away to school Samuel lived in Portland, which was considered "Down East" from Boston and Cambridge where he spent his University years and a good part of his later life. The logic behind "Down East", instead of up north as many people say when looking at a map, is that ships sailed down the prevailing easterly winds from Massachusetts' ports to reach Maine.

Portland, Maine was originally called *Machigonne* (Great Neck) by the Native Americans who first lived there. It was settled by the British in 1632 as a fishing and trading settlement and renamed *Casco*. In 1658 its name was changed again, this time to *Falmouth*.

In 1675 the city was completely destroyed by Indians during King Philip's War. The city was rebuilt, to be destroyed by the same Indians again several years later. In 1775 the city was destroyed yet again, this time by bombardment by the Royal Navy during the American Revolutionary War.[8]

Samuel enjoyed his life in Maine, which, as mentioned earlier, became a state not long after Samuel was born. In effect they grew up together. The District of Maine was made up of the three easternmost counties of Massachusetts, but the "Downeasters" found it difficult and expensive to send their political representatives to Boston. In addition they felt they received less than their due attention from state government. Therefore many Maine residents wanted to be separate from Massachusetts and put the question of statehood on the ballot in 1780. It failed then as well as the next three times it was voted on over the years. Finally, on June 19, 1819 Massachusetts passed legislation separating the District from the State and on July 19, 1819 Maine put it on the ballot and it won 17,001 to 7,132. In October 1819, the Massachusetts legislature accepted this and forwarded it to the U.S. Congress with the proviso that Congress had to recognize Maine as a state by March 4, 1820 or it would revert to its previous status as district.

Also in 1819, Missouri submitted a request to Washington that it be considered for statehood. At the time there were 22 states, 11 with slavery legal and 11 where it wasn't. Maine had no slave owners, but had a significant number of abolitionists. On the other hand, Missouri had a number of slave owners.

Under normal circumstances, the addition of a new state would not have a significant effect on a child growing up. However, Maine became a state as a result of the Missouri Compromise and since his father was a congressman this meant he would have heard about the debate on the issue.

Originally Congress treated the two proposals as a package. This made the central issue federal control, where slavery should be dealt with on a national level, versus state control, allowing individual states to decide on the issue of slavery themselves. Thus, slavery was inserted into the federalist-states' rights argument. This was a situation that incensed long-time federalists such as Stephen Longfellow.

By the time that Samuel was a child, the issue of slavery had been argued for many years. Prohibition of slavery had even become an issue in the writing of the Declaration of Independence when Thomas Jefferson included references to the active support of slavery in America by King George III in his draft:

> He has waged cruel war against human nature itself, violating it's most sacred rights of life and liberty in the persons of a distant people who never offended him, captivating and carrying them into slavery in another hemisphere, or to incur miserable death in their transportation hither.[9]

However, because of pressure from both northern and southern slaveholders, it was not included in the final version of the Declaration of Independence. Nevertheless, this only postponed the final clash on the issue.

A Maine statehood bill finally passed both houses without being attached to the Missouri bill and the President signed the law creating Maine as the 23rd state on March 3, 1820, just one day before the deadline. Missouri's request was included in the "Missouri Compromise." This legislation established that there could be no slavery in any state above latitude 36° 30', with the exception of Missouri. The bill passed and Missouri became the 24th state and once again the balance was equal with 12 free and 12 slave states. Despite achieving statehood, the residents of Maine, including the Longfellow family, were not happy being forced into the position of pawns in this conflict that resulted in an increase in slave states.

Over the years Maine continued an anti-slavery tradition and Bowdoin considered its connection with the Civil War stronger than other schools in New England. Among the people and actions linking Bowdoin and the Civil War, two stand out. Many assert that the war started at Bowdoin with the writing of *Uncle Tom's Cabin* by Maine resident Harriet Beecher Stowe. The end of the Civil War was connected to Bowdoin through Joshua Lawrence Chamberlain. He was a hero at Gettysburg and recipient of the Congressional Medal of Honor and was the soldier selected to receive the formal surrender of the Confederacy at Appomattox. He was a professor at Bowdoin, governor of Maine and later president of the College.

This created a situation that fixed itself in the memory of the population at the time, and Samuel surely was exposed to discussions both at home and at school about the Missouri Compromise and the moves to advance slavery. The feelings toward the events surrounding Maine's statehood were further emphasized as the events in the 1840s and 1850s leading to the Civil War became more serious and consequently made Samuel's dedication to the Abolitionist movement stronger.

In the following section are comments by acquaintances and family of Samuel Longfellow that describe his personal character.

Despite the fact that they were written at different times in his life and in different circumstances, there is a consistency in the descriptions.

Placing them together here provides an opportunity for the reader to decide what in Samuel's personality was influenced by his upbringing. It also provides a place where the opinions of his friends can be compared and a point to refer to when Samuel as a person is described in the remainder of the book.

Samuel Longfellow was not an easy person to characterize clearly. However, the way his friends describe the way he lived and related with others provides enough information to say that he was kinder and calmer than other persons that they knew. Joseph May, in his *Memoir*, quotes Thomas Wentworth Higginson and Octavius B. Frothingham about Samuel.

> "He was a difficult person to delineate," writes Colonel Higginson, "from the very simplicity and perfect poise of his character. He was, in the old phrase, 'a very perfit gentil knight.' He had no exceptional or salient points, but an evenness of disposition which, from boyhood onward, kept him not only from the lower temptations, but the higher ones. This was true of him when I knew him in college, and true at every later period. One could not, for a moment imagine him vexed or petty, or ungenerous. Few men have led a life of such un-broken calm and cheerfulness. At the same time, he was equal in strength of character, to any emergency, and would have borne himself firmly upon the rack when more boisterous men failed. ...He went about your, as a lady once said, 'mur-muring little charities;' for every book, every picture, he had a work of kindly apology, making the best of it; but he had his own standard of right and adhered to it with utter fearlessness. He did not strive, nor cry, nor did any man hear his voice in the streets; but on any question requiring courage, he held the courageous side." [10]

> He was a man of men, one of ten thousand, – a man the like of whom for infusing a pure and liberal spirit into a church

has never been surpassed; full of enthusiasm of the quiet, deep, interior kind; worshipful, devout, reverent; a deep believer in the human heart, in its affections; having a perfect faith in the majesty of conscience, a supreme trust in God and in the laws of the world; a man thoroughly well instructed, used to the best people, used to the best books and the best music, with the soul of a poet in him and the heart of a saint; a man of a deeply, earnestly consecrated will; simple as a little child with the heart of a child; perpetually singing little ditties as he went about in the world, humming his little heart-songs as he went about in the street, wherever you met him. ...He was one of the rarest men; in intellect free as light having no fear in any direction, able to read any book, able to appreciate any thought, able to draw alongside any opinion; hating nobody, not even with a theological, not even with a speculative, not even with a most abstract hatred; he did not know in his heart what hatred meant; he loved God, his fellow-men. ...He was always in an attitude of belief, always in an attitude of hope, brave as a lion, but never boasting, never saying what he meant to do or what he wished he could do, but keeping his own counsel and going a straight path, ploughing a very straight furrow through a very crooked world. He was as immovable as adamant and as playful as a sunbeam. He wrought here, as the oldest of you know, with a singleness of purpose and a singleness of feeling that knew no change from the beginning to the end.[11]

In his description of Henry Wadsworth Longfellow, Frank Preston Stearns provides a comparison of the personalities of Henry and Samuel in his *Cambridge Sketches*.

He [Henry] did not believe in a luxurious life except so far as luxury added to refinement, and everything in the way of fashionable show was very distasteful to him. His brother Samuel once said, "I cannot imagine anything more disagreeable than to ride in a public procession;" and the two men were more alike than brothers often are. We notice in the poet's diary that he abstains from going to a certain dinner in Boston for fear of being called upon to make a speech. Craigie House gave

Longfellow the opportunity in which he most delighted, – of entertaining his friends and distinguished foreign guests in a handsome manner; but conventional dinner parties, with their fourteen plates half surrounded by wine-glasses, were not often seen there. He much preferred a smaller number of guests with the larger freedom of discourse which accompanies a select gathering. Many such occasions are referred to in his diary, – as if he did not wish to forget them.[12]

Edward Everett Hale was one of Samuel's best friends and they maintained an enduring friendship throughout their lives from when they met as students. Hale was always full of praise for Samuel, and here describes how strong Samuel was despite his modesty and kindness, as well as how his effectiveness was in good part due to his being straight-forward and advocating that all we desire is possible. He also describes how Samuel was drawn to young people and they to him.

For me, I have never seen so remarkable an illustration of what Dr. Putnam used to call "the wrath of the lamb," – the strength of a person whose personal life was so tender and modest and gentle that you were half afraid to trust him out of doors, showing itself, when there was any need, in vigor amounting to audacity, and in moral control of every one to whom he had to speak.

He was of a sensitive and analytical nature which made him detest, as much as St. Peter ever did, anything that was common and unclean. But he, too, had seen the vision, and he knew very well that what God had cleansed he was not to call common. There is not a dainty critic of them all who could go beyond him in pointing out inelegancies. And yet, if you saw him with a dirty gutter-boy of the Cambridge streets, whom he had drawn into the boys' club of an evening, you would see that his was that greatest privilege, the intuitive sympathy and love of untutored children.[13]

He was no play-actor; he meant what he said, and said what he meant, without fear or mental reservation, as for "popular noises," he seemed not to heed or hear them, so attentive was he to the still, small Voice, which out-thundered them all. Nor did he come into the field of controversy, or appear as the assailant of error and evil, with weapons drawn from the armory of the old Adam. He was a champion of truth in the spirit of truth, and of goodness in the spirit of goodness; never hostile or antagonistic in temper. He acted on the principle that the best way to get rid of darkness is by bringing in the light. If any custom, opinion, or phrase ceased to serve or satisfy him, he simply dropped it and forgot it, or went along without it, leaving the dead to bury their dead.[14]

Samuel Longfellow was a prophet of the new time, mightily believing that the best things are possible, if we will but live for the best. The past with all its treasures of good is ours; but it is our servant, not our master. We do highest honor to all great souls, "not by following them, but by following what they followed.[15]

He was very fond of little children, especially of boys, and frequently enlivened his solitary bachelor quarters by inviting some urchin to share his lunch. Once, at a house where he was a guest, he spent a long time on the veranda with a little fellow whose mother afterwards asked, "What did Mr. Longfellow say to you?" – "Oh, he didn't say much, he kept kissing my hair." A Portland gentleman says that his children were accustomed to speak of Mr. Longfellow as "the *kind* man."[16]

Joseph May also confirms Samuel's work with children in the *Memoir.*

For children he had always an especial love and care, and won their affections as he did those of their elders. Their love for him was instinctive; they trusted him, and clustered about him, by a natural impulse which it scarcely required words for him to excite. His gentle manners, grave but genial, his pleasant humor, the quickness of his sympathies on all sides, the transparency of his religious emotions and moral instincts, the quiet wisdom of his practical thought, won the confidence of growing youth, of the sorrowing, the doubting, the troubled in mind, and prepared them to accept inspiration, guidance, or comfort.[17]

Another of Samuel Longfellow's Divinity School classmates was Ephraim Nute, the first Unitarian minister in Kansas with a church in the city of Lawrence. He was a strong opponent of slavery during the bloody battles in the 1850s between "free-staters" and "slave-staters". Although Nute initially thought that Samuel did not pay attention to the "darker side" of human activity, he found that this was because Samuel focused on the positive point of view.

> Another classmate in the Divinity School [the Rev. Ephraim Nute] writes of him, as he knew him at that period: "He was singularly quiet and undemonstrative. He made no professions of friendship, no display of knowledge, never argued or dwelt on differences of opinion, uttered no uncharitable imputations. Himself the soul of sincerity and truth loving, he seemed to assume that all were similarly disposed. At first, he appeared to me utterly oblivious of the darker sides of human character, as if he did not recognize that there was any such thing as sin in the world, or any occasion for a struggle against evil in our own souls. This I found afterwards, was my own mistake. It came from his disposition always to look upon the bright side, both in his estimate of others and in his own experience, By his clear, optimistic faith, he discerned, beyond the struggle, the final victory and peace. I felt deeply his superiority of character, his Christ-like spirit. Among the advantages of the school, I esteemed his influence one of the richest. There was a nameless calm, a gentleness mingled with earnestness and strength, a fine poetic spirit. He filled a large place in my remembrance as one to whom I owe much which yet I cannot clearly define.[18]

As a minister, Samuel was famous for his preaching. There is a collection of some of his sermons and writings, *Samuel Longfellow, Essays and Sermons*, which provide us a chance to read some of his material. The quantity of Samuel's writings is limited to a certain extent because his health affected his ability to publish, as Octavius Brooks Frothingham, leader of the Free Religious Association, stated.

> Like his friend [Samuel Johnson], Longfellow is quiet and retiring – not so scholarly, not so learned, but meditative. His sermons are lyrics; his writings are serene contemplation, not white and cold, but glowing with interior and suppressed radiance. A recluse and solitary he is, too, though sunny and cheerful; a thinker, but not a dry one; of intellectual sympathies, warm and generous; of feeble intellectual antipathies, being rather unconscious of systems that are foreign to him than hostile to them. He enjoys his own intellectual world so much, it is so large, rich, beautiful, and satisfying, that he is content to stay in it, to wander up and down in it, and hold intercourse with its inhabitants; yet he understands his won system well, is master of its ideas, and abundantly competent to defend them, as his essays published in the "Radical" during its short existence testify. He has published little; ill health has prevented his taking a forward place among reformers and teachers; but where he has ministered, his influence has been deep and pure. Not few are the men and women who ascribe to him their best impulses, and owe him a debt of lasting gratitude for the moral faith and intellectual enthusiasm he awakened in them.[19]

> He was no play-actor; he meant what he said and said what he meant, without fear or mental reservation. As for "popular noises," he seemed not to heed or hear them, so attentive was he to the still, small Voice, which out-thundered them all. Nor did he come into the field of controversy, or appear as the assailant of error and evil with weapons drawn from the armory of the old Adam. He was a champion of truth in the spirit of truth, and of goodness in the spirit of goodness; never hostile or antagonistic in temper. He acted on the principle that the best way to get rid of darkness is by bringing in the light. If any custom, opinion, or phrase ceased to serve or satisfy him, he simply dropped it and forgot it, or went along without it, leaving the dead to bury their dead.[20]

Samuel Longfellow was a prophet of the new time, mightily believing that the best things are possible, if we will but live for the best. The past with all its treasures of good is ours; but it is our servant, not our master. We do highest honor to all good souls, "not by following them, but by following what they followed."[21]

Although Samuel Longfellow was very liberal in his beliefs in peace, women's rights, and against slavery, he was not an active participant in the activities that took place to support them. This is most likely due to his lifelong opposition to participation in groups. He was willing to write articles and to speak at conventions, but left active demonstrations to others. His friend Thomas Wentworth Higginson in particular was well known for his sometimes too active participation in Abolitionism and while Samuel was not as outspoken, he was definitely opposed to slavery.

Higginson was thirty-four years old, a tall, belligerent clergyman who liked "to pitch right into people and show them how foolish they are thinking and acting." Although he was now one of the angriest and most outspoken abolitionists in New England. Higginson had been a shy and introspective youth. He, too, had grown up in a world of books, had entered Harvard at the age of thirteen and graduated in the class of 1841. At Harvard, he befriended Theodore Parker and Samuel Longfellow, younger brother of the poet and a truly "beautiful soul."[22]

But the ethical element was always the deepest of all in Samuel Longfellow, and was becoming prominent in his thought, his preaching, and his views of professional duty. To the reforms of the day, especially the antislavery reform, he was giving an ardent sympathy and increasing attention. The "funnier things yet" which, a few years before, he had expected to see, were now the grave subjects of his most earnest thought and sense of duty. In political affairs, at this time so agitated and ominous, he took the eager and serious interest of a patriot and a moralist, hesitating never to refer to them, in his mild but emphatic and persuasive way, in his Sunday discourses.[23]

This antislavery question comes, as Christianity came, into an unbelieving age; comes judging, dividing, separating family, church, political party, precisely because it is the question which now in this country tests the fidelity and sincerity of individuals, and church, and party. And therefore you are right in holding your ground, feeling that the question is one quite beyond persons. We do not doubt what the result will be in the end. And the end will come the sooner, and bring the peace which shall endure, the more faithful every man is in his place.[24]

One final comment is from someone who did not know Samuel very well, but was acquainted with his brother Henry and some of his friends. As a result we have an opportunity to see how Samuel was viewed within the general milieu of the Boston intellectual community.

A lesser light of this time was the Rev. Samuel Longfellow. I remember him first as of a somewhat vague and vanishing personality, not much noticed when his admired brother was of the company. This was before the beginning of his professional career. A little later, I heard of his ordination as a Unitarian minister from Rev. Edward Everett Hale, who had attended and possibly taken part in, the services. The poet Longfellow had written a lovely hymn for the occasion. Mr. Hale spoke of "Sam Longfellow" as a valued friend and remarked upon the modesty and sweetness of his disposition. "I saw him the other day," said Mr. Hale. "He showed me a box of colors which he had just purchased. Same said to me, 'I thought I might have this now.'" He was fond of sketching from nature. Years after this time, I heard Mr. Longfellow preach at the Hawes Church in South Boston. After the service, I invited him to take a Sunday dinner with Dr. Howe and me. He consented, and I remember that, in the course of our conversation, he said: "Theodore Parker has made things easier for us young ministers. He has demolished so much which it was necessary to remove."

The collection entitled *Hymns of the Spirit*, and published under the joint names of Samuel Longfellow and Samuel Johnson, is a valuable one, and the hymns which Mr. Longfellow himself contributed to the repertoire of the denomination are deeply religious in tone; and yet I must think that among Unitarians of thirty or more years ago he was held to be something of a skeptic. Thomas G. Appleton was speaking of him in my presence, one day, and said: "He asked me whether I could not get along without the idea of a personal God. I replied, 'No, you —— ——.'" Mr. Appleton shook his fist, and was very vehement in his expression; but his indignation had reference solely to Mr. Longfellow's supposed opinions and not at all to his character, which was esteemed of all men.[25]

The last sentence above summarizes how Samuel Longfellow's was perceived throughout his life – while people did not always agree with his ideas, nobody ever questioned his sincerity, honesty and character.

Notes:

[1] Letter, Zilpah Longfellow to Stephen Longfellow, Sr., Jan. 10, 1824, ZLP, LNHS.

[2] Letter, Zilpah Longfellow to Henry Longfellow, May 7, 1829, LP.

[3] Greenleaf and Hubbard, Business Records 1850-1860. Mss: 761, 1850-1860, G814. Cambridge Baker Library, Harvard Business School.

[4] Letter, Samuel Longfellow to Henry Longfellow, April 25, 1828, LP.

[5] Peterson, Gayle. "On being the youngest child."

[6] May, Joseph, *Memoir.* p. 4-5.

[7] Longfellow, Samuel. *Henry Wadsworth Longfellow, Vol. I.*, 1886. p. 1.

[8] en.wikipedia.org/wiki/Portland_Maine.

[9] "Rough Draft of the Declaration of Independence" Boston Public Broadcasting System – WGBH Educational Foundation, www.pbs.org/wgbh/aia/part2/2h33.html. 1999.

[10] May, Joseph, *Memoir.* p. 106.

[11] Ibid., p. 211-212.

[12] Stearns, Frank Preston. "Longfellow," *Cambridge Sketches.*

[13] Hale, Edward Everett, *Five Prophets of Today*, p. 15.

[14] Ibid., p. 43.

[15] Ibid., p. 46.

[16] Ibid., p. 55.

[17] May, Joseph, *Memoir.* p. 110.

[18] Ibid., 107

[19] Frothingham, Octavius Brooks. *Transcendentalism In New England: A History,* p. 348.

[20] Hale, Edward Everett. *Five Prophets of Today* p. 43.

[21] Ibid., p. 46.

[22] Oates, Stephen B. *To Purge this Land with Blood,* p. 189.

[23] May, Joseph, *Memoir.* p. 109.

[24] Letter Samuel Longfellow to Samuel Johnson, June 26, 1851, SLP, LNHS.

[25] Howe, Julia Ward, "Reminiscences of Julia Ward Howe", *The Atlantic Monthly. Volume 83, Issue 499,* p. 711.

CHAPTER 3 – SCHOOL DAYS

Young Samuel began school under "the guiding care of two female teachers."[1] Not having information about the specific age Samuel began school, it is reasonable to assume that he began at about the same age as his brothers Stephen (at age 5) and Henry (at age 3). It is also likely that Samuel attended the same school in Portland as his brothers, which was that of Mrs. Fellows, better known as "Ma'am Fellows." Assuming that she was still there ten years after his brothers attended and the school curriculum had not changed, Samuel was taught "his letters and respect for elders, if nothing more."[2]

He spent a couple of years learning his lessons in his first school and "at the proper age" he was ready to pass to the next level. Again he followed the lead of his brothers Stephen and Henry and entered the Portland Academy in order to prepare for college life.[3] As with his first school, the "proper age" was not specified, but it was probably about the age of five like Henry. Unlike Stephen and Henry, however, he was not sent to public school first. This was most likely due to Henry's experience in public school, where relating to some of the rougher boys was objectionable to him and he ended up staying only a week before his parents transferred him to private school.

The headmaster of Portland Academy during the time Samuel attended was the "able and irascible" Mr. Bezaleel Cushman. Mr. Cushman had been the first headmaster at Bridgton Academy, located about 40 miles west of Portland, and began his tenure at Portland Academy in 1817 while Henry was studying there. Correspondence from Mr. Cushman to Samuel Longfellow indicates that the two were on friendly terms.[4]

Samuel was diligent in his studies of the classical course, which was the same as when Stephen and Henry were there. Nevertheless, like many young boys, he had his "lapses" and was tardy or missed classes. Among his reasons were seeing his brothers who were home for a visit from school or wanting to play with a visiting baby, about, which he said, "he is a little dear."

The Portland Academy was different from schools in many parts of the country at the time because it was co-educational. This feature of the school was not just "discussed, but practiced without question." In Samuel's biography of his brother Henry he provides an amusing description of a co-educational class at Portland Academy.

> In the Portland Academy the girls and boys were duly placed apart on either side of the aisle that ran from the door to the teacher's platform; but these two sets of desks faced each other. Imagine the lessons that were learned above the grammar and the arithmetic, the romances that were composed but never submitted to the teachers for criticism! There is even a trust-worthy tradition that some of the shyer, or more ardent, boys cut peep-holes in the lids of their desks to be furtively used in the prolonged intervals of putting away a slate or getting out a writing-book.[5]

However, by the time Samuel started the Academy,

> it admitted boys only, but a girl's school was kept in the room above. Opportunity for romance was thus not entirely wanting; and the older boys who sat in the upper seats under the eastern windows were sometimes known to spend their recess in watching the girls at play in the yard below.[6]

In a manuscript written in 1892 and republished in 1945, Samuel describes his study program at Portland Academy. Mr. Bezaleel "was very fond of talking" and sometimes went on at "great length." Samuel felt "it did not do us much good for we had lessons to get, and after a while we turned to our books and heard no more."[7] In addition to the subjects mentioned below they read and wrote French, which Samuel liked, as well as studied other subjects.

My study of Latin began at eight years with Adams's grammar and a primer which truly began at the beginning, for its first words were: *In principio Deus creavit coelum et terram intra sex dies.* ...Into English grammar our way was made pleasant by the use of a small text-book in the form of conversations, which relieved the dryness of the subject. Our Arithmetic, besides the "four rules," taught us the "Rule of Three," "Practice," and "Alligation," terms now unknown to schoolboys. ...Of English literature we had nothing beyond what we got in our reading-book, *Scott's Lessons.* This gave us specimens of English writers under the headings, "Eloquence of the Bar," "Eloquence of the Senate," "Eloquence of the Pulpit." ...Our preceptor was our writing-master. He set the copy for us at the head of the page, and on writing day he went round from desk to desk, mending our quill pens, steel pens being then unknown. He looked over our writing-books and marked with a pencil the bad places. ...Of course we drew pictures on the blank leaves – heads, caricatures, etc. I remember our teacher said, "I see by your books that you have a talent for drawing: now if you will draw some pictures on sheets of paper, not in your books, I will give you marks for them." I remember, too, with what disappointment I found myself receiving only "4" for an elaborate and brilliant water-color of a cottage, a lake, and a grove of trees. The boys who could not draw nicknamed us "The Fine Arts."[8]

Throughout his life Samuel enjoyed drawing and a number of his drawing books still exist. He also drew pictures in some of his letters, usually of places he describe in the letter. It also appears he enjoyed painting and continued to paint at least into his college years as indicated by a letter to his father shortly after entering Harvard in which he asked his father to have "Mary send my paintbox by John."[9] In the collection of his drawings and his journals there are a few painted in watercolor.

Besides their academic education, children were expected to attend church and Sunday school regularly. As a result, Sunday was not a day off from studying, but a day for "religious culture."

The two services of Sunday were a matter of course. But there is a trace of positive interest in them, in Samuel's record of the texts and intelligent comments on the sermons. One or two may have made a lasting impression. The minister of the First Parish was Rev. Dr. Nichols, revered and beloved by his people through many years, and some of whose writing were as household words among the Unitarians of the period generally.[10]

Samuel was attentive to the sermons and religious texts during the church services. He often made comments on them in his journal and gave his opinion about the lesson or the manner in which it was presented. Besides church, "Sunday-school had now been established, but it made, perhaps, little impression on the boy's mind..."[11] and he made almost no comments on this aspect of his religious education. Sometimes Dr. Nichols held Sunday School classes at his house so "he might become acquainted with the children." One particular lesson that stuck in Samuel's mind was one that fit in with his interests in science. After the children had finished their recitations, Dr. Nichols "showed us a microscope and gave us a shock with an electrical machine."

School and church were not Samuel's only sources of knowledge and culture. As an adolescent he mentions in his journal that he attended "courses of lectures on natural science" more often than those on any other topic. He went with his schoolmates, but sometimes alone. Among the lecture subjects he noted in his childhood journal were "Attraction," "Properties of Matter," "Steam" and "Mechanical Properties of Air." He made comments in his journal regarding his reactions to the speakers and the topics and also showed an ability to understand the concepts presented and was able to describe them clearly.[12] Sometimes on Saturdays he would go to "court to hear some noted pleader," but it is not clear if this was his father's suggestion or his own interest in what his father did. In any event he liked going and, as was his custom, he made comments in his journal on the "artifices of the rhetoricians." He also visited an artist's studio and attended band concerts, again making observations about what he did and did not like. As Joseph May, editor of Samuel's *Memoir*, points out: "In these sincerities and refinements the boy was the father of the man."[13]

After his instruction and experiences were completed at Portland Academy, his family considered him ready to go to College. In the summer of 1835, Samuel traveled alone from the quiet, rural life of Portland to the intellectual diversity of Cambridge and entered Harvard University at the age of 16.

> [He] brought to college the reputation of a fine scholar; a love for good literature and for the beautiful in all its forms; an inquiring mind; a sensitive conscience; a strong will for the right; and a heart which was to open erelong, with singular responsiveness, to religious impressions and the suggestions of spiritual things.[14]

In keeping with family tradition, Samuel was supposed to have entered Bowdoin like his older brothers, especially since Henry had become a professor there in 1829 and his father served on the governing boards. However, there had been some changes in the religious character of Bowdoin that affected the decision about which university to choose.

Even though Bowdoin College was officially non-denominational, there were ongoing quarrels on the Board about the college's religious leaning. The balance of power shifted back and forth between the Congregationalists, who were mainly from the inland areas of Maine, and the Unitarians and Episcopalians, who resided primarily along the coastal area where the Longfellows lived. Many members of the early governing boards of Bowdoin were religious liberals, but, in the 1820s the more conservative Congregationalists began to take control of Bowdoin away from the liberal Unitarians and Episcopalian Board members. In addition, the religious changes were accompanied by outside changes toward a more conservative political viewpoint. After being under state control for a period, the college returned to private control, however, it lost its state subsidies. In effect, Bowdoin had become a secular institution with Congregationalist financial support and leanings.

On the other hand, Harvard's religious history demonstrated a movement in the liberal direction away from its Calvinist Origins through Congregationalism and finally became a majority Unitarian. In 1805, the Unitarian Dr. Henry Ware was appointed to fill the Hollis Divinity chair at Harvard. The Congregationalists at the University were unhappy with the decision, resigned their positions and founded Andover Theological Seminary. With these changes in the religious character of Bowdoin and Harvard, the result was that Harvard was much more in keeping with the religious convictions of the Longfellow family.

Another possible reason for Samuel's family agreeing to his move to a university so far from home was because his brother Henry would also be living in Cambridge. Henry had started teaching at Bowdoin in 1832 and after three years began to feel the need to extend himself beyond the possibilities available at a small, rural university. Added to this were the aforementioned religious, financial and political problems that affected Bowdoin.

In late 1834 the position of Professor of Modern Languages at Harvard became available and Henry Wadsworth Longfellow was nominated for the position, which he accepted. However, before he took up residence in Cambridge and began teaching, Harvard allowed him a trip to Europe to study some of the languages he would be teaching.

In April 1835, Henry and his wife Mary Potter Longfellow, whom he had married in 1831, and two of her friends, Mary Goddard and Clara Crowninshield, set sail for Europe. Mary announced that she was pregnant while they were in Stockholm in the summer. Unfortunately, she had a miscarriage when they were in Amsterdam in October and was greatly weakened from loss of blood. In Rotterdam her condition worsened and she died in late November 1835. Henry shipped his wife's body back to America, and despite his grief he continued his trip accompanied around Europe by Clara Crowninshield.

In the Swiss Alps Henry and Clara met the Appletons, another Boston family. Among the family members he met was Frances Appleton who would eventually become his second wife. However, it would take several years of a practically one-sided pursuit by Henry before she would agree to marriage. Henry's European trip came to an end in the latter part of 1836 and he returned to the U.S. and "established himself in Cambridge."[15]

At long last Samuel once again had a family member close at hand. In addition to having the friendship of a brother, he would come to know the people who made up the milieu in which Henry worked and socialized. Some of the people Samuel met through Henry would become important in his own life in the future.

During his four years as a Harvard undergraduate, Samuel had only a few intimate friends with whom he exchanged "visits" and debated the issues of the day. Nevertheless, among his schoolmates Samuel "was well-known, never recluse or unsocial, and took a hearty interest in all college affairs."[16] As his friend Nichols, son of his Portland Pastor, said, "I can only recollect that my regard and affection for him were daily increased by this closest contact which one young man has with another."[17] Some of his closest friends are described in the following paragraphs.

A lifelong friend was Edward Everett Hale. In a small book published in 1892, Edward describes how close their relationship was from their time at Harvard continuing till the later years of life.

> Mr. Samuel Longfellow... was my daily companion and friend from the time when I was thirteen, for many of the earlier years of life. And when, in after years, we were personally parted more, the old tie was never sundered, and with half the world between us, we loved each other as we always shall.[18]

Edward Everett Hale was grand-nephew of the Revolutionary period hero Nathan Hale and became a Unitarian minister and author. He was an abolitionist before the Civil War and in 1909 became U.S. Senate Chaplain. He is best-known today for his story *The Man Without a Country* (1863)

Another close friend of Samuel's, Thomas Wentworth Higginson, was two years behind him at Harvard. However, because of Samuel's year in the Azores, they ended up in the same graduating class at Divinity School. Higginson was a radical theologian and participated in the social reform movements in the mid-19th century. His major roles were as secretary of the Massachusetts Temperance Society, as a member of the Woman's movement arguing for the rights of women and as an abolitionist leading organized resistance to the Fugitive Slave Law, during which he was involved in violent actions. In the literary field he was the first to publish the work of Emily Dickinson.

When the Civil War started, Higginson carried through with is abolitionist position and became a Colonel in the Union Army. In 1862 he became commander of the 1st South Carolina Volunteers, the first regiment of African Americans, which was made up of freed slaves. This was a year before the better-known Massachusetts regiments were formed. Higginson's regiment was later named the Thirty-third U.S. Colored Troops.

Another of Samuel's good friends, and an acknowledged poet, was James Russell Lowell who was born the same year as Samuel. In addition, he was a friend of Samuel's brother Henry and was a regular member of the Dante Club that formed around Henry while he was translating *The Divine Comedy*. His own contribution to literature is his poem *The Vision of Sir Launfal*, which is a retelling of the Grail legend with a democratic viewpoint.

As with many of Samuel's friends, Lowell was involved in the abolitionist movement. Despite Lowell's small involvement in the political arena, President Hays appointed him Resident Minister to Spain in 1876, perhaps because he spoke Spanish and was well-versed in Spanish literature. In 1880 he was appointed American Minister to Great Britain, a position he held until 1885. An official function he performed in Britain was being present when Henry Wadsworth Longfellow's bust was unveiled in Westminster Abbey, something he surely felt was a personal honor. Lowell was paid respect by several European universities, and when he returned to America he received recognition from Harvard. Back home he began to work on his poetry, which was published in 10 volumes in 1890.

Unfortunately, not all of Samuel's relationships with his classmates were positive. He gives an example in his journal from the years he was at Harvard.

As I was going down for some water, saw Pope helping himself to Williams's coal which is in the entry. It seems he makes a practice of doing this. They don't like him at all – hardly any body does here. He is the greatest egotist extant & we have given him the cognomen of "the great Gustavus"! or more shortly, the great Gus.[19]

Samuel describes another incident that shows how silly roommates can get when they have different ways of doing things.

Took a short walk with Hayes before dinner & called in to see Williams. – Hale came up, in the aft, to get his French with me. I like to read it with him, but was rather sorry that he came, as it disturbs Hayes to have us read aloud. But what could I do? So we sat down to Moliere which we began last Wednesday. Whereupon Hayes shut up the book he was writing in & began to read aloud but finding that this did not disturb us he came up & putting himself between us read on and bawled at the top of his voice so as almost to prevent our going on with the lesson; but we were determined not to let him interrupt us & we read on till recitation time taking scarce notice of him; he all the while trying to disturb & vex us by all sorts of mean tricks – It was a scene of rudeness which perhaps I should have done better not to have attended to here; very likely it was done in fun, but even then it showed an utter want of propriety & consideration, which I have often observed in H. in similar cases.[20]

Samuel also had exceptionally close relationships during his life. As an undergraduate he had a relationship with a student who was in the same year about whom he says little. This friend was William Drew Winter, but Samuel does not describe how they met nor the times they were together, and apparently they did not see each other often. However, sometimes when he was working he

...fell into a most sentimental reverie about W.W. The scenes of last spring came back to me with sadness – in short

I mused myself into a most romantic melancholy. I have thought a good deal about him of late in my musings – and sometimes feel as if I should go crazy when I think of last year. I don't think I ever made a greater sacrifice of inclination to a sense of duty – but it was not a hearty one – I was reluctant then; I have been sorry at times ever since. It was a strange infatuation. And yet after all my fears might we not have been happy together – I loved him & think he liked me – He had a good heart – might I not have exerted a favorable influence upon him? But I was afraid the influence might be the other way. I have got along very well with my chum; but, in fact I began almost with a determination but to like him. It may seem strange that with such feelings I should take him for a chum; but the choice between *[illegible]* & him; the first I didn't feel enough acquainted with; W. I was advised not to take as a chum. I thought I could see him a good deal if I did not room with him. But he has not been to see me this year, but once. – After all I don't know but this affair is one of imagination and sentiment more than reality. I have weaved around him a web of Fancy and – Enough of that.[21]

Samuel describes a meeting with Willie that took place in church in 1838

Willie Winter came in & staid awhile. For whom my passion is revived. I sit next to him at table & look into those eyes of his full of fun.[22]

The relationship between Samuel Longfellow and William Winter was probably over by 1850 when Samuel became pastor at the Unitarian Church in Brooklyn. Winter went on to become a lawyer and met Sarah Stirling when he was working as a lawyer in St. Louis. They got married at her family's plantation named Myrtles in Mississippi in 1852.

A few years later William Winter was involved in an unusual incident that ended up in his death. At this time he and Sarah were the parents of six children and living on plantations near her family. He had spent the Civil War in Mississippi and in 1865 his wife's mother, who was a widow, was having problems managing her properties and hired Winter to act as her attorney and agent and turned Myrtles over to them. After the war they had financial problems, went bankrupt and had to sell the property in 1867. Two years later Winter's wife, as her father's heir, was able to repurchase the property. How they lost their money and then regain their fortune is unknown. On January 26, 1871, Winter was teaching a Sunday School lesson at the Myrtles and heard a horseman approach. The rider called him to come out because he had business with him. When Winter went outside he was shot and died on his porch. A suspect was arrested, but there is no record of what the outcome was. Today the Myrtles is a Bed & Breakfast Inn and considered "one of America's most haunted sites" with one of the ghosts alleged to be William Drew Winter.

Relationships such as this between Samuel Longfellow and William Winter were not exceptional during this period in Boston. It also was not the only such relationship of this type that Samuel would have in his life, the best known being that with Samuel Johnson after they met in Divinity School. Among the numerous intimate male relationships in Boston, there were some worth noting among Samuel's friends, which are discussed in more detail in the book *Improper Bostonians.*

Ralph Waldo Emerson, in considering man and God, developed the idea of a Platonic love that was used by others to justify a strong emotional involvement. As a college senior, Emerson himself was attracted to freshman Martin Gay, a relationship that lasted about two years. Following along similar relationship lines were Herman Melville and Nathaniel Hawthorne, although Hawthorne rejected Melville early on, and also Leverett Saltonstall and Charles Dabney, Jr., both in the Harvard class of 1844. Samuel may not have been aware of this last relationship because he was in the Azores as tutor to Charles Dabney's younger brothers and sisters (see Chapter 6).

As discussed in *Improper Bostonians,* it was not uncommon for men to write letters to each other as if they were writing to someone of the opposite sex, however, same-sex intimate relationships among women were more widespread than among men.

In fact two women living together was called a "Boston Marriage". Two reasons have been conjectured for fewer affectionate relationships among men. One is that self-discipline was an important aspect of masculinity, thereby limiting how close men were allowed to get. The other was than an intimate relationship was seen as unnatural and could lead to sodomy, an act that the early colonists punished by death. To avoid accusations of indecency, the concept of "special friendships" was created. Although expressions of affection between men were acceptable, any hint of physical intimacy was evaded. As a result of the care taken in writing letters, journal entries or poetry, exactly what was involved in the relationship between two men falls mainly in the area of speculation.

Samuel was a good student at Harvard and his study habits "though not highly methodical were diligent and attentive and gave him both good standing in his class and the repute of ability and promise."[23] Among the subjects he studied were the Classics, English literature and history, mathematics, mechanics and French. In addition, he began to study German, which he enjoyed and in which he did so well he was able to substitute for the instructor when he was absent from class. Harvard still required attendance at chapel, but Samuel did not pay a great deal of attention as he shows in his journal for Sunday, September 25, 1836, "After church this morning (where I was sleeping as usual & did not hear the sermon at all – Dr. Ware is dull and soporific, there is no doubt of it) After church I say, to get an appetite for dinner & enjoy the fine air I walked with Kebler – the little German – who has of late been quite frequently my companion."[24] His friend Kebler was born in Germany and later became a prominent lawyer in Cincinnati, Ohio.

One subject that had interested Samuel since his childhood in Portland, and through which he never slept, was natural science. His love of plants led him into botany. Throughout his life many of his letters to his sister Anne contained discussions of plants, especially when he was in the Azores, and he often took clippings and bulbs for the gardens at Craigie House and in Portland and was an early member of the Natural History Society in Cambridge.

In writing about his early life in 1892, Edward Everett Hale talks about Samuel's scientific interest in botany.

> Our tastes were similar, and the close intimacy which then began has continued through life. Longfellow and I were both fond of flowers, and Cambridge was still good botanizing ground.[25]

Samuel also had a great interest in astronomy and he and seven of his friends created a natural sciences study group they called "The Octagon". They prepared papers to be read at their meetings, studied the skies from the Harvard Observatory, and they watched meteors streak across the sky and admired the beauty of the Northern Lights from the tops of their houses.

He was anxious that he not miss anything of interest, as he indicates by a letter to Edward Everett Hale in which he asked about an aurora The Octagon had observed, but which he had happened to sleep through. In the same letter he also discussed what he considered to be a reasonable hypothesis that sea-serpents were reptiles that had survived from primordial times.[26]

Sometimes Samuel's inquisitive character took him to the leading edge of discovery in science. In 1839 Sir John Herschel coined the word "photography," in which Samuel took a particular interest, "it being the subject, which now appears to occupy the attention of the scientific world."[27] In January 1839 Daguerre announced the photographic invention, still associated with his name, to the world, but kept the details secret. He later sold his completed process to the French government.

On January 31, 1839 William Henry Fox Talbot, a British researcher in photography, read his paper entitled "An Account of the Art of Photogenic Drawing or the process by which natural objects may be made to delineate themselves without the aid of the artist's pencil" to the Royal society. Unlike Daguerre's announcement, his paper gave details of the process, which was called Talbotype and later Calotype (kalos meaning beautiful in Greek). As a result, this process, which was also less expensive than the Daguerrotype, was the first attempted in New England.

Samuel along with Edward Everett Hale started working on the Calotype process very shortly after it had been presented by Talbot and may have been the first in New England to try the process. The Calotype process requires a "photogenic mixture," or silver nitrate, with which the two had been experimenting. One day Samuel visited his friend Alexander Washburn in Divinity Hall to get some "photogenic mixture."

> Staid there some time eating crackers& talking about various matters in the usual desultory way – that is a pleasant room of his by the by – & then came home and photogenised, working away in my darkened closet with nitrate & salt-&-water till dinner. Having dispatched that I tried some of the prepared paper which produced a very good man's-hand-with-a-belt-in-it upon a chocolate ground, which I pride myself upon as being the first distinct picture we have accomplished.[28]

Edward Everett Hale describes a more sophisticated experiment he and Samuel performed during the same period.

> Mr. Samuel Longfellow ...and I were intimate friends in Massachusetts Hall in Cambridge. We ...followed Talbot's directions as closely as possible. With these directions, and with an artist's camera, which I have still, I took a picture of the windows opposite, in Harvard Hall. In especial, there was a bust of Apollo in the window, which came out very well, black on white ground, the bust being itself white on the black of the room beyond. I thought at the time, and I think now, that this was the first experiment in a Talbotype, which was made in this country.[29]

It wasn't until 1840 that Talbot discovered how to convert his negative images to positive images. The negative images produced by the two friends were unfortunately lost over the years and there is no indication that they continued their experiments much beyond these first attempts at the new process of photography.

Some of Samuel's friends took classes his brother Henry taught as professor of Modern Languages. Hale took a German class with Henry Wadsworth Longfellow on which he remarked in his *Atlantic Monthly* article "A New England Boyhood":

> He [Henry] made a long introduction to the matter at hand, very flowery and bombastical indeed, which appeared to me very much out of taste. I believe, however, that it was entirely extemporaneous and that he was carried away by the current of his thoughts. In fact he appears to say just what comes uppermost. The regular translation and explanation part of the lecture was very good.[30]

Thomas Wentworth Higginson also had a class with Henry. He commented on Henry's class in his book *Old Cambridge* (1899):

> I had the good fortune to study French under him... His lectures which were to us most interesting, were sometimes criticized as too flowery by our elders, who had perhaps been accustomed to gather only dried fruit; and I remember how he fixed in our memories the vivid moral of any French books that happened to be provided with that appendage...[31]

His classmates considered Samuel the best writer in the class. One of his classmates said, "What he did not know about belles-lettres seemed to us not worth knowing."[30] He often included poems in letters and in his journal, however they were collected after his death in the collection *Hymns and Verses*, but he never achieved the reputation for his poetry that his brother did. Nevertheless he was recognized for his poetic skills among his peers and his friend Thomas Wentworth Higginson said of him that "he was also a genuine poet, like his elder brother."[31] Because of his writing skills, he was often asked to provide verses and songs for meetings of various campus groups or general university festivities or ceremonies.

Edward Everett Hale describes Samuel's writing in an article published in the year Samuel died and also describes the reaction to Samuel's writing by writer and Harvard professor Edward Channing, the son of William Ellery Channing.

> He was perhaps too delicate and self-critical with regard to the work of his light and easy pen. I have always wondered why he was not a more frequent writer for the periodical press, his touch was so delicate and his view of all passing life so sympathetic and imaginative. I fancy he wrote a good deal which he never read to anybody, and which never saw the light. This is sure: that a life so unselfish, so generous, so wide in its range, and so delicate in its observation, has been of inestimable value to thousands of other lives.[32]

> He was a favorite of Edward Channing, – and well he might be, – his themes always receiving the highest mark of that sympathetic and appreciative critic.[33]

Having become acquainted with Henry Longfellow as a professor, Hale stated that

> in our own joking talk with each other we always called him [Henry] "the brother of the poet." For we recognized our Sam Longfellow as the member of all our number, whose reading, whose imagination and fancy, and whose delicate appreciation of Nature in all her best work made him our poet; and we knew he would be a poet through his life.[34]

Even though Samuel Longfellow was respected for his writing ability, he did not consider his skill at public speaking very good.

> When therefore my turn came I rose having hardly an idea in my noddle about the matter. I spoke on however, scarce knowing what I said. My voice trembled much of which I was quite ashamed as all the others spoke with so much confidence & ease, but I could not help it. I found however that words, & perhaps thoughts came, much easier than I had expected. I spoke but once that even tho' the debate became animated. I tho't I was on the wrong side.[35]

Despite being disturbed by his problem speaking in public, Samuel was aware that he only needed to work on it. After one of the meetings of the "Institute," where Samuel and his school-mates debated a variety of issues that were assigned to each one by the group, he remarked on his presentation.

> In fact tho' I said quite a deal – it was rather poor I know. But I dare say, after some practice I shall be able to speak decently.[36]

Considering the comments by his contemporaries about his skill in speaking in the pulpit in later years, he certainly demonstrated that he was most successful in resolving any problem he had speaking in public.

Samuel was also an active participant in certain of the important campus organizations. Among these was Alpha Delta Phi, the first Greek-letter fraternity at Harvard, which was established there in 1837 as an adjunct of the Yale society. It focused on intellectual and literary activities, but also had a social side. The society was reportedly disbanded in 1861, but activities continued under a new organization called the A.D. Club, which still exists today.[37]

> He was an early member of Alpha Delta Phi, which means that he was one of the group of men specially interested in literature. He read everything and remembered everything that was worth reading.[38]

Samuel was also a member, and secretary, of the Hasty Pudding Club, which had "patriotic and friendship" aims, as well as its well-known dramatic presentations. Another fraternity he belonged to was Phi Beta Kappa, which focused on philosophical and political questions. However, Samuel was not a supporter of most university groups with their secrets and symbolic proceedings.

> The idea of invisible bonds and secret leagues, and swearing eternal friendship to hundreds of people one has never seen,

is better suited to chivalric times than to these days of ours when everybody chooses to go on his own hook.[39]

Samuel Longfellow completed four "happy and useful years" at Harvard and graduated in 1839, 8th in a class of 61. In his later correspondence he indicates that, "it was a formative period, of earnest thought and feeling and real growth." [*Memoir*, p 13] Joseph May adds to this in saying, "But the maturing of his mind was to be the work of a period still a few years in advance."[40]

Notes:

[1] May, Joseph, Ed.. *Samuel Longfellow: Memoir and Letters.* Cambridge: The Riverside Press, 1894. p. 5.

[2] Longfellow, Samuel, Ed. *Henry Wadsworth Longfellow, Vol. I.*, 1886. p. 16.

[3] May, Joseph, *Memoir.* p. 5.

[4] Ibid.

[5] Longfellow, Samuel, Ed. *Henry Wadsworth Longfellow, Vol. I.*, 1886. p. 24-25.

[6] Longfellow, Samuel, "The Old Portland Academy: Longfellow's 'Fitting School'." *New England Quarterly*, p. 248.

[7] Ibid., p. 249.

[8] Ibid., p. 249-250.

[9] Letter, Samuel Longfellow to Stephen Longfellow (father), January 8, 1835., SLP, LNHS.

[10] May, Joseph, *Memoir.* p. 6.

[11] Ibid., p. 7.

[12] Longfellow, Samuel. *Samuel Longfellow, Journal January 1, 1833 to March 26,* 1833. No publisher.

[13] May, Joseph, *Memoir.* p. 9.

[14] Ibid., p .10.

[15] Longfellow, Samuel, *Henry Wadsworth Longfellow, v 1*, p. 200-242.

[16] May, Joseph, *Memoir.* p. 10.

[17] Ibid.

[18] Hale, Edward Everett, *Five Prophets of Today*, p. 12.

[19] Longfellow, Samuel. *Journal, September 24, 1836 to May 30, 1839*, p. 11.

[20] Ibid., February 23, 1837.

[21] Ibid., Feb. 24, 1837.

[22] Ibid., Jan. 28, 1838.

[23] May, Joseph, *Memoir.* p. 12.

[24] Longfellow, Samuel. *Journal, September 24, 1836 to May 30, 1839*, Nov. 4, 1836.

[25] Hale, Edward Everett, Jr. *The Life and Letters of Edward Everett Hale, Vol. II.* Boston: Little, Brown, and Company, 1917. p. 17.]

[26] May, Joseph, *Memoir.* p. 13.

[27] Longfellow, Samuel. *Journal, September 24, 1836 to May 30, 1839,* May 30, 1839.

[28] Ibid.

[29] Robinson, William F. *A Certain Slant of Light: The first hundred years of New England photography.* Boston: New York Graphic Society, 1980. p. 4.

[30] May, Joseph, *Memoir.* p. 12.

[31] Higginson, Thomas Wentworth. *Cheerful Yesterdays.* Boston: Houghton, Mifflin and Company, 1898. p. 38.

[32] Hale, Edward Everett. "Samuel Longfellow." *Commonwealth Weekly.* October 8, 1892. Boston. p. 508.

[33] Ibid., p. 507.

[34] Ibid., p. 508.

[35] Longfellow, Samuel. *Journal, September 24, 1836 to May 30, 1839,* Nov. 8.

[36] Ibid., p. 38.

[37] Betinck-Smith, William, Ed. *The Harvard Book, Selections from Three Centuries, Revised Edition.* Cambridge: Harvard University Press, 1982. p. 389-91.

[38] Hale, Edward Everett. "Samuel Longfellow." *Commonwealth Weekly.* p. 507.

[39] May, Joseph, *Memoir.* p. 12-13.

[40] Ibid., p. 13.

CHAPTER 4 – T IS FOR TUTOR

After Samuel Longfellow graduated from Harvard in the summer of 1839, his first job emerged more from his lack of making a choice of a particular direction rather than committing to a plan to follow in his life. The idea of continuing on to Divinity School had not become a definite idea to follow, and may not have even seriously entered his mind yet judging from the lack of its mention in either his letters or journal entries.

In April 1839 Samuel was debating about whether to find some work in Cambridge or to see what was available elsewhere. One of the activities he took up during this period, aside from reading, was architectural design.

> I made to-day a very nice plan for a "cottage of gentility." I should like one of these days to see some of my numerous 'fancies' in something more substantive than ink & paper. But I don't think I should care to live in them – not because they wouldn't be convenient & elegant above most others – but all the pleasure would be in the contriving. The rest would be but hare-soup after the hunt was over – to borrow an illustration from Scott.[1]

Samuel never spoke much about his architectural interests, but he designed at least one house in Plymouth that a friend he visited lived in. He also put architectural drawings of buildings and other types of structures in some of his letters. In addition, some of the letters he received from others have architectural doodling in the margins or on the back.

He could not find work in Cambridge and was leaning toward looking for something outside of the Cambridge area, despite the regret he would feel in leaving Cambridge and his friends. As he told his father in a letter in June 1839,

We have but little more to do, however, the term closes in four weeks; & now that I have written my last theme, read my last forensic & performed my last declaration. I feel as if there were little left. And in truth now that the times of leaving approaches, I feel somewhat impatient to get free. It will certainly be painful to part with some of the friends with whom I have formed intimacies here, & I am attached to the place itself & to the quiet & pleasant life of a student. Yet after four years one gets a little restless under the restraint of hours & bells.[2]

Even before graduating, Samuel was considering a job as a tutor at a school at Roxbury in the Boston area. As tutor he would "teach a little of everything – Greek, Latin, Mathematics, French and to take charge of the school when the headman is absent. Then besides five hours in the day, he is occupied an hour in the evening in school so that he had but little leisure for reading."[3] In the end, he did not get the position because they needed him to be there before the end of the term and he did not think it proper to leave college before graduation. Samuel also did not get a private tutoring position he thought he had, or positions in Burlington and Tuscaloosa, which Henry had made contact about.

In the letter to his father about the job at Roxbury, he also described other possibilities he was considering.

Mr. Wheeler recommends to me to stay in Cambridge as a resident graduate & says that I could get private students here. I should prefer this plan on some accounts. I should have more time for reading which is one of my principal objects; & have the advantages of the Library. But on the other hand I should rather leave Cambridge for a while & see some other side of the world than the groves of Academy. What do you think of a private tutorship in a family? Such things are not very difficult to get at the South.[4]

In the fall of 1839, Samuel applied for a job as a teacher in a home school belonging to a "Southern gentleman" at Rockburn in Elk Ridge, Maryland about ten miles southwest of Baltimore. However, he was not completely confident about getting the job.

> I count as confidently upon going to Balto., I behave as if the matter were all settled. Hope no danger at least no extinguisher will come tomorrow morning.[5]

However, a week later he was still looking for news and had started thinking about options in the event that the offer fell through.

> No letter from Baltimore this morning which disappointed me. Hope they won't "bake a scunner" to me. I don't think though, that I should feel very bad if they did. The result of the Burlington business rather gave me a disgust to the whole matter of pedagogy – & as that was so nice a situation others seem not very attractive in comparison. Up on the whole, though I shan't be more occupied in point of time with these fifteen than with those two – & these will I dare say prove more tractable. Uncle says the Murrays are a fine family – which is rather more than the Bishop Doanes had the credit of being. Still I had formed so many air-castles at Burlington that the result has rather destroyed my spirit & interest in the business.[6]

In keeping with his lack of assurance, he states in his journal that, "Meanwhile I hold on to the Augusta affair." He hung on to this job offer in case the Elk Ridge job fell through at the last moment or he changed his mind after arriving. Though he does not clarify what "the Augusta affair" was, it is probable that it was a tutor's job in the St. Mary's Hall School at St. Mary's church where William Doane was Bishop in the Augusta – Burlington area of New Jersey, between Trenton and Philadelphia. Samuel talks about this in a later letter in which he mentions passing it on his way south. The Doanes were Boston relatives of the Longfellow family and Bishop Doane later was involved in the founding of Columbia University. Despite his concerns, Samuel finally received confirmation of the job with the Murrays at Rockburn in Maryland.

Just before Samuel left Cambridge for Maryland, he wrote a letter to his friend Edward Everett Hale in which he said, "I'm off, as the inhabitant of the mysterious mustard pot said, on my way to Elk Ridge, Maryland, to take charge of a dozen or so boys and live in the family of Mr. Daniel Murray."[7] The "mustard pot" was a reference to a whimsical short story with an unexpected ending, published in the first edition of the "New-England Journal" (1831). To some extent, the story was indicative of his unexpected move to the south to be a tutor as a resolution to his search for work. Going to Elk Ridge was also a move away from a northern metropolis with its easy access to culture to a rural southern setting isolated from his family, friends and the opportunity to indulge in his usual intellectual pastimes.

After his trip south, during which he stopped in New York where Samuel "walked three or four times nearly the whole extent" of what he called "the Babylon." In addition he made stops in Philadelphia and Washington, D.C. In Washington Samuel visited his Uncle Commodore Alexander Scammel Wadsworth. The Commodore served in the Navy for more than 40 years and was on the *USS Constitution* during the War of 1812, receiving a medal for his action on the ship. At the time Samuel was at Elk Ridge the Commodore was Inspector of Ordinance in Washington.

After visiting his Uncle "who has been very kind," he went on to Elk Ridge and his new teaching position.

> I met Mr. Murray just as I turned into the road leading to the House & he led me as I thought a tremendously long way through the woods. The house is very pleasantly situated & the people very pleasant too & I feel quite at home already. Mrs. M. received me very cordially & I found that I was in very good season as the pupils do not assemble till the day after tomorrow. Tomorrow he invites me to go to Balt°. with him.[8]

The school was a two-story, brick farmhouse near a brook that ran through a glen giving the house its name, Rockburn. The boys' schoolroom was in the basement, but it was "a sunny room and if it had a little higher ceiling & were not heated by the stove would be as pleasant as one ought wish." The girls were taught in the adjacent room, also in the basement. The room Samuel lived in was on the ground floor "just back of the front entry & over my school room." It had previously been the dining room, but it was furnished well enough for him to do his school work, as well as his own personal reading.

His class consisted of 12 boys, mainly from Maryland, although the class was later increased by four more students, all of them between the ages of nine and fifteen. Of the original twelve students, eleven were "all related to each other & one of them is uncle to half the rest. He is the son, by the way, of the author of 'The Star Spangled Banner,' Mr. Somebody Key of W[ashington, Georgetown]." This, of course, was Francis Scott Key, who was 60-years old at this time, who apparently was not yet well known. Samuel found his students to be "mostly bright boys & all of good dispositions i.e. amiable, but some of them are dreadfully backward in their studies."9

Samuel's schedule required him to teach "Latin, Geography & Arithmetic, beginning French" plus other subjects as necessary eight hours a day, but his "main difficulty [was] to keep them still." Throughout his life Samuel was known for being sensitive to the feelings and needs of boys and told his mother, "I can hardly find it in my heart to blame remembering the difficulty I used to have on that score when I was a schoolboy myself."10

Samuel spent a year at Elk Ridge, and his stay turned out to be more pleasant than he had anticipated. Although Samuel did not write in his journal during the entire year he was at Rockburn, he did maintain correspondence with his family and friends. In a letter to his father, he mentions that he had

> ...found the country pleasanter than I expected. Indeed the time has passed very quickly, as it always does when one is constantly employed. And I do not think I could have found in the city so pleasant a family as this. I do not think rural simplicity altogether a fiction. In town there must always be ceremony and etiquette and where these are there must follow if not deception at least concealment of feeling and loss of naturalness and truthfulness.11

Mr. Murray was pleased with Samuel's work and asked him to return to Elk Ridge after the summer and teach the following year. However, what attracted him to the school and its situation were outweighed by the combination of things that he did not like about Elk Ridge plus the family, friends and activities he missed in Massachusetts and Maine.

> I believe that I wrote you that Mr. M. is desirous that I should stay another year. Of course I shall not think of making any engagement as yet. Indeed, I do not think I shall be willing to stay longer than this year – at least I had not expectation of doing so when I came. I do not like being in the same house with the boys all the time. I do not think it is much advantage to either party, but rather the reverse. Then I should prefer either teaching a much smaller number or confining myself to some single branch. As I have no room to myself – which College life rendered quite necessary for study – I have not been able to pursue my own studies as I had hoped – besides the little leisure I have comes when I feel quite wearied with schoolroom duties – which I am rather too nervous to bear well. Nevertheless, in a different season I may find things changed. I know I shall be sorry to leave the place & shall not like to give up my boys to any body else.[12]

Even though he was looking forward to returning north, Samuel's plans for what to do when he arrived home were still as nebulous as before he took the Elk Ridge job. It seems that he returned to Cambridge in late spring for a short period and then returned south. During this short stay Cambridge did not live up to his memories of it, and in a letter on his way back south to Edward Everett Hale he describes his reactions on returning.

> Cambridge – shall I say it? – did not, after all, appear to me quite the paradise I had fancied. I did not feel quite so glad to get back as I had thought I should do. Ever since I left, I had looked forward with some hope of returning there for a year or perhaps more. It was the height of my ambition, when in

college, to remain as a resident-graduate, and avail myself of the opportunities there so fully offered, of pursuing further and more thoroughly such general studies as my inclination prompted. The reason why the place appeared less charming is no doubt obvious enough. Class feelings and college feelings form so essential a part of the college student's life and are so woven into all its pleasures that a return under different circumstances could not but give things quite a changed aspect. Nevertheless, as I was asked to come back and take three or four little shavers to teach, I think, if I can arrange matters to suit at C., I shall say good-by to dear Mr. Murray next fall.[13]

Samuel returned to Cambridge and wrote a letter to his father describing the ideas he was considering for his life there. A number of these ideas were about the same as he had written to his father over a year before, and had probably become more prominent in his mind during the year at Elk Ridge because of his reflections on his undergraduate experience at Harvard. However, he still made no mention of the possibility of entering the Divinity School.

You ask why I should not take ten or twelve boys at Cambridge? Because I do not wish to have a school. My main object is to avail myself of the literary opportunities of Cambridge – its library & lectures in the production of my studies. I could not but feel when I had finished my college course, how far from complete it had been in some departments. This must necessarily be the case from the variety of studies & comparatively limited time. Our colleges indeed do not pretend to make finished scholars, but only to lay the foundation. This is but one development of our national character. Our people are in so much haste – young men in general press forward so eagerly into life that they cannot spare time for making themselves thorough scholars. That must not be thought of, or must be left for the leisure hours which after life may afford. In the situation which I selected for myself this year I had hoped to do a good deal toward this, but have been disappointed as to time & opportunity – and this is the reason why I wish to make teaching at Cambridge a subsidiary thing.[14]

Samuel was willing to take the risk of making his living with a small number of students whom he would teach in his room in Cambridge. However, he thought he would have to limit the number of students or he would need an additional room. He also believed that even an increase beyond just a small number of students, though not requiring more teaching hours, "would materially increase the trouble and vexation of spirit" and affect his health.

He anticipated his father's reaction to this proposal, and at the end of his letter cited above he adds "I think I shall take the risk of finding something to do at Cambridge – or perhaps I should take a seat in your office for the winter."[15] Doubtless, his father knew the last comment was an empty "threat", and that it was Samuel's way of emphasizing that he was going to stay in Cambridge at all costs.

Samuel's brother Henry was agreeable to helping him if he returned to Cambridge and went as far as arranging for students. This was the type of work that Samuel wanted and also seemed to allow him to follow his other plans.

Letters from home tell me that you have been making some arrangements for me at Cambridge in the way of pupils. Many write that you have engaged the three sons of Mrs. Otis, but farther than this professes ignorance, & though it is very satisfactory as far as it goes, I, of course should like to get all the additional information, which you as fountain head in the matter may be able to furnish. You have as I understand already made the engagement, which I am glad of as I had resolved to come to Cambridge the next year at any rate & try my fortune, with or without any other visible means of support than those obtained by my labors here – which will leave me about 300 dollars – still it will be pleasant little fund untouched. Besides I am convinced that I should accomplish as much in my studies & be rather more industrious, were a part of my time regularly occupied in some other employment not too engrossing or fatiguing. So that the arrangements you have made suit me exactly so far.[16]

Samuel's plans changed and instead of returning to Cambridge in the fall after his year at the Murray School had ended, Samuel left and took a trip farther south. This time he was headed to Charlottesville, Virginia, to visit the University of Virginia about a tutoring position in modern languages. He describes this opportunity in a letter to his father.

> You will doubtless already have heard from Cambridge of a new plan that has offered itself to me for the next year – if not longer. I am now on my way to Charlottesville to make enquires in regard to an appointment or appointments which are about to be made in the University of Virginia in the department of Modern Languages. A professor is to be appointed next July meanwhile one or more Tutors. If a suitable person applies competent to teach the French, Spanish & German none other will be appointed & he will receive the full professor's salary, 1000 dollars, besides fees from the students, about 5 or 600 more. Unfortunately my knowledge of Spanish is very limited, although with my present acquaintance with it & the other languages I could soon master it. This probably would not suit their views. With the other languages I am sufficiently well acquainted & they might be willing to substitute Italian for Spanish. These things however I shall enquire into.
>
> I hardly like to give up my plan of residence at Cambridge the next year, but this situation is too eligible to be neglected.[17]

On his way to Charlottesville he stopped in Washington and got a letter of introduction from his uncle. Nevertheless, he was pessimistic about getting the job despite the letter of introduction to Mr. Bonny Castle, a Mathematics professor at the University. He spoke with the professor, who "shook his head very solemnly & slowly"[18] when Samuel said he couldn't speak the languages the professor asked about. The professor repeated the action when Samuel revealed his age. Nevertheless, in the end the Professor invited Samuel for dinner and wrote him a letter of introduction to Professor Davis, the Chairman of the Department.

Contrary to the mathematics Professor's reaction, the Chairman told him he thought that speaking a foreign language wasn't necessary in order to teach it. Samuel describes his language abilities to his brother Henry and expresses some doubt about getting the position.

> In the French, German & Italian I am well versed & should consider myself perfectly competent to teach, & lecture if required. But unfortunately, I have studied the Spanish but little & though I am acquainted with the pronunciation, I cannot translate it with any ease. No doubt with my present knowledge of it & the other languages I could soon make myself familiar with it; but they would have a right to expect more than this; at any rate would find it in others.[19]

Unlike the Mathematics teacher, the Chairman did not believe that Samuel's age was a problem given the characteristics of the University. However, the Chairman gave him the idea that there were other candidates who were more likely to be offered the job. Despite not getting the position, he had a pleasant trip and finally "bid adieu to the South with a tear in my eye."[20]

On his way north he stopped off in Washington for a week. His Aunt and Uncle wanted him to return and spend the winter with them, which he didn't. Continuing his trip he made a stop in Elkridge to "bid adieu to the South with a tear in my eye." Some time after he left he received a letter from one of his ex--students, Francis Key Howard who described what was going on in Rockburn and went into some detail about their debating club and what some of the students were dong.

In his memoir of Samuel, Joseph May states, "It is strange that no reference to slavery occurs in his letters which remain from his visit to the south, yet it would hardly seem possible that he was not in contact with it." [*Memoir*, p. 14.]. However, Samuel was not a person who pushed his ideas and opinions on others, and would be less likely to talk about controversial issues with people he did not know well. He also considered it not wise to confront the people he had to work and live with for an entire year with the potential of making his stay difficult. It is also a possibility that the Murrays were also against slavery and did not express their beliefs to outsiders, which Samuel probably would have known.

Always observant of what was going on around him, he was sure to have been aware "of [slavery's] evils and shames." On his return to the north he would be able to recall the reality of slavery when he went to hear the Abolitionist speakers and talk with his anti-slavery friends. Joseph May stated that "his deep abhorrence and profound opposition"[21] to slavery would become very strong in the years to come.

There was another possible reason for Samuel's lack of response to the slavery in Maryland. In the years immediately after Samuel Longfellow graduated from Harvard, he still had not developed strong opinions on the ideas that were to become important to him in later years. This is borne out in an article on Samuel Longfellow written by Oscar Fay Adams for *The New England Magazine* in 1894, just over fifty years after Samuel's stay in Elk Wood. In the article, Adams presents his opinions on the development of Samuel's convictions.

> It does not appear that in these three years [between leaving Harvard and starting Divinity School] the controlling feelings of his after life – opposition to slavery, strong religious convictions – manifested themselves. But his was a nature that matured slowly. His quiet, refined tastes sought their gratification at this time in music and other forms of art, and his natural reserve perhaps prevented his speaking to his friends upon themes which as yet were but partially apprehended by him. But the pause thus made before taking up the definite work of life was not in itself a bad thing. He broadened and expanded during this period; and when, in 1842, he entered the Divinity School of Harvard College, he had reached a period of development where judgment had full play.[22]

On his return to Cambridge, Samuel considered his options and had some ideas that he was seriously keeping in mind, Henry was willing to help and his father sent a letter with suggestions. Samuel responded, providing the first indication that he might enter Divinity School.

> The subject which you mention in your letter is one of which I have not been unmindful. The only one of the three professions to which my inclinations would lead me is Divinity. At the same it is one which requires such peculiar qualifications and involves such heavy responsibilities that I almost shrink from engaging in it. I should therefore prefer, if it could be obtained, some collegiate professorship; for which situation, indeed, I think I should find myself better suited than for either of the professions. Still there is this difficulty that such a situation does not depend upon one's own choice.

> My plan, therefore, has been this; to stay here, as at present, till the next year, and then, if nothing better has offered meanwhile, to enter the Divinity School. The idea has occurred to me of entering one year in advance, which I might perhaps do by studying the next six months.[23]

In the same letter Samuel mentions that "On Friday I had the pleasure of breakfasting at Henry's with Mr. Dickens," an experience that was surely among the advantages Samuel considered for living in Cambridge. At this time in 1841, Charles Dickens and his wife were on a trip to America, during which Dickens was received enthusiastically. However, he was disillusioned by the country and some of the people he met. Despite this reaction, he met some people in Boston with whom he got along well, including Henry Longfellow, Cornelius Felton, Charles Sumner and the historian William H. Prescott. It is probably with this group that Samuel had breakfast. Dickens became especially good friends with Felton a good friend of Henry and a professor at Harvard and later its president. Two years later Samuel wrote a letter to his sister Anne in which he told her that Felton had received a letter from Dickens in which Dickens stated he was disgusted with the established church and said,

I have fulfilled a long cherished idea & joined the Unitarians who would do something for human improvements if they could and who at least practice charity & toleration.[24]

Later in the spring after Samuel's consideration of the Divinity School, his father told him about a job as the head of a private school that he was unexpectedly told about. Although the name of the school was not mentioned, a good possibility was the Thornton Academy in Saco, Maine, where Samuel's father Stephen knew members of the Board of Trustees from Bowdoin and his experience in politics

The Trustees of our Academy had a meeting last evening on the subject of procuring a Preceptor, and they are very desirous that you should take charge of the Institution. By their direction I now address you on the subject. They wish to know whether you are willing to become the Instructor, and when you would be able to assume the duties.[25]

Samuel's immediate reaction was to turn the job down and he sent a letter stating his feelings to his father to be forwarded to the Trustees. His father disagreed with Samuel's opinion, and even his brother Henry thought "that the offer is too good to be rejected."[26] Nevertheless, Samuel would not change his mind. He explained to his father why he turned down the position and provided us with an idea of how he viewed his previous teaching experiences and his concern with his physical and mental exhaustion.

I have considered the subject of your letter, but do not see reason to change my former decision. I still feel unwilling to undertake the charge of the Academy, & must therefore respectfully decline the request of the Trustees. I cannot leave here before July at least the soonest; that is, before the end of the college would leave some one at leisure to supply my place. And furthermore I do not feel that the charge of such a school would suit me – its duties would be too wearying to body & mind. I used to feel nervous & tired after my school duties last year, with the comparatively small number of scholars & though no more time would be occupied, yet the increase of number brings much increase of care & hurry & bustle. The crowding of the many & various recitations into the hours of school, the constant attention to individuals & at the same time a general care of the whole make necessary either very peculiar qualifications in the preceptor or else the influence of long habit to prevent their producing much bodily weariness & vexation of spirit.[27]

Samuel Longfellow was subject to bouts of ill health throughout his life, which sometimes required him to withdraw from activities or to even seek treatment. Writing in 1892, Edward Everett Hale comments on Samuel's health.

He was a man of delicate physical health, so delicate that you wondered that he attempted any professional calling which requires a man to call upon himself regularly for his work, and gives him no opportunity for lying back for refreshment.[28]

Samuel did not think that his health problems were hopeless and in a letter to his friend James Richardson, a classmate he met Divinity School and later a Unitarian minister, he describes his views on how one recovers strength and health.

I ought not perhaps to omit five verses of Hebrew read one very virtuous morning, in the dawning of new resolutions. People may talk of rest for the mind, & returning to study with renewed vigor; and if the relaxation be of the right sort, keeping the mind active though in a different, & so to speak more physical & outward direction, no doubt there is truth in the idea, but the mind cannot, I believe, be prepared for study by idleness & dissipation, any more than the body in like manner for a race or pugilistic encounter.[29]

After the initial shock on his return, Samuel settled down into a quiet life in Cambridge in keeping with his natural preference for peace and quiet and entered into learning subjects as they presented themselves to his attention. This is the life that he had kept as a goal in the back of his mind while he considered other options available.

Considering what he accomplished in his life, it is surprising to learn that Samuel considered himself the type of person who needed a little urging in order not to be lazy.

> But I am afraid a lazy man, like me, who should nominally devote his whole time to private general study, wouldn't accomplish much; some external force is needed, such as is supplied, in studying a profession, by the definite aim in view. At any rate, I should prefer, in my own case, to have some regular engagement a part of the day.[30]

An example of why he considered himself lazy is in the way he studied at Harvard. As he describes in his journal, he put himself into a position of being pressed for time, not unlike the way that many students still do their school work.

> After dinner sat down to write my theme, having adopted the fashion lately of writing it at the last moment & then but one copy. I know it is too bad thus to put them off but I cannot summon energy to do them earlier indeed I need the spur of the moment to make my ideas flow.[31]

To overcome his lack of energy, he needed to make his time limited to give the "spur of the moment" push, but not work too hard in order to leave him "abundant resources" to devote to "his love of literature and philosophy and in the cultivation of his tastes." He limited the time he had for doing the things he wanted by tutoring and then went on to do what he enjoyed.[32]

In the beginning, he became the tutor for "my little 'Otis loves'," as had been arranged by Henry. The following year Samuel took two students recommended to him by Charles Sumner, who told him, "Mrs. Ritchie [sister-in-law of Mrs. Otis] is desirous that they should be examined by some competent person, who will be able to form an opinion as to the class which they should enter, &, if necessary, superintend their studies till next commencement."[33]

Charles Sumner was one of Henry Wadsworth Longfellow's best friends and an ardent abolitionist. He was selected as Senator from Massachusetts and was an outspoken opponent of slavery on the Senate floor, which resulted in his having the dubious distinction of being assaulted and seriously hurt while seated at his desk on the Senate floor in 1856. Sumner's attacker was pro-slavery Congressman Brooks from South Carolina who entered the Senate chamber and savagely bludgeoned Sumner until he was bloody and unconscious on the Senate floor.

Along with his tutoring activities, Samuel Longfellow took advantage of the cultural activities available in Cambridge and Boston. This was an important part of his life in which he could not partake during his year in rural Maryland.

> Music was, lifelong, his unfailing resource. He enjoyed it in its classical forms, and had a great love for simple and expressive melodies. From Cambridge, recourse to the musical privileges of Boston, and he constantly availed himself of them. All other forms of art attracted an equally appreciative attention.[34]

During this period, Samuel also took on some duties that kept him in close touch with Harvard. In late summer 1841, the university appointed him as Proctor. Among his duties was to attend chapel each morning and evening and "to put down any riot." Toward the end of September 1841, the University President announced during prayers "that Mr. Proctor Longfellow had been appointed Instructor in German pro. tem." and Samuel "tried to look like he didn't mean [him]." However, Samuel began teaching the afternoon of the President's announcement. [*Journal,* entries in August and September.]

At this time he was living as described above and he still had not made a definite decision on what to do in the long term. This lack of decision was something that concerned his parents who wanted him to be more definite about what he planned to do with his life. His father points this out in a letter he sent to Samuel in November 1841.

It is difficult to advise you respecting the expediency of taking one pupil at $250, without knowing your future plans. If it is your intention to remain at Cambridge for the purpose of pursuing your studies, it would be desirable to have one pupil, if more could not be obtained. I have hoped that you would be disposed more fully to develop your plans that we may have a view of the whole ground, and be able to advise you – You have arrived at that age, when it is desirable that your intentions for future life should be formed, and it is always desirable to advise your parents & friends on that important subject. We should like therefore to know your views & intentions.[35]

It is not easy to know what Samuel Longfellow was thinking about at this point because he did not write many letters or make many entries in his journal during this period. In addition, what he did write did not specifically refer to his career choice. In a letter to his father he indicated his relief that school was almost over for the year and also asks for money for support as he did periodically. He was fortunate in having financial support from his father, which allowed him to have the time to carefully consider his opportunities and not have the need to work.

For myself I am glad that quiet again reigns, even the perfect quiet of vacation which is of the superlative degree – I do not live very well to stay here I must confess; but I do not feel at liberty to leave my pupils – they have little enough time.[36]

Some of his letters do contain discussions about religious subjects, but many do not, although it may have been his intention all along to enter the Divinity School. However, the comments he did make on religious subjects in his journal and in letters leave no doubt that religion was a major focus in his life. Samuel had definite opinions about which religious concepts moved him, which did not edify him, which he disagreed with, etc., in addition to those that he believed could lead many people to doubt their beliefs or strongly cling to one in particular. This is summed up in his conviction: "Can God's truth be put in jeopardy by mans words?"

As Joseph May says, "It may be that entrance upon the ministry was, for him so natural a step and so well understood among his friends as to call for little particular mention."[37] Even though his personal character was very open on topics, he may not have completely established in his mind what his principle interests were. Furthermore, Samuel may have thought that his friends or family may not have fully agreed with his ideas and he recognized that "it is impossible for me to speak of such things unless I am sure to meet with sympathy."[38]

However, nine months later, in August 1842, he wrote a very short letter to his father stating, "For myself, I have entered the Divinity School, having commenced recitations there yesterday."[39] Despite "the somewhat dilettante interval of his resident-graduate years,"[40] the time he took for reflection had not been a useless exercise in Samuel's life. In all likelihood, it allowed his thinking to open up and out and help in making a definite decision about his life. He, thus, was finally able to reach a position where his thoughts had a more complete view of what was really possible and desirable. At the age of 23 he had at long last started on the path that would occupy the rest of his life.

Nevertheless, even after making this major decision Samuel was considering taking a trip to Europe for a year with his friend Parker. However, he had no money and his father refused to pay for the trip. Samuel was also concerned about starting the new course because of his health, as he states to his father.

> I do not indeed feel myself in a condition advantageously to begin a new course of study – My bodily weakness reacts upon the mind depriving it of energy & activity – My nervous system is out of order – Any considerable degree of bodily or mental exertion exhausts me. I cannot but think that if I could for eight months or a year break away entirely from this place and these occupations & recruit myself by a voyage & visit

abroad, I should return quite another man, & be able to re-commence my studies with vigor & a chance of success.[41]

In spite of all the indecision and the barriers, some real some created, to choosing a career, Samuel Longfellow had finally decided on the direction for this life.

Notes:

[1] Longfellow, Samuel. *Journal,* October 13, 1839 to April 26, 1843, Oct. 15, 1839.

[2] Letter Samuel Longfellow to Stephen Longfellow (father), June 22, 1839, SLP, LNHS.

[3] Ibid., April 9, 1839, SLP, LNHS.

[4] Ibid.

[5] Longfellow, Samuel. *Journal,* October 13, 1839 to April 26, 1843, Oct. 17, 1839.

[6] Ibid., October 19, 1839.

[7] May, Joseph, Ed.. *Samuel Longfellow: Memoir and Letters.* Cambridge: The Riverside Press, 1894. p. 14.

[8] Letter Samuel Longfellow to Stephen Longfellow (father), November 4, 1839, SLP, LNHS.

[9] Letter Samuel Longfellow to Zilpah Longfellow, November 15, 1839, SLP, LNHS.

[10] Ibid.

[11] Letter Samuel Longfellow to Stephen Longfellow (father), February 7, 1840, SLP, LNHS.

[12] Ibid.

[13] Letter, Samuel Longfellow to Edward Everett Hale, June 5, 1840, *Memoir and Letters.*

[14] Letter, Samuel Longfellow to Stephen Longfellow (father), June 28, 1840, SLP, LNHS.

[15] Ibid.

[16] Letter, Samuel Longfellow to Henry Longfellow, September 16, 1840, LP.

[17] Letter, Samuel Longfellow to Stephen Longfellow (father), October 10, 1840, SLP, LNHS.

[18] Letter, Samuel Longfellow to Mary Longfellow Greenleaf, October 13, 1840, SLP, LNHS.

[19] Letter, Samuel Longfellow to Henry Longfellow, October 22, 1840, LP.

[20] Letter, Samuel Longfellow to Anne Longfellow Pierce, October 28, 1840, SLP, LNHS.

[21] May, Joseph, *Memoir.* p. 15-16.

[22] Adams, Oscar Fay. "Samuel Longfellow", *The New England Magazine,* v. 17, n.º 2, pp. 205-213, Boston, October 1894.

[23] Letter, Samuel Longfellow to Stephen Longfellow (father), February 7, 1841.

[24] Letter, Samuel Longfellow to Anne Longfellow Pierce, April 8, 1843, SLP, LNHS.

[25] Letter, Stephen Longfellow (father) to Samuel Longfellow, April 8, 1841, SLP, LNHS.

[26] Letter, Samuel Longfellow to Stephen Longfellow (father), April 11, 1841, SLP, LNHS.

[27] Ibid., April 29, 1841.

[28] Hale, Edward Everett, *Five Prophets of Today,* p. 15.

[29] Letter, Samuel Longfellow to James Richardson, February 21, 1843, SLP, LNHS.

[30] May, Joseph, *Memoir.* p. 16.

[31] Longfellow, Samuel. *Journal September 24, 1836 to May 30, 1839*, February 2, 1838.

[32] May, Joseph, *Memoir.* p. 18.

[33] Letter, Charles Sumner to Samuel Longfellow, May 17, 1842, SLP, LNHS.

[34] May, Joseph, *Memoir.* p. 18-19.

[35] Letter, Stephen Longfellow (father) to Samuel Longfellow, November 14, 1841, SLP, LNHS.

[36] Letter, Samuel Longfellow to Stephen Longfellow (father), July 16, 1842, SLP, LNHS.

[37] May, Joseph, *Memoir.* p. 20.

[38] Ibid., p. 20-21.

[39] Letter, Samuel Longfellow to Stephen Longfellow (father), August 31, 1842, SLP, LNHS.

[40] May, Joseph, *Memoir.* p. 23.

[41] Letter, Samuel Longfellow to Stephen Longfellow (father), September, 1842, SLP, LNHS.

CHAPTER 5 – THE DIVINES

After God had carried us safe to New England, and we had builded our houses, provided necessaries for our livelihood, reared convenient places for God's worship, and settled the civil government, one of the next things we longed for and looked after was to advance learning and perpetuate it to posterity; dreading to leave an illiterate ministry to the churches, when our present ministers shall lie in the dust.[1] [*In respect of the College (1643)*, *The Harvard Book*. Ed. William Bentinck-Smith. Harvard University Press, Cambridge, MA, 1986, p. 3.]

In order for the "founding fathers'" to achieve their priority of advancing learning, they founded Harvard University in 1636. The school buildings were constructed on the north side of the Bay Colony village in an area named New Town. The site of the school was on a plain that was "smooth as a bowling green" and reminded many of the Cambridge University graduates of their alma mater on the Cam River and the village was renamed Cambridge. The bequest of one half of the estate of John Harvard, as well as his library, gave the impetus to carry out development of the project. Additional funds came from others interested in the College as well as the government, and the University was completed and the first class of 12 students began their studies in 1638.

The introductory quote of this chapter specifies that the major function of a College in early America was to train ministers to ensure that the people would have their religion presented in the manner approved by the church. With the entire university serving a religious purpose, there was no need for a separate Divinity School at Harvard. This situation also held true for other Colleges created during this period. However, by the first quarter of the 19th century, Puritan religious beliefs had become more liberal and the relationship between the church and the university had changed.

The first generations of Europeans to come to America all had strong convictions in their religious beliefs and had had to struggle to be able to practice their beliefs. As a result, they made the decision to leave their homeland for an unknown land that allowed them the freedom they desired. However, even by the second generation after their arrival, church attendance had decreased to some extent. This generation had been born in the Colonies and grew up in an environment without religious persecution. Nonetheless, they had not chosen their religious community and they were not as committed to following all the church's tenets as closely as their parents.

Another factor contributing to the decrease in church attendance was the growing merchant community that had extensive contact with cultures in other countries and their less rigorous systems of religious belief. This resulted in a conflict with the Puritan leaders, who in their extreme anxiety tried to control trade and "profiteering", but in the end the Puritans were unsuccessful.

The new immigrants who arrived were more often seeking the benefits of business activities in New England than religious freedom. In addition, a large proportion of them were Anglicans. Therefore, by the beginning of the 18th century, the Puritan leadership had not only lost its power to control business activities, and was also losing in its attempts to control changes in the religious beliefs of the New England population. Throughout the 18th century, there were waves of religious revivals occurring as responses to the development of more liberal religious congregations. Much of this religious seesawing was a result of the conflict between the rational and emotional approaches to religious belief. However, liberal theology gradually took its place as the predominant conviction.

By the close of the 18th century many of the largest churches, especially but not exclusively in eastern Massachusetts, had become markedly liberal in their theology. Their ministers and lay members were openly though not confrontationally, Arminian and Unitarian. To these liberals, freedom of the human will was both a reality of common experience and a necessary corollary to the goodness of God, without which the justice of God would be meaningless. They rejected as unbiblical the traditionally held Calvinist doctrines of original sin, total depravity, predestination and the trinity. They adopted positive doctrines of the nature of humanity and the possibility of continuing moral, spiritual, and intellectual growth.[2]

Naturally, the changes in church doctrine had their effect on the teaching of religion in the universities. At Harvard, the Hollis Chair of Divinity became vacant in 1803 upon the death of the strict Calvinist Dr. Tappan. After remaining unfilled for two years, Harvard made a crucial decision in 1805 that affected its future direction. The Board appointed Unitarian Henry Ware, Sr., to the Hollis Chair over his Calvinist rival John Appleton, and as a result, the Calvinists broke from Harvard and founded the Andover Theological Seminary in 1808. The ongoing changes during the 17th and 18th centuries gradually led to the establishment of a liberal, non-sectarian divinity school program at Harvard in the 19th century. However, it was not until 1811 that Dr. Ware initiated "a course of definite theological instruction."

In 1815, University President Kirkland made a request to alumni and friends of Harvard "soliciting subscriptions for a theological education fund." They raised nearly $30,000, "and lo! John Adam's name led all the rest." The next step was the formation of a society for fund collection and establishment of the Harvard Divinity School as a non-sectarian institution.

> It being understood that every encouragement be given to the serious, impartial and unbiased investigation of Christian truth, and that no assent to the peculiarity of any denomination of Christians be required, either of the students or professors or instructors.[3]

In 1824, the Divinity School society was reorganized and in 1826 it became a corporation. At this point Divinity Hall was constructed, and the students, who referred to each other as "divines", moved into their rooms and began their lessons in the new classrooms

The location of the Harvard Divinity School was somewhat to the northeast of the other campus buildings. However, a large amount of the space between the Divinity School and the main campus was filled in by the huge structure of the Peabody Museum and its associated science laboratories, which opened in 1866 after a 35-year construction period.

> The most prominent person associated with the Museum was Louis Agassiz, who was internationally respected and whom many considered America's leading scientist in the mid-19th century and some of his work influenced Darwin in developing his theory and accepting its truth. Interestingly, Agassiz never believed in Darwin´s theory. His closest non-scientific friend was Henry Wadsworth Longfellow and he was not infrequently a guest at Craigie House on Brattle Street where Henry lived. Samuel also frequented Craigie House and lived there for a good part of his life and was, therefore, sure to have known Agassiz.[4]

An unanticipated result of the Museum being so close to the Divinity School was that some of the students in scientific studies lived in vacant rooms of the Divinity School. This led to interesting discussions between the "divines" and the scientists resulting in the former absorbing some of the rational science of the day into their theological thoughts. A number of the divines even ended up agreeing with Darwin's theory that was proposed shortly after mid-century, but not widely believed among many in the religious community.[6]

Although Samuel Longfellow had graduated long before this period, he would surely have appreciated these interchanges with the science students. As mentioned previously, he had a great interest in natural science and his membership in the Octagon Society at Harvard further documents this.

The religious split that occurred in 1805 was not the end of the changes in church doctrine. Some churches even split into separate congregations and the various ministers and theologians often went in directions that were more their own than those of a particular "church." In addition, it also was not uncommon for ministers or congregations to change theological directions, and some time later change back to their original tenets. For more than another two decades the controversy within and among churches continued with the variations in beliefs becoming continually more set in concrete.

At Harvard, the liberalization of beliefs continued and extended to the Divinity School, which became a Unitarian-run facility, even though the program they taught was still officially non-denominational. After years of the Unitarian Church influencing the curriculum at Harvard, the situation reversed in the 1830s and the Divinity School became important in setting the direction of Unitarian belief. Harvard's influence was solidified by a speech Ralph Waldo Emerson made at Harvard Divinity School.

> So it happened that July 15, 1838, the place became a temple witnessing the most sacred scene in all its history, the delivery of Ralph Waldo Emerson's famous "Divinity School Address," the most lyrical and spontaneous utterance of his life, and the most epoch-making in the history of Unitarian thought.[6]

Although there is no comment in Samuel Longfellow's letters or journal about Emerson's lecture, he surely was aware of it and must have discussed it with his friends even if he didn't actually attend it. In his *Memoir* of Samuel Johnson, Longfellow gives his view on Emersons' Divinity School lecture: "That address, which had been a sunburst to so many young minds, was to most of the elders an ominous and baleful meteor, 'portending change.'"[7]

Ralph Waldo Emerson (1803-1882) was one of the most important people in America in the development of Unitarianism and Transcendentalism and the relationship between them. He had become a Unitarian pastor in 1829, but he resigned in 1832 after antagonizing his congregation because of his beliefs regarding Jesus. He then took a trip to Europe and his interest in Transcendentalism developed after he spoke with Carlyle, Coleridge and Wordsworth. A few years later he also became involved with anti-slavery and women's suffrage movements.

In the 1830s he began a career as lecturer and writer and in 1836, based on some of his lectures, he published the book *Nature* in which he set out the main principles of Transcendentalism. He was a sought after speaker, but not all his presentations were well received. The prime example is the "Divinity School Address," which many people considered to be his refutation of Christianity. It created such an uproar that he was not invited to Harvard to speak again and almost excluded from the Unitarian Church. However, there were those who had problems understanding what Emerson was trying to say and Samuel expresses his understanding of the reasons.

> Mrs. G. has been reading R.W. Emerson's little book "Nature." She said there were some beautiful passages – but that as a whole it was rather 'too <u>sublimated</u> for her comprehension' – That's the word. It is written in the true German spirit of idealism, and only the favored few who are all spiritual can comprehend it I should imagine.[8]

Among the "elders" who reacted against Emerson's speech was Henry Ware, Jr., who became professor at the Divinity School in 1830, ironically, leaving his church in the hands of his younger colleague Ralph Waldo Emerson. It was the appointment of Ware, Jr.'s father to the Hollis Chair in 1805 that created the religious split at Harvard. After the "Divinity School Address" Ware wrote a letter to Emerson and followed up on it with a sermon entitled "The Personality of God". In the sermon Ware alleges that some of Emerson's statements aimed at overthrowing the authority and influence of Christianity, were pantheistic and also needed the addition of personality to the abstractions of his philosophy.

Emerson responded in a letter that drew almost as much attention as his speech. In it he granted that Ware had the right to present his thoughts as long as Emerson could present his and could express his beliefs without having to have the arguments to support them. He said this because he did not know How one could argue with someone's thoughts. From this point on he let the others on both sides argue about the speech and stayed out of the conflict.

There were some important supporters, who carried Emerson's ideas forward. Among these was Theodore Parker who was so taken by the ideas in Emerson's "Divinity School Address" that

> ...as he walked home that night over Charles River bridge, saw everywhere in the moonlit sky and water visions of high duty beckoning him and heard mysterious voices that bade him gird himself in solemn haste for an adventurous quest![9]

Theodore Parker was one of the figures whose ideas Samuel Longfellow considered worthy of great attention and, in return, Parker was an early supporter of the hymnbooks by Samuel Longfellow and Samuel Johnson. Parker was considered on the level of Channing in importance and influence in the Unitarian church. After the "Divinity School Address," Parker was inspired to speak out on church and social reform and also became a major supporter of Transcendentalism. However, Parker denied the miraculous aspects of Jesus and the Bible and, as a result, many Unitarians did not consider him a Christian and he was not allowed to speak from the pulpit in most churches. His own church in West Roxbury continued to support him and the publicity helped his career as a public speaker.

The development of Samuel Longfellow's life paralleled the establishment of the Divinity School and the transition to a new more liberal Unitarianism in addition to the blossoming of Transcendentalism. There was a period of slow growth, not without some difficulties, and then suddenly they came to fruition and were ready. At the time Samuel Longfellow entered the Divinity School of Harvard University, it was not well funded or equipped, and there were only two men responsible for the school, who Samuel said were doing "the work of four professors."

One was the Reverend Convers Francis, who was appointed professor of pulpit eloquence and pastoral care in 1842, thus beginning the same year Samuel did. Joseph May describes him as

> ...an encyclopedic scholar; refined, genial, and sensitive; full of sympathy and help for any student who showed signs

of real scholarship; opening the stores of his own learning and the contents of his library, freely and kindly, to any such who sought his aid; conservative in temperament and cautious in expression, but thought to be broader in his esoteric views than in his public utterances; formal and reserved, yet cordial, in personal intercourse; fluent but prosaic in his public offices; a true gentleman and thoroughly a clergyman of the old school.[10]

The other professor was the Reverend George Rapall Noyes, whom the students nicknamed "the Rabbi" because he was an outstanding Hebrew scholar. He was celebrated for his translations of the Old and New Testaments and his writing on many other religious subjects. May describes Noyes as

...of quiet and even shy manners, but incisive in speech, and of a dry and occasionally caustic wit; rigidly upright; as an exegete and translator having no views of his own, but devoted with unqualified singleness of mind to identifying the meaning of his author.[11]

The two professors were both dedicated to teaching their students the truth and encouraging their continued search for it. However, despite the move toward liberal Unitarianism for which Harvard was recognized, the two professors

...belonged, especially Dr. Francis, to a former time; their methods were scholastic and antiquated; in later days, at least, their exercises were tedious and uninspiring in the extreme.[12]

In addition to attending classes, Samuel Longfellow and his classmates supplemented their school lectures by listening to the sermons and speeches by the well known Unitarians and Transcendentalists in Boston and the surrounding area. Besides their assigned reading, they sought out books that went beyond their assigned texts and read others by local, as well as European, primarily German and French, and Asian authors and philosophers.

Besides their schoolwork, the students discussed the hot political issues of the day. Among these were antislavery and the debates about Texas and the Mexican War. All of these were fodder for the habitual discussions among Samuel and his friends, which sometimes became a little hot. Their debates sometimes extended beyond the student group with the professors not exempt from being put on the defensive.

Samuel Longfellow had his own unique approach in the regular debates, and he was well known and respected throughout his life for the way he dealt with controversy.

> He was never an eager, nor even a willing, disputant; but he was singularly clear and firm in his convictions, which he expressed with positiveness and gravity, but preferably as intuitions rather than argumentatively. Unkind he could not be, yet he was not quite incapable of prejudices, in these early days, nor of something like partisanship, as his references to typical conservatives sometimes show. His opinions, thus far, were apparently little modified from those of the Unitarianism in which he had been brought up. But he was a radical and a transcendentalist by nature, and these traits were fast determining him to views in religion much in advance of the prevailing Unitarian thought.[13]

There were several students in the Divinity School entering class of 1842 that Samuel associated with more frequently than others. Joseph Henry Allen, became a minister and a writer on classical and religious themes; he did not like the new concept that the structure of a church was important relative to the sacredness of what took place in a congregation. William Rounseville Alger, a minister in a number of churches, going as far west as Denver, was also an author of several books; some considered him more talented than his cousin Horatio Alger, with whom he collaborated on the biography of the actor Edwin Forrest. Charles Henry Brigham became a minister and spent most of his life as a pastor in Michigan. Thomas Hill was a Unitarian minister who succeeded Horace Mann as president of Antioch College in Ohio, following which he was appointed President of Harvard and served in this position from 1862-1868. In addition, Hill was a writer and an accomplished mathematician who invented a number of "mathematical machines," including one that predicted eclipses visible west of the Mississippi for a four-year period. Octavius Brooks Frothingham became a prominent Unitarian minister in Boston and New York and by 1864 was recognized as the leader of the radical branch of Unitarianism and the first president of the Free Religious Association.

Samuel Longfellow had other friends, but Samuel Johnson was his closest friend and the most important relationship in his life. Longfellow describes Johnson in the "Memoir" he included in *Lectures, Essays, and Sermons by Samuel Johnson,* which he edited after Johnson's death.

> The first time that I remember seeing Samuel Johnson was in the old College Chapel at Cambridge. It was the "Class-day" of 1842; and he was giving the class oration. It was poetic even to rhapsody; certainly very unlike ordinary college orations. I remember only one passage, and that indistinctly: it was something about the warrior's shields sounding upon the walls, – some illustration, very likely, from Ossian. But I recall, as if it were seen yesterday, the dark, animated countenance, the flowing hair, the earnest, musical tones, the light quick movement from one foot to the other, – the whole air of inspiration. It was as fascinating as it was unlooked for. This must have been in July. In the autumn of the same year, when I entered the Divinity School, I soon found him out among my classmates. The same fascination drew me toward him, and then began a friendship which continued for forty years.[14]

> Meeting Johnson in the school, I was very soon attracted to him by certain similarities of taste, and more by the peculiar earnestness, ideality, and the spirituality of tone which marked him out among the rest.[15]

> Johnson was a transcendentalist by nature, a born idealist; the cast of his mind intuitive rather than logical. He instinctively sought spiritual truths by direct vision, not by any processes of induction; by immediate inward experience, rather than by any inference from outward experience. God, Right, Immortality,

were to him realities of *intuition*; that is, of direct *looking upon*; shining by their own light, spiritually discerned, the affirmations of the soul. But his transcendentalism, which was later to become a carefully-weighed *rationale of thought*, was now a nature, a perception, a sentiment, an inward, unargued faith. It began soon to take on a *mystical* phase, which led him into some deep experiences.[16]

Samuel Johnson was a conservative Unitarian at the time the two met and was in the congregation that heard Henry Ware's response to Emerson's "Divinity School Address," in his sermon "The Personality of God." Johnson listened to the sermon with "great delight," however, his views became more liberal later in college. He expressed his revised beliefs in a letter to his sister.

> May 28, 1841
>
> Is not this a strange world that runs thoughtlessly on through all this living, speaking loveliness, which seems to point every moment toward the God whose hand is forming and fashioning all before all eyes? How few there are who seem to have any but a theoretical belief that there is something at work around us besides the trees, the flowers, the clouds and the sun! We see them at work, and ask no further; ask not who makes them work, who gives them all their loveliness and liberty and life. ...What should we do but fall down and adore before this visible creation of an invisible and all-pervading Being?... Thank Him that you are able to read in the flowers the poetry of His love.[17]

The relationship between the two Samuels lasted from their meeting at Divinity School until Samuel Johnson's death in 1882. They lived in different places, but between their correspondence and occasional meetings they were able to maintain a strong relationship that accepted their differences and criticisms of the other. They are best known for the hymnbook they wrote in Cambridge and later modified on a trip they took to Europe.

Joseph May believes that for Longfellow, who had such a genius for friendship, the relationship between the two Sams was the most important condition in the development of Samuel Longfellow's character and thought." May also describes a number of differences and similarities between the two men and concludes this discussion with the statement: "In moral fervor and firmness, and in the radical quality of all their thought, these men, so congenial to each other, were indeed 'nobly peers.'"[18]

In his article on Samuel Longfellow, Oscar Fay Adams also describes the relationship between Longfellow and Johnson.

> While the two men shared the same poetic nature and the same intense spirituality of thought, there were many points of unlikeness. Longfellow, who was the elder by three years was a man of wide sympathies and social disposition, desultory rather than continuous in his methods of thought and study, and ever and always serenely patient. Johnson's sympathies, on the other hand, were restricted, and he was far more of the recluse than the man of the world. He was naturally ascetic in his tastes while his habits were those of the systematic, tireless student, and where he felt deeply he was disposed to be dogmatic and aggressive. Dissimilar as the two men were on so many points, their friendship, was, as Mr. Chadwick [Divinity School alumnus from 1864] has said of it 'the most rare and perfect satisfaction of their lives'"[19]

As their friend Edward Everett Hale said, "there existed for forty years an intimacy which could hardly have been understood by David and Jonathan."[20] This statement refers to the Old Testament book I Samuel 18 that describes the meeting between Jonathan, son of Saul, and David just after he killed Goliath. To emphasize Hale's comment on the extreme closeness of this relationship, it is worth citing I Samuel 18:1-3.

> After David had finished talking with Saul, Jonathan became one in spirit with David and he loved him as himself. From that day Saul kept David with him and did not let him return to his father's house. And Jonathan made a covenant with David because he loved him as himself.

Samuel Longfellow's first year in Divinity School must have been very busy since he wrote very few letters and did not even take the time to make entries in his journal between September 1842 and April 1843. He was involved in meeting new friends, starting new studies and participating in the activities at school. These all took their toll on Samuel so at the end of the academic year he found his health had declined and he needed a break from teaching.

During his time in Divinity School, Samuel continued to be concerned with his health. However, Samuel describes how he thought one recovers strength and health in a letter written in February 1843, to his friend and classmate James Richardson, later a Unitarian minister.

> People may talk of rest for the mind, & returning to study with renewed vigor; and if the relaxation be of the right sort, keeping the mind active though in a different, & so to speak more physical & outward direction, no doubt there is truth in the idea, but the mind cannot, I believe, be prepared for study by idleness & dissipation, any more than the body in like manner for a race or pugilistic encounter.[21]

As a result, he looked for an opportunity to take part in an activity that would not have a great deal of stress and yet be significant to him.

Notes:

[1] Betinck-Smith, William, Ed. "In respect of the College (1643)", *The Harvard Book*. Harvard University Press, Cambridge, MA, 1986, p. 3.

[2] Wesley, Alice Blair, Peter Hughes and Frank Carpenter. "The Unitarian Controversy and its Puritan Roots. Unitarian Universalist Historical Society.www.uua.org.uuhs/duub/articles//unitariancontroversy.html 2004.

[3] Chadwick, John White. "The Harvard Divinity School," *The New England Magazine*, v. 17, n.° 6, pp 740-756. Boston. February 1895, p. 747.

[4] Howell, Charles D. The Fortnightly Club of Redlands, California, Meeting # 1407. March 13, 1986.

[5] Chadwick, John White. "The Harvard Divinity School," p. 747.www.redlandsfortnightly.org

6 Ibid.

[7] Longfellow, Samuel, Ed. *Lectures, Essays and Sermons by Samuel Johnson*, Boston: The Riverside Press, 1883, p. 8.

[8] Longfellow, Samuel. *Journal, September 24, 1836 to May 30, 1839*, p. 29.

[9] Chadwick, John White. "The Harvard Divinity School," p. 747.

[10] May, Joseph, Ed.. *Samuel Longfellow: Memoir and Letters*. Cambridge: The Riverside Press, 1894. p. 25.

[11] Ibid., p. 26.

[12] Ibid.

[13] Ibid., p. 29.

[14] Longfellow, Samuel, *Lectures, Essays and Sermons by Samuel Johnson*, p. 1.

[15] Ibid. p. 13.

[16] Ibid. p. 14.

[17] Ibid. p. 9.

[18] May, Joseph, Ed.. *Samuel Longfellow: Memoir and Letters.*, p. 23-25.

[19] Adams, Oscar Fay. "Samuel Longfellow." *The New England Magazine*, October 1894, v. 17, n.º 2, p. 205-213. Boston., p. 207.

[20] Hale, Edward Everett, *Five Prophets of Today*, p. 40.

[21] Letter, Samuel Longfellow to James Richardson, February 21, 1843, SLP, LNHS.

CHAPTER 6 – MID-ATLANTIC ADVENTURE

With the decision made to look after his health and not take on anything very stressful, Samuel Longfellow found himself doing very little. He clearly talks about this in a letter to his friend James Richardson in February, 1843.

> I have accomplished just about – nothing. See what I have done, one ball, three lectures, one oratorio, one concert, four parties, one dinner party, I have regularly eaten my three meals a day and slept my —— hours o'night. I have attended Church twice each Sunday & heard Sunday School Classes after Church – I have read Mrs. Lee's Life of Jean Paul and Frederica Bremer's "Neighbors." Swedenborg's Heaven and Hell, with uncounted quantities of newspaper & magazine stuff. I have written three or four letters – three or four sheets of manuscripts – some calls – a good deal of piano-drumming & day-dreaming – no small quantity of pottering & "desperate loafing" – Voila Tout![1]

However, an offer of work that appealed to Samuel and met his requirements for dividing his time between work and his personal activities appeared unexpectedly. He described what happened in a letter to his father in April.

> Here has something new turned up. Dr. Webster came to me yesterday morning & asked how I would like to go to Fayal. A friend of his residing there writes to engage an instructor for his children. There are four children two boys of 16 & 13 and two girls. The family is a most delightful one, I am assured, cultivated and hospitable & with them the instructor resides. The climate is one of the finest in the world. The last instructor, who is the son of Mrs. Clarke with whom I board, tho much of an invalid when he left here two years ago, has not had a sick

day on the island. The salary is about $400 a year, with a free passage out & back in the *Harbinger*, Mr. Dabney's brig which runs between Fayal and Boston.

Now of course my only inducement to go is the advantage to my health. And in this respect I cannot but think that the voyage & residence of a year in the Island would be of immense benefit. I really need something of the kind. I am sure nothing else would induce me to break up here & go off so far. And if I should get health & a vigorous body the time would certainly not be lost even in view of my profession.[2]

In his journal from that date he talks about his reaction to the meeting with Charles Dabney, Sr. and what he did after his encounter with Dr. John Webster, a Harvard professor and family friend.

This of course threw me into great excitement. I rushed over to Mrs. Clarke's & had an interview with Miss Parker to learn about Edw. Clarke. Then to Dr. Webster for further particulars – then to Henry's who was not at home. ...Henry came in, in the aft. & strongly advised my going for a year. I suppose it will be the best thing for me & I am strongly inclined to go.

I went into town in the aft. to see Mr. Cunningham. Had a short interview with the wife & then went down to his counting room, thro' all sorts of noisy & dirty streets in a dark cloudy aft. My visit to the wharf & the trip made me dismal enough – did not learn much from Cunningham & found I might have got all & more from Chas. Dabney at Cambridge. But I thought I wd. for once be prompt & energetic & rushed into town.[3]

It appears that although Samuel had never met Charles Dabney, Sr., he was acquainted with his son Charles, Jr., who was a student at Harvard at the time. Samuel mentions him in his February letter to James Richardson, "Your account of the snow storm chorus & the encounter with D'Aubigne, amused me highly." D'Aubigne was the original French Huguenot name of the Dabney family who were descendents of Huguenots who had fled France to England and then to America.

Charles Dabney, Sr., was the United States Consul to the Azores, succeeding his father John Bass Dabney, who was the first U.S. Consul in the Azores and had served as Consul from 1806-1828. Charles Dabney, Sr. was followed by his son Samuel Wyllys Dabney, Consul from 1872 to 1892, the year the family returned to America. As a point of interest the U.S. Consulate in the Azores still exists, although on another island, and is the oldest existing U.S. Consulate in the world.

The Consul and his family were also the most important merchants in the Azores during the time the U.S. still allowed Consuls to have their own business. Their Boston representative was Mr. Charles Cunningham, a cousin of the Dabneys, who Samuel Longfellow went to visit after he received the offer to teach in Faial. In his *Memoir* of Samuel Longfellow, Joseph May describes Charles Dabney, Sr.

> That gentleman, by enterprise, force of character, public spirit and benevolence, had become, as it were a feudal chieftain on his island. Surrounded by a large circle of his relatives and descendants, he lived with them a charming life of refinement, bounty, hospitality, and usefulness, in the midst of the half-tropical loveliness and balmy atmosphere of (as Longfellow calls it in the words of some other) "the green and breezy isle."[4]

Dr. Webster, who approached Samuel Longfellow with the job offer, was a Harvard professor and he and his family were friends of Henry Wadsworth Longfellow and many in the Boston Brahmin community. His wife was a daughter of the Hickling family who had lived on the island of São Miguel in the Azores since 1769, with Thomas Hickling having been appointed a consular representative in 1795. Two of Webster's daughters, with whom Samuel was acquainted, married Dabney sons – Sarah to John Pomeroy Dabney and Harriet to Samuel Wyllys Dabney, the future U.S. Consul.

The story of Dr. Webster and his family took a tragic turn a few years after Samuel returned from Faial. In 1850, Dr. Webster was arrested, tried, convicted and executed for the murder of another Harvard Professor, Dr. George Parkman, also a Boston

Brahmin and friend of the Longfellow family. Webster's trial involved many of Boston's social and intellectual elite such as Dr. Oliver Wendall Holmes and Judge Lemuel Shaw, Herman Melville's father-in-law. The outcome of the trial caused the Brahmin community to turn inward and share their opinions and reactions only within the group. It was considered the trial of the century and laid the legal basis for the use of circumstantial evidence that is still in effect today. The Webster incident also had an effect on literature produced at the time when Melville used this trial as a basis for the trial of Billy Budd in his book of that name.

Samuel did not take much time to reflect and made his decision to go to Faial almost immediately. Within a couple of weeks the Dabney ship the *Harbinger* set sail from Boston for Faial carrying Samuel to new experiences in life. The *Harbinger* sailed the second Sunday in May 1843 and they "rounded the headland and were in the bay of Horta" on May 26. However, Samuel did not have the most pleasant voyage, as he describes in a letter to Edward Everett Hale.

> Don't let any of your friends persuade you, as some of mine tried to do (I did not believe a word of it, though, and so was not disappointed), that there is any *enjoyment* in a sea voyage. I deliberately declare that I did not have more than two hours of positive pleasure in the whole nineteen days. I was seasick, more or less, for a week, and, after that, so dull and listless, so guiltless of thought, feeling, or fancy, that it seemed as if I must have returned to that state of oysterdom in which, according to Dean Palfrey, I once learned patience. What would I have given, what would any of us have given, for a hearty laugh! I was not moved, either, by any sublimity in the ocean, and in this I was much disappointed. In fact, I think it needs to be seen from the shore, with a fine rocky foreground, or a strip of silver sand.[5]

On May 26, Samuel gladly set foot on solid land in Horta, the main town on the island of Faial. He told his father that he thought the town of Horta "a pleasant one – everything about it, houses, churches & people, shops, donkies & sedan chairs, having a very 'foreign' and picturesque appearance." He goes into a little more detail to his friend James Richardson.

> It is a pretty place situated on a semicircular bay between two headlands. The streets are narrow and paved with round uneven stones painful to unaccustomed feet; the houses are all of stone, which look so picturesque in views in Italy and Portugal. In the streets you meet the barefooted men in various odd dresses & women covered up in blue cloth cloaks with immense hoods which they wear all summer – others with hats or handkerchiefs on their heads. Everything is odd & foreign & one seems as he walks along to be turning over the plates of the landscape annual. Everything too looks solid and most things old & respectable if not gray and moss grown.[6]

Although he had never met most of the people who greeted him, he was glad to "see the familiar faces of the Miss Websters," daughters of Dr. Webster, whom he knew from Cambridge. The daughters of Dr. Webster were just visiting at the time, but in later years Sarah and Harriet Webster would marry two of Charles Dabney's sons. Because of the Webster girls and other visitors, the Dabney's house was full at the time, and Samuel had to make his "lodgings at the English Board." [letter to father, 8 June 1843] After the *Harbinger* left with several of the Dabney guests, Samuel took up residence in their house named "Fredonia"; the house also functioned as the U.S. Consulate to the Azores. He was happy with the move and the room in which he stayed.

> The day after [the *Harbinger's*] departure, my trunks were brought over from the boarding house & I had the satisfaction of unpacking & establishing myself in my own sanctum – and a great satisfaction it was, & a very nice & pleasant sanctum – The left corner window in the little sketch which I sent Mary & which I suppose she will transmit to you, will indicate the situation thereof – one window looks out upon the flower

garden & the hills beyond, and "commands a view" of the bay & Pico – the other opens upon two great orange gardens & by stretching your head out of it you can see the Carmelite Convent & a part of the town – all which makes perhaps as pleasant a look-out as one could have the fact to ask for – not to say the eyes to see.[7]

Initially Samuel did not feel well even after getting off the ship, but he had plans for improving his health, which he describes in a letter to James Richardson.

I have not felt well enough to enjoy myself very much since I have been here. I find this warm, damp weather rather enervating, but when I finally get settled – I hope by a splendid system of daily bathing and exercise which I have in my mind to get as stout and hearty as the best of you.[8]

However, he got along well with the family and kept busy after his arrival by joining them "in seeing the place, & in various walks and excursions into the neighboring country." These walks could be quite strenuous, such as climbing to their customary picnic area 2-3 miles up the hill behind the town, or even eight miles to the top of the crater in the center of the island. The hills behind the town of Horta had fantastic views of beautiful valleys, the sea and nearby islands, particularly Pico a little over 5 miles away with a volcanic peak rising from the coast to over eight thousand feet. He describes two of the major walks he and the family made and gives an overall picture of the island's charm.

Last Monday we went on a pic-nic to Sant'Amaro, a large garden two or three miles off, belonging to Mr. Dabney, & where the family usually go on Sunday afternoons. It is a famous place covering two sides of a hill, a perfect wilderness of trees & labyrinth of winding steep walks bordered with roses; full of grottoes & jutting rocks clambered over by vines, & rustic seats meeting you in all sorts of unexpected nooks. On the summit is a tower of white stone from whose top (I am almost distracted with this obdurante pen and muddy ink) is a fine view of the sea & distant islands on the one hand & the "Happy Valley" of the Flemingos spotted with villages & farmhouses, on the other. That beautiful valley! I have seen nothing that so charmed me – while the dinner was unpacking. I wandered away by myself till I came to little cave on the side of the hill the shade of whose rocky roof hung with vines and feathery ferns invited me to enter – I sat down upon a twisted root & gave myself up to the beauty of the scene. The soft wind came tempered from the sea. Before the entrance was a light arbor of ivy & through its arched front as in a frame I saw the picture of the treetops & the undulating hills patched with varied green & beyond, the ocean meeting with the sky. From the town came now & then the softened jingling of the bells of the convent churches ringing a merry peal – for it was one of the Whitsuntide holidays – & occasionally music from the little hamlet at the foot of the hill, & always the songs of many birds, for the first time I was perfectly happy. ...It was on our return from the garden that I first visited the Valley of the Flemingoes which has so enchanted me that I would fair take up my abode there for the rest of my life.[9]

The most important excursion we have taken was our visit, last Tuesday, to the Caldeira, or crater, in the centre of the island. No longer ebullient, it has not even smoked within the memory of man. A large party we were, of ladies and gentlemen, on horses, donkeys and feet. I found a walk of eight miles up a constant and very rough ascent, in the middle of a hot day, not a little fatiguing and perhaps for this reason was little moved by a scene which is expected, I believe, to put strangers into raptures. In the midst of a steep and barren common, covered with moss and heath, you come, all at once, upon a huge cup, five miles in circumference and perfectly regular; so deep that the sheep feeding at the bottom looked no larger than white mice; its sides channeled with rains, and within it a gloomy Stygian lake and a smaller cone and crater. The whole scene was wild and gloomy, but had little beauty.[10]

In a letter to his father he describes the Dabney family and the town of Horta

The family I find extremely pleasant, easy & kind. Mr. Dabney is a man of very polished manners, his wife one of the most excellent of women. There are three sons at home – the two youngest of whom, one eighteen & the other fourteen will be under my charge, together with two of the daughters one sixteen the other eight. One other daughter completes the family. I have not yet commenced my duties.[11]

In another letter to his family, Samuel describes his daily life once he had settled in with the Dabneys and his young students.

We breakfast at eight o'clock, which will perhaps strike you as a pleasant arrangement, though full late for summer, at nine I join my four pupils in the schoolroom, where we remain with short intermission, till twelve. The two hours before dinner, since it has become too hot to walk, I spend in various light relaxations – reading, playing on the piano, billiards, or turning in which last two, my education in these branches having been neglected in early youth, my skill is not so great as it will be – now confess, didn't you laugh at the idea of my playing billiards? Frank laughs to see me play. We dine at two or half past, & generally have by way of company one or more whaling captains (the whale ships from New Bedford generally stop here) and sometimes the captain or other officers of her Majesty's steamship Styx, who are engaged in a survey of the islands. From four to six I am in the schoolroom again with Sam & Frank & Mrs. Savage's two boys, who come down to have the benefit of my instructions half the day. We do not have tea till eight o'clock, so that all the twilight strolling so pleasant in summertime has to be done before tea instead of after, as at home, and after shutting the school room door I generally set off for a long walk, either alone, or with some of the ladies, while another party takes a sail or row, or a ride on horseback or donkey-back. Mrs. Dabney has tried hard to make me ride a jack, but I have not yet made myself ridiculous in that way. I mean to try it one of these days. After tea we adjourn to the saloon or drawing room. This is a very large & pleasant, but rather incongruous apartment. Incongruous, for a drawing room, because the billiard table is here & because, for the sake of dancing, it has no carpet. Generally some of the Bagatelle family come in (Bagatelle is the name of Madam Dabney's place, about a mile from our house) or other visitors; the gentlemen play billiards, others waltz to the music of the piano, others read, talk, or play a game of Dr. Busby. Or if there is no company we read aloud, perhaps, or have music from the young people. Altogether it is a very pleasant way of living. Everything is in handsome style. Not unlike, I fancy, an English gentleman's country seat – assuredly very much like one of Miss Edgeworth's novels.[12]

The Dabney's religion entered all aspects of their life. They were Unitarians, but because of the strength of the Catholic Church in Portugal the islands lacked any protestant churches. As a result, the family conducted services in their home. During their services they read a sermon or an essay by one of the New England Unitarian ministers, which not infrequently led to family discussions, some of which could be heated. A number of the sermons were very recent, as were the books they read because the Dabney Company ships operated almost a shuttle between Boston and Faial. It also helped that the Dabneys were part of the same circle as the Longfellows and their friends in the Boston Unitarian and Transcendental communities. Among these was Ralph Waldo Emerson, whose daughter Ellen spent several months on Faial and visited the Dabneys.

During his year on Faial, Samuel sometimes attended mass at the Catholic churches. He mentioned going to mass to his family and some of his friends, but told them to "have no fears – or hopes – of [him] becoming a Catholic here. The formality is too bald & glaring." He considered attending these services as part of his own learning experience and evaluation of religious concepts.

I have been interested in visiting the Catholic churches and witnessing their ceremonies. There is a sentiment of the poetic and a sentiment of the past hanging about them which appeals to my ideality and reverence. Still it is very sad to see how dead and lifeless a shell these forms have become. The lower classes are sincere and devotional, but those who have such a degree of intellectual development enough to put a new life *into* the form are in bad condition. And this is the case with most of the "better class" of people here (particularly the men), and with some at least of the priests. If I could make a reform I would not begin by doing away with the Catholic religion, – for the mass of the people, at least. If one could reform the priests, and by that I mean as much as anything, open their eyes, now blinded by the dust which falls from every crevice of their ancient pile, and show them the mighty responsibility which rests upon them as the guardians of the people, and moreover show them *how* to begin a moral regeneration that would be the best way.[13]

Their children's education was very important to the Dabneys. Initially they had sent all their children to America for schooling, some with well-known teachers. Charles Dabney's oldest daughter Clara studied at the Beecher's School where her teachers were Catherine Beecher and Harriet Beecher (later Stowe). In the mid-1830s the family began to hire tutors to come to the island and stay for a year or two. The tutor on Faial just before Samuel Longfellow was Edward H. Clarke, who had been recommended by Dabney family friend and Harvard President, Josiah Quincy.

Samuel replaced Edward H. Clarke, who was a Longfellow family friend and the son of Mrs. Clarke with whom Samuel boarded in Cambridge. Edward Clarke left Faial to study medicine in Europe and later became one of the most respected physicians in Boston. On December 16, 1872, Dr. Edward Clarke, who was now at the Harvard Medical School, was the invited speaker at The New England Women's Club in Boston and talked about the problems women could have if they were provided education. Naturally this created a stir in certain circles and Dr. Clarke published a book expanding on his ideas and clarifying what he meant in defense of his statements to the Women's Club. He provided a detailed explanation of his statements and what he saw as problems for women, and not just in education.[14]

Dr. Clarke went on to publicize his "ideas" in popular books and talks in which he inspired others in his profession to prescribe "rest cures" for ambitious women. However, members of the club who heard the speech included a number of women's rights activists including club president and poet Julia Ward Howe, writer Louisa May Alcott, the vigorous abolitionist and suffragist Lucretia Mott, as well as Lucy Stone, an Oberlin College graduate, who had started a trend by keeping her own name when she married. These outspoken reformers disputed Dr. Clarke's views and physician Mary Putnam Jacobi wrote a response providing clinical evidence that menstruation was evidence of health, not debility and argued that the ability of women in all areas had been greatly underestimated.

Samuel Longfellow started his classes with students who were somewhat reserved in their acceptance of a new teacher who was replacing one they had liked so much and had so recently left. However, it didn't take them long to warm up to Samuel Longfellow and welcome him into their family. One of the children who commented on the change in teachers was 16-year old Roxana Dabney.

> I confess to feeling some antagonism at first towards Mr. Longfellow, for I was very much attached to our former tutor, Mr. Clarke, as indeed we all were.

> Who could help liking Mr. Samuel Longfellow, and I became from the first, when he started me with Italian, so charmed that I sorely regretted that I was to lose his tuition, when it was decided that I was to accompany my grandmother and Aunt Annie to the United States to go to school, either in Boston or Philadelphia. ...Mr. Longfellow's especial favorites were S.W.D. [Samuel Wyllys Dabney] and your Aunt Fan, of whom Mr. Longfellow wrote a friend that "she was a sunbeam that lighted on the earth nine years since."[15]

In addition to the family homes on Faial, the Dabneys had a residence on the island of Pico facing the town of Horta on Faial. Pico was covered with vineyards, including those of the Dabneys, and the grapes from these produced a wine similar to Madeira

wine that was a favorite of the Czars of Russia. In 1853 a grape
blight struck the island and almost destroyed the economies of
Pico and Faial. As a result a number of the residents took up
whaling from the shore in small boats introduced into the islands
by the Dabneys.

Besides its agriculture and whaling, Pico was also a summer
retreat for people on Faial and the Dabneys spent several weeks
there every year. During Samuel's year on Faial he was taken
over to Pico with his students and enjoyed the stay and the different activities. However, even this short voyage across the five-
-mile wide channel was a trial for Samuel and his inclination to
seasickness. The house the Dabneys owned on Pico was called
the Priory because of its previous use that ended in 1834 with
the liberal victory in the Portuguese Civil War and the closing
of the convents and monasteries in Portugal.

> The house is oddly constructed, a one story house. On a high
> basement – & – this is the odd point, all the rooms open at
> the top, that is, without any ceiling, so the first thing on waking
> was a general conversation, from one cell to another, a wishing
> of good morning, enquiries as to the weather & as to the dis-
> position of certain individuals to take a bath before breakfast,
> which disposition was observed to be much more ardent during
> the first few days.[16] [*letter to Anne Longfellow Pierce,* 29 October
> 1843.]

Life on Pico was a break from the routine of Horta and Samuel
told his mother, "It is the kind of life that suits me exactly."[17]
He described one of these idyllic days on Pico to his sister Anne.

> After breakfast, the ladies read Yucatan while I & my two
> pupils kept school, a sort of "play school" it was. In recess we
> played battledore or jumped rope in a way in which perhaps
> you never figured – a sociable game – two people swinging
> the rope while the rest ran round & jumped over it. I never
> quite conquered my dread of that fearful rope & we always got
> into a great gale, after dinner, to which it was very comfortable
> to come in a dressing gown or blouse & after a slight siesta,

I generally read aloud, till it was time for our evening walk. Pico looks from the shore like a mass of ragged black rocks with here & there a tinge of green, but get up into the country & look down & the green quite predominates; we found some really verdant little nooks. I sometimes took my sketch book with me & tried to draw the picturesque looking women whom we saw at the wells, dressed in blue jackets & full skirts, with flat straw hats, or met coming down the road, with water buckets or baskets on their heads, & a step firm & free as Elsker's. We got home by dark & the two hours before our late tea were spent in various amusements, such as dancing scotch reels & strathspeys or the Portuguese national dances, which are very graceful, when well danced, but very monotonous. Then after tea, (we had famous appetites, & drink Pico well-water like heroes, or Washingtonians) we read or talked Portuguese, by way of a lesson on the part of Miss Jessie Paterson & myself, or else wrote a newspaper which we sent to our friends in Horta twice a week.[18]

Among the material that he taught to his pupils were the concepts that his group of friends in New England adhered to, but which many people did not accept. One of these ideas was Transcendentalism that most of the Dabneys considered something objectionable. Samuel appears to have enjoyed presenting something to his pupils and having them like the idea and then taking them off guard by telling that it is something they thought they shouldn't like.

Mrs. Child's letters, which I have read with much delight, as have the ladies, who did not know & were surprised when told that it was transcendental to the considerable (inward) triumph of Miss Olivia & myself. The same was the case with "words in a Sunday school" which they were all charmed with & said if that were transcendentalism they had always been in a mist & it was a better thing than they had taken it for. Is it not the office of such writers as these to lead down Transcendentalism in the common mind (which cannot take it in its condensed Emersonian form) through the medium of the affections

& sympathies & the simpler poetic emotions, and is it not beautiful to see how through various channels it is tinging the thought & literature of the time?[19]

There were three events that occurred during the time Samuel was on Faial that caught his attention. One was the surprise visit by Dr. Webster, several years before his trial, who brought something that was sure to interest Samuel because of his experiments with photography.

> On going down to breakfast I found Dr. Webster in the parlor, who had appeared to the great surprise of all, in the Harbinger. What a sky rocket he is! A pleasant man, too, to keep one alive & stirring in a quiet place like this. The quantity of news he contrived to give out before breakfast was over, was perfectly astonishing, as was also the quantity of luggage he brought with him for a three weeks visit, great box, little box, band box & basket. He brought a Daguerrotype apparatus among the rest, and such a funny time as we had at Dr. Davis's (not Gilman's) one afternoon, when he was trying to take a view of Pico; It was a total failure as were all the other attempts he made here, which he attributed to the fact that the air was three per cent moister here than at Cambridge.[20]

Shortly after the *Harbinger's* arrival, the *U.S.S. Missouri* sailed into the bay of Horta. The appearance of a warship from any country was always a major event in Horta, and particularly if it was an American vessel.

> Shortly after the Harbinger came in, we had a visit from the Steamer Missouri which was taking Mr. Cushing on his way to China. They staid here two days & a half, and you may imagine what a pleasant episode it was in our quiet life, & what an excitement it created, the visit of an American national vessel at Fayal being an extremely rare occurrence. Our house was full of officers – they came to breakfast, to dinner & to tea, and in the intermediate times to walk in the gardens & play billiards. Altogether as Americans we had reason to be proud of the ship

& her officers, who were remarkably fine looking & intelligent men, & contrasted favorably with the English naval officers who have been here. Mrs. Dabney gave them a party.[21]

Perhaps the most important event for Samuel was the marriage of his brother Henry to Frances Appleton, known as Fanny. He learned about the nuptials from a New Bedford newspaper before any letters from his family arrived with the news. While Samuel does not express any problems with learning about the wedding secondhand, his curiosity was surely piqued.

One piece of news, however, you will not surprise me with – though I have not yet quite got over the astonishment with which I read in a New Bedford newspaper the other day of Henry's marriage to Miss Fanny Appleton, altogether the most sudden & unexpected thing that I have met with. One of the last things that Miss Lowell told me was, that Henry had assured her that his heart was entirely free, & that he could now meet Miss Appleton without any emotion. I am extremely curious to know how it all happened, and not a little so to see the lady, which I have never done. I do not feel quite sure yet that it is not all mistake.[22]

Henry's engagement & marriage – altogether the most romantic & entirely sudden thing on record. Odd, too, that I should have learned it first from a New Bedford newspaper. I was glad to hear the details from you & Anne, being, naturally, curious on the point, and very glad to hear that she has so won your love.[23]

A few months later, Samuel received his first letter from his new sister-in-law as an addendum to a letter from Henry. Shortly after that he wrote to Fanny and sent her a present of local handicrafts.

Dear Sammy, my dumb duties of amanuensis being over, I must say a few words for myself. If they are my first to you, it is not my fault & I shall be grieved if I find you have been looking at this while for my sisterly greeting. At this late day I send you, in case this may have happened, & I assure you that although the sea is between us, I have learned to love you, & I shall count your friendship as enriching a happiness already so great as mine is. *now* I have no time at present for more than these brief sentences, but wishing you all pleasure & health in yr sunny Island, remain very affly. yrs Fanny Longfellow.[24]

My dear Sister – Your letter thro' England <u>was not</u> received. But it will be along one of these days from St. Michaels or Lisbon. Meanwhile, I hope to answer it by an American barque, which sails in two or three weeks & will bear to America all my sins of omission, in the way of correspondence. I send you two or three Fayal baskets, such as I could get in a hurry. Will you send one of them to Caroline Greenleaf – I wish I could fill them with Fayal Flowers.

Affectionately yours,[25]

Samuel began to notice changes for the better in his health as the year progressed on Faial. The Azores were famous for their health-giving climate and a number of travelers of the period went there for this purpose alone. Combining this with the low--stress work he enjoyed and the chance to walk and swim year round, it is not surprising that Samuel found himself feeling better.

I certainly feel much better than when I first arrived. I was miserably off the first few weeks after the voyage & feared they would think me the most stupid of beings; I had not energy enough for thought or speech. I bathe in the sea almost every day, & walk every afternoon, after school, one or two hours. One gets a great deal of exercise, too, out of a walk here – the roads are so roughly paved & so steep. There are many beautiful places near the town & I have already some favourite walks. I often take my sketch book with me – that, with my cane generally my only companion, the young people here not being fond of walking. I find entertainment enough, however, in my own thoughts & in observing the odd people I meet, some very picturesque & some very ragged. Then I make great friends of the little boys who come begging for "cinc reisin" or five mills (a modest sum) with such merry voices & such beautiful eyes, that I forget how ragged & dirty they are, & in default of money show them my sketches & try to talk Portuguese with them. I have learned a little of the language, & take a lesson every morning before breakfast, with Sam Dabney.[26]

Physical well-being was not Samuel Longfellow's only concern and he also made an effort to improve his mental and emotional state. In a letter to his best friend Samuel Johnson, he provides some insight about how he did this and provides us with an idea of his approach to life.

For myself, I have scarce written anything of prose or verse since I have been here – save letters. Indeed I have thought but little; less, much less, than I hoped and expected. Still, I have lived some beautiful hours and had some revelations from the world around me, – revelations which have given peace to my soul and which I hope may prove nourishing dews to the germs of spiritual life within me. And yet, at times, – I feel sad and depressed at the consciousness of my want of intellectual development. You cannot tell how much I suffered when I first came here. I was very dull, and silent, and stupid, and then much ashamed and mortified at being dull, and stupid, and silent. This made me very unhappy, more so than my words convey. I felt as if I had nothing which was wanted here. Then it was that, in my solitary walks, nature whispered, "Peace! vex not thyself because though art not as others! Be content to be that which thou art; manifest thyself according to the laws of the individual being. The flower at thy feet hopes not to be a star, nor strives to be aught but a flower. Be calm, and fear not but thou wilt find thy place. Believe that thou wast not for nothing sent into the world. Obey thy nature, and fear not but that thou wilt do the good thou wast sent to do." Such lessons did the trees and rocks and waters, the green hills and that calm, majestic mountain breathe into my heart. Nor were words of man wanting, and in the pages of Emerson I found strength and reassurance. I am content now to be silent when I have nothing to say. Indeed, I begin to think silence better than words. ...I cannot tell how much comfort I have had from *one* source; how happy I have felt in the consciousness, as I never felt it before, of the near presence of friends absent in the body. Often, my friend, have you come and walked beside me in my evening ramble, or opened the door of this chamber, as you used to do that of my room in Massachusetts Hall, and this, not as a thing of fancy but a reality.[27]

Samuel Longfellow had given himself a year to stay on Faial, and as the end of this period approached he began to consider his return and his options in Cambridge. His improved health and the free time he had available allowed him to think about the direction of his life. Some of his ideas were among those that he had considered before he left for Faial and had not completely discarded. In letters to his brother Henry and friend James Richardson, he expresses some of his thoughts about his future on his return.

You ask about my plans. I shall be able to write you more decidedly about them by the next Harbinger – only; as to the Professorship, I have given up the idea – as to the European tour I should like to take a turn through England, Germany & France on my way home next summer, but I am sure I should not enjoy it without a companion. If therefore you can persuade any of my friends to meet me in England I should be happy to make the said tour with them.[28]

I am somewhat troubled, James, not to know what you are doing in the school, and a little so about my connection with it & my probable return to it. I wish you would enquire whether & on what conditions I can go on with the class on my return. I should not exactly like to join another class, & have you all getting on a year before me. And yet I don't know that it would matter much, for I should see you & be with you as much as ever out of the recitation room. However, I have something further to say. Which is that I have doubts about going back to Cambridge at all on my return. I have thought whether I might not pursue my Theological studies as advantageously elsewhere. More advantageously in some respects. I did not, I must confess, find Divinity Hall all that I expected. I did not find a band of brothers seriously & earnestly devoting themselves to a great religious work – building up each others souls into a simple piety & encouraging each other to every good work. I found triflings & contentious & jealousies, & hard words. I do not doubt that there was much more good than I saw, but I did not find it by my own fault perhaps, but so it was, & I was disappointed & dispirited. I have thought of two plans – one the good old fashioned way of studying with some clergyman in private – say my own good pastor Dr. Nichols, – the other is what I used to talk to you about sometimes – that is to retire to the Brookfarm Community & study with Mr. Ripley. I have felt at times much inclined to this latter course. It would have peculiar advantage of including the necessity (if I joined the Com.) & offering the opportunity (if I merely resided there) of physical labor, which would be a great thing for me. I am stronger & more vigorous than when I left Cambridge, but I am not well yet, as how should I be? Now dear James these three plans are in my mind but have not taken very definite shape yet. I do not like to fluctuate, but I should not hesitate to change where I was pretty sure of finding the rest I seek.[29]

In a letter to Fanny he announces his return and the elimination of one of his choices: "I shall return in the H.[arbinger] the next time & be with you in early August, having given up the trip to Europe – set it forward, that is, a little farther into the future."[30]

In the summer of 1844, Samuel returned to America on the Dabney ship *Harbinger*, a voyage that took 28 days, "no longer than we expected, yet tedious enough on all hands." Joining him on the voyage were several members of the Dabney family who were going to the graduation of Charles Dabney, Jr., from Harvard. It was "the most hot, dusty & bustling" time of the year in Cambridge and one Samuel Longfellow found "disagreeable."

In a letter to Samuel Dabney, with whom he maintained a lifelong correspondence, he expressed regret that he had seen so little of Charles, Jr., and "the rest of my Fayal friends at this time."[31] Several times throughout his life Samuel found himself under stress and feeling in poor health, and at these times he told his friends that he was planning a trip to Faial to recover. While he took off other times for health reasons, his dream place to recover when he was feeling worst was the island of Faial with its peace and beauty.

Samuel arrived back in Cambridge, well rested, in better health and prepared to set out on the next phase of his life. He moved into the Craigie House in Cambridge where he lived with his brother Henry and sister-in-law Fanny. The Craigie House had been built in 1759, used by George Washington as his headquarters during the siege of Boston and bought by Andrew Craigie in 1791. Henry Longfellow rented rooms there from Mrs. Craigie while he was a student and also a new professor at Harvard. After his marriage, Fanny's father, Nathan Appleton, bought the house for the young couple and Henry and Fanny lived out their lives there, with Samuel Longfellow as their not infrequent houseguest.

Notes:

[1] Letter, Samuel Longfellow to James Richardson, February 21, 1843, SLP, LNHS.

[2] Letter, Samuel Longfellow to Stephen Longfellow (father). April 24, 1843, SLP, LNHS.

[3] Longfellow, Samuel. *Journal, October 13, 1839 to April 26, 1843*, April 24, 1843.

[4] May, Joseph, Ed.. *Samuel Longfellow: Memoir and Letters*. Cambridge: The Riverside Press, 1894. p. 30.

[5] Letter, Samuel Longfellow to Edward Everett Hale, June 11, 1843.SLP, LNHS.

[6] Letter, Samuel Longfellow to James Richardson, June 8, 1843. SLP, LNHS.

[7] Letter, Samuel Longfellow to Stephen Longfellow (father) and Anne Longfellow Pierce. July 7, 1843. SLP; LNHS.

[8] Letter, Samuel Longfellow to James Richardson, June 8, 1843. SLP, LNHS.

[9] Ibid.

[10] Letter, Samuel Longfellow to Edward Everett Hale, June 11, 1843. May, Joseph. *Memoir*.

[11] Letter, Samuel Longfellow to James Richardson, June 8, 1843. SLP, LNHS.

[12] Letter, Samuel Longfellow to Stephen Longfellow (father) and Anne Longfellow Pierce. July 7, 1843. SLP; LNHS.

[13] Letter, Samuel Longfellow to John T.G. Nichols, 26 February 1844. May, Joseph. *Memoir.*

[14] Clarke, Edward H. *Sex in education, or, A fair chance for the girls.* James R. Osgood and Company. Boston.1875.

[15] Dabney, Roxana Lewis, *Annals of the Dabney Family in Fayal.* n.p., 1912. p. 455-6,

[16] Letter, Samuel Longfellow to Anne Longfellow Pierce, October 29, 1843. SLP, LNHS.

[17] Letter, Samuel Longfellow to Zilpah Longfellow, October 7, 1843. SLP, LNHS.

[18] Letter, Samuel Longfellow to Anne Longfellow Pierce, October 29, 1843. SLP, LNHS.

[19] Letter, Samuel Longfellow to James Richardson, February 16, 1844. SLP, LNHS.

[20] Letter, Samuel Longfellow to Mary Longfellow Greenleaf, September 7, 1843. SLP, LNHS.

[21] Ibid.

[22] Letter, Samuel Longfellow to Zilpah Longfellow, August 15, 1843. SLP, LNHS.

[23] Letter, Samuel Longfellow to Mary Longfellow Greenleaf, September 7, 1843. SLP, LNHS.

[24] Letter, Henry W. Longfellow to Samuel Longfellow, January 12, 1844. LP.

[25] Letter, Samuel Longfellow to Henry W. Longfellow, February 18, 1844. LP.

[26] Letter, Samuel Longfellow to Zilpah Longfellow, August 15, 1843. SLP, LNHS.

[27] Letter, Samuel Longfellow to Samuel Johnson, November 21, 1843. May, Joseph. *Memoir.*

[28] Letter, Samuel Longfellow to Henry W. Longfellow, February 18, 1844. LP.

[29] Letter, Samuel Longfellow to James Richardson, February 16, 1844. SLP, LNHS.

[30] Letter, Samuel Longfellow to Fanny Longfellow, May 11, 1844. SLP, LNHS.

[31] Letter, Samuel Longfellow to Samuel Dabney, September 5, 1844. ADF.

CHAPTER 7 – RE-DIVINED

After an enjoyable and restful year on the island of Faial, Samuel Longfellow once again took up his theological studies at Harvard Divinity School, this time with renewed vigor and direction. His initial residence after he returned to Cambridge and returned to school was the Craigie House where his brother Henry and his wife Fanny lived. "Through the devoted love of the two brothers, it was, at intervals, the home for long periods, of Samuel Longfellow also."[1] He returned to the Craigie house periodically whether he was living elsewhere in Cambridge or living in other towns where he had his ministry.

Samuel's stay at Craigie House had the benefit of allowing him to enjoy being part of a family. He got along very well with Fanny and adored their children. Of course, he also had his household duties. In a letter to his sister Anne, he describes how he assisted Henry with some of his routine daily work.

> I am finishing my letter in the morning and Henry has just called me to my Secretarial labors. Do you know the grand plan how I act as his amanuensis, in answering letters from a half hour to an hour before breakfast while he is shaving & dressing. The greatest saving of time it is that has ever come in fashion.[2]

His strength having been restored Samuel applied himself to his second-year studies. The two-year Divinity School program at Harvard was divided into a theoretical and a practical curriculum. The theoretical curriculum comprised a variety of topics and they were the focus of the studies during the first year. During the second year, the practical tasks that would be needed in the working ministry became more important in the students' coursework. Among these were the writing and presentation of sermons.

In a letter to his sister Anne, Samuel mentions his first experience in writing a sermon.

> I carried in my first sermon, this week to Dr. Francis – we are to write one a month during the year. He expressed himself pleased with it. I wish you would send me by Mary the MS which you have of mine.[3]

Samuel was considered a better writer than speaker, at least when he first began preparing sermons. To improve themselves, Samuel and his classmates practiced presenting their sermons to each other. His good friend Edward Everett Hale provides a comment on Samuel's preaching ability and confirms his skill in writing sermons.

> As a preacher, he did not excel in popular power. As a rule, his speech was neither eloquent nor magnetic, nor were his discourses rich in illustration. Yet they were impressively serious. He held attention by the spell of his fine personality, and because he always *aimed at the centre*. Righteousness was as great a word to him as to any Hebrew prophet. And his sermon material was always of the best, – not merely literary or critical, but mind-illuminating, motive quickening, life helping.[4]

That his congregations felt the same is demonstrated by a comment that Edward Everett Hale overheard from one of the congregation members and about which he adds his own comments.

> "Mr. Longfellow could say anything in that pulpit which he chose. We might not agree with a syllable that he said, we might wish that he was saying something else; but we never thought of anything which you can call antagonism to him, and never thought of limiting in any way his right to say it again and again, as often as he chose."
>
> For me, I have never seen so remarkable an illustration of what Dr. Putnam used to call "the wrath of the lamb," – the

strength of a person whose personal was so tender and modest and gentle that you were half afraid to trust him out of doors, showing itself, when there was any need in vigor amounting to audacity, and in moral control of every one to whom he had to speak.[5]

Samuel Johnson also returned to Divinity School in early 1845 after a trip to Europe with Washington Very, whose family he knew from Salem.

> In 1845 [Samuel Johnson] is back again in the Divinity School, joining the class below that which he had first entered. As we had each been absent a year, we were again together. He returned much refreshed in mind and body, though he was never thoroughly free from the bodily ailments belonging to his bilious temperament.[6]

Samuel Longfellow was glad that Johnson had returned and even more pleased that they would be in the same class in Divinity School.

> Of course you will come back to the school one of these days & join my class. I can hardly call it ours. I hated to leave the old one, but shall feel better if I can get you back again. But you must not come till you are well & then we will keep up a magnificent system of diet & exercise. At any rate you will make us many visits in the Spring & Summer.[7]

At the end of the school year in 1845, Samuel's original Divinity School class graduated. In a letter to Mrs. Dabney in the Azores, he not only expressed his feelings about being close to his former classmates, but remarked on how he felt about his own preparation for the ministry.

> Today is the Valedictory of the Senior Class. Tomorrow my friends of the Divinity School should have their parting exercises. It is my own class and I feel as if I should be among them. I have nearer and dearer friends in that class than in the class which

I joined on my return, and as long as they remained here I felt as if I were still one of them; but now they are going out to their work and leave me behind. Still, in view of my own poor preparation for so great a trust, I cannot for a moment regret that I have a year longer for girding myself for the task. At times my feeling of unfitness is painful and discouraging; but I try to keep such thoughts from me. I do not care so much for any intellectual disabilities or short comings, but I fear I shall never have devotion and earnestness enough, purity and holiness, and spiritual life enough to break the bread of life to a hungry and waiting world.[8]

Even though he still had doubts about himself and what he wanted to do, Samuel had matured since graduating from Harvard. During his second year in Divinity School, his ideas became more fully crystallized and he chose a direction for his life. His friends soon became aware of the change in his way of thinking and considered him a step ahead of the generally accepted beliefs.

The Unitarianism in which the Longfellow family had been trained was that of the early leaders of that faith, and according to the testimony of his brother Samuel, Henry Longfellow seems never to have essentially departed from its conclusions. But the younger brother was a radical by nature, and though up to the time of his entrance upon the study for the ministry his views may not have undergone much change from those in which he had been brought up, his radical and transcendental tendencies soon manifested themselves, and at the time of his graduation he stood far in advance of the Unitarianism of half a century ago. But though he never concealed his convictions, they were never aggressively put forward, and people listened to him gladly even when their own views were not in perfect accord with his.[9]

Joseph May describes how Samuel Longfellow applied himself in his classes. Now that he had made his decision regarding his life's calling, he was wholeheartedly occupied in becoming as well prepared as possible. As a result, his beliefs and attitudes matured and became better defined. He was no longer the boy, but was becoming the man Samuel who would have so much influence in various areas during the period.

> The growth and maturing of Longfellow's character reflect themselves clearly in the remains of his correspondence. His interest in social reforms deepens visibly. His radicalism of thought becomes more and more distinct, although he parts slowly with the forms of opinion and modes of expression in which he had grown up. The question of moral and intellectual fitness for the ministry agitates his mind, alongside the anticipations of its various forms of duty and visions of places of settlement, which are common to students in the last year of their theological course. There appears always that mixture of extreme modesty as to his powers and attainments, with the firmest quiet self-confidence where a distinct moral or intellectual issue presents itself, which was characteristic of the man throughout his life.[10]

One of Samuel's most important activities was to prepare and present his first sermon in public.

> It was the custom at that time to "allow" the members of the senior class to preach in the neighboring churches as a "labor of love." They were to try their 'prentice hand, but without money and without price, so as not to interfere with the graduates of the school who were not yet "settled."[11]

However, Samuel had some reservations about his abilities to preach. He expresses his concern in a letter to his father

> I feel some hesitation about beginning to preach, this vacation. Still I am anxious to make the experiment that I may have some idea what the reality is, & how far I am fitted for it. I am sure, too, that I shall be better able to write sermons after having preached from the pulpit a few times.[12]

One of the reasons for Samuel's concern was that he believed he had problems in the way he spoke. Consequently, he wanted to take elocution lessons, but did not have the money for it. He asked his father for some help in paying, which he was willing to do.

> I shall see immediately what can be done about the lessons in Elocution. I am not insensible to the importance of a well cultivated voice to the preacher, & I regret that better provision is not made in the department at the school. The only exercise of the kind there is one in reading during the first two years, but this amounts to very little.[13]

Samuel Longfellow's first sermons, as well as Samuel Johnson's, were at Dedham in the pulpit of Dr. Lamson, a classmate of Samuel Johnson's father. In a letter to Johnson, Longfellow describes what must have been one of the most important days in his life.

> Dear Sam
> I have preached, and like it very well! But the strangest thing must come first; strangest because it was least of all expected or premeditated; yet came about in the most natural manner. I am to preach next Sunday for Theodor Parker, at West Roxbury, which society it seems, he still supplies (preaching there himself in the afternoon) till February. So you see I have quite got the start of you in that matter...
> But first about Dedham. You know the melancholy storm on Saturday. I went to D. in the evening train, and, getting out of the cars, soon encountered a little man whom I knew at once must be Dr. Lamson. I introduced myself, and we trudgd up through the snow to his warm house, where I was in five minutes entirely at home, so informal and kind were they... We sat up till eleven o'clock, talking. But oh! Sam, all night I dreamed haunting dreams about my first preaching. I cannot remember them know, but one was that when I got into the pulpit I found that my sermon was entitled Lalla Rookh [an oriental romantic poem by Irish Poet Thomas Moore], and

I was afraid to preach it. The last phase of the dream was that I awoke and went down, and found that it was six o'clock of Sunday *evening:* that I had, in fact slept all day, and that the doctor had preached in my place!

After breakfast I selected my chapter and hymns. The doctor's collection proved to be the old "New York collection," unlike any I ever saw, and I could not find one of the hymns I wanted, except "While Thee I seek," for the opening in the afternoon. The sexton came for the hymns, the bell rang the knell (of parting Sam), and we went through the snow to the church. To my great joy it had cleared off and was a glad, bright sunshine. At the head of the broad aisle (which is a short one), the doctor bowed to me to go up on one side, while he ascended on the other. We went up the pulpit stairs like Moses and Aaron, "in the sight of the congregation," which consisted, as it seemed to me, of about *ten* people. I suppose the real number was fifty or so. I would have waited for more to come, but presently the doctor, who knew better, motioned to me to begin, and I arose and made the opening prayer. It seemed just like the School. Then I stepped down and would have taken the hymn-book, but the doctor told me the Scripture must be read next. (N. B. I had been studying the order of the services all the morning!) So I opened the Bible, and made no blunder, except reading the wrong chapter, mistaking xviii, for xvii. The long prayer I made myself and made it short, I suspect. Then the sermon. I was not in the least embarrassed or nervous, but felt rather stiff and not altogether at ease; moreover without a spark of enthusiasm I was glad to find that I could see the people and I discovered one young man listening intently... But in the afternoon I looked and he came not. Sam, the sermon of "Suffering," I am sorry to say, moved rather heavily. In the afternoon I gave them the sermon of "Reforms." I felt now entirely at my ease; the discourse is more animated and I was myself quite lively. At its close the doctor said quite heartily: "I like your sermon very much. I should not wish to alter a word of it." So ended my first preaching; and on the whole I liked it very well, as I said. Still, I felt no seriousness or solemnity about the matter, *that* I must tell you. In the prayers, indeed, I did at times lose myself and felt something of earnestness. I found not the least difficulty or fatigue in speaking. It must be a remarkably easy church to speak in, and I am glad you are going to begin there.[14]

The evening after his first sermon, Dr. Lamson took him to hear Theodore Parker speak on slavery at the Boston Academy of Ministers. Parker spoke about the duties of the north, filled his speech with irony and sarcasm and took a swipe at the Academy. While Samuel liked what Parker had to say, he told Johnson that, "I cannot quite like that man. I feel that we are not of spiritual kin."[15] Later Dr. Lamson introduced Longfellow to Parker, who invited Samuel to speak at West Roxbury, a congregation for which he arranged substitute ministers and sometimes spoke himself.

Samuel Longfellow was strongly opposed to war and supported the peace organizations. Henry's friend Senator Charles Sumner was also a strong supporter of peace and spoke on the subject in Boston at a time most speakers spoke against slavery. In a letter to his sister Anne, Samuel considers the difference between a minister preaching peace and a layman talking about the same topic.

> Henry & Fanny have gone into Boston to hear Mr. Sumner's Oration. I shall defer my visit till the afternoon. Mr. Sumner, I am glad to say, is going to utter a strong protest against war, & show its [unreadable word] inconsistency with Christianity & with the true policy & the true glory of a country. These will be strange words in the ears of many who have never strayed into a Peace Society meeting & who think such words from the pulpit are only professional cant. Coming from a man in Mr. Sumner's position I think they will have a good effect in opening the minds of many who have never thought about the subject before to the wickedness & barbarity, or at least the absurdity & miserable policy of the whole system founded on that heathenish maxim "in peace prepare for war."[16]

Almost a year and a half after the above letter, Samuel had a chance to act on his beliefs when he voted in the 1846 Congressional elections. This was the first time that he had voted. He was opposed to President Polk's policy toward the Mexican--American War and the support the war had in Congress. Although not fully supporting the party, Samuel voted for Whig candidate John Gorham Palfrey. Palfrey won the election and served from 1847-1849. The Whigs supported a congress that was stronger than the executive branch of the government, however, some of their actions were contrary to what Samuel and his friends, as well as his brother Henry believed. They changed their support to the Free Soil party, which had its first party convention in 1848. As a result, during the next Congressional elections Palfrey ran as a member of the Free Soil Party, which had a platform stating: "We inscribe on our banner, 'Free Soil, Free Speech, Free Labor and Free Man,' and under it we will fight on and fight ever, until a triumphant victory shall reward our exertions". Unfortunately, Palfrey lost this election. Prior to entering politics, Palfrey had been a Professor of Sacred Literature at Harvard while Samuel was an undergraduate. After the election, Samuel describes his political feelings to Samuel Johnson.

To-day I voted, for the first time in my life & for Palfrey as Rep. to Congress. I have been reading some facts about the War to-day, & it is lamentable to see how those weak Whigs, all but 16 in both houses were panic struck, frightened, cajoled into assuming & supporting the war – a cunning trick of a despotic president who first assumed a power, to which he had no shadow of claim & then duped the Congress into taking the thing off his hands. It seems that they need not have done anything even to rescue [Zachary] Taylor, first because any assistance from them must necessarily be too late & secondly because he already had authority to demand aid, as he did, from Louisiana & Texas. Here is a thing to be reached by political action. Mr. [Daniel] Webster says in that weak speech of his "If the voting for the war-bill" stained a man's hand with blood, then is the whole Whig party red with blood up to the chin." True Daniel. Think of it, Sam, only sixteen men straight forward enough to cut through a "complicated question" by a simple fidelity – to conscience – not even acute politicians enough to keep out of the trap of their opponents.[17]

Notes:

[1] May, Joseph, Ed.. *Samuel Longfellow: Memoir and Letters.* Cambridge: The Riverside Press, 1894. p. 46.

[2] Letter, Samuel Longfellow to Anne Longfellow Pierce, April 24, 1845. SLP, LNHS.

[3] Letter, Samuel Longfellow to Anne Longfellow Pierce, Thursday night, 1845. SLP, LNHS.

[4] Hale, Edward Everett. *Five Prophets of Today.* Boston, 1892. p. 53-54.

[5] Ibid., p. 14-15.

[6] Longfellow, Samuel, Ed. *Lectures, Essays and Sermons by Samuel Johnson,* Boston: The Riverside Press, 1883, p. 26.

[7] Letter, Samuel Longfellow to Samuel Johnson, January 18, 1845. SLP, LNHS.

[8] Letter, Samuel Longfellow to Mrs. Charles William Dabney, July 18, 1845. ADF.

[9] Adams, Oscar Fay. "Samuel Longfellow." *The New England Magazine,* October 1894, v. 17, n.° 2, p. 205-213. Boston., p. 207.

[10] May, Joseph, Ed.. *Samuel Longfellow: Memoir and Letters.* Cambridge: The Riverside Press, 1894. p. 56-57.

[11] Longfellow, Samuel, *Lectures, Essays and Sermons by Samuel Johnson,* p. 27.

[12] Letter, Samuel Longfellow to Stephen Longfellow (father), December 16, 1845. SLP, LNHS.

[13] Ibid.

[14] Letter, Samuel Longfellow to Samuel Johnson, January 19,1846. SLP, LNHS.

[15] Ibid.

[16] Letter, Samuel Longfellow to Anne Longfellow Pierce, July 4, 1845. SLP, LNHS.

[17] Letter, Samuel Longfellow to Samuel Johnson, November 9, 1846. SLP, LNHS.

CHAPTER 8 – "THE BOOK OF SAMS"

Samuel Longfellow – Samuel Johnson – *The Book of Hymns*: mention one and the other two are very likely to come to mind for people most familiar with the work of these two men.

> The most important incident of Samuel Longfellow's remaining years at the school was the somewhat remarkable one of his undertaking, in conjunction with Samuel Johnson, to prepare a new book of hymns for the use of Unitarian congregations.[1] [*Memoir*, p. 48-49.]

The Unitarian churches of the period did not lack a choice of hymnbooks for use in their services. However, people like Joseph May considered them "dreary," even though they were great improvements over editions that predated Dr. Greenwood's published 15 years earlier, and which more than half the congregations used. May believed that "while it contained many noble and beautiful hymns, it was encumbered with a mass of sadly prosaic and antiquated ones."[2]

The Reverend Frank Appleton, a friend and former classmate of Longfellow and Johnson, had a pastorate in Danvers, Massachusetts where he "was using a very antiquated and to him unsatisfactory hymnal."[3] So they "told him one day that [they] would make a new one for his use."[4]

Longfellow and Johnson were concerned that the religious doctrine presented in contemporary hymns was "that of the conservative Unitarianism of the period."[5] "They had both grown into loving acceptance of a pure Theism, and their faith longed to set itself to music, the music of a religion at once natural and universal."[6] Others also felt the same way and produced hymnbooks that competed with those that contained what was considered the customary collection of hymns.

Joseph May describes what he thinks was the reason behind the two students wanting to produce one more hymnbook,

> Was largely a poetical one, but it was still more the desire to provide a body of hymns in which the religious attitude of the worshipper should be that of a more natural and immediate relation with the Divine Spirit, and in which, especially, the dignity of humanity, the hopefulness of being, the obligations of rectitude and brotherly love, should have more adequate expression.[7]

They thought that a new hymnbook was needed that would include hymns that were "aimed to attune the spirit of worship to pure thought, cleared of irrational tradition."[8]

Once the two friends had decided that a new hymnbook was needed, they set about producing it "with the greatest zeal and thoroughness and with a business energy hardly to be looked for in theological neophytes,"[9] "who knew nothing of the practical needs and administration of churches... But it was also another illustration that youth is the courageous original inventive period of life."[10]

They gathered hymnbooks and hymns from a variety of sources, including some from other denominations. They read thousands of hymns, compared them and came up with judgments on their acceptability for the hymnbook they had in mind. They also looked through poetry in newspapers and adapted what they could for their book.

In a letter to Johnson, Longfellow describes how he had been working on reading and selecting hymns and what he considered in evaluating them.

> I have not been idle about the Hymns. I have copied several new ones, and read over those I had already copied, a good many of which will have to be rejected – we must sift carefully, and not put in any new ones that are not really good – better than those we omit. My sister thinks we had best have quite a small, & a choice collection.[11]

A number of the hymns and poetry they used had already been written by friends and included one prominent poet brother named Henry. Among their other friends who were authors of the poetry they used were John Greenleaf Whittier, Sarah Flower Adams, Edmund Hamilton Sears, Richard Chenevix, Trench William Henry Furness, Edward Clarke, Jones Very, James Russell Lowell, Theodore Parker and Ralph Waldo Emerson. A letter from Emerson gives an idea of how he prepared his material for the hymnbook.

> I have recovered the old hymn which you ask for, & send a copy of it. In transcribing it, I have mended it & hope, a little; Yet it is easy to see that a little lavour would make it much better. But I am constrained today to let it go as it is, or not at all, and you shall print it or leave it, as you will.[12]

However, not all the ideas they wanted to express were to be found in the existing literature. As a result, they asked some of their friends to write new work with the specific purpose of meeting the needs of the hymnbook. In addition, the two friends wrote some of the hymns themselves with virtually all of these hymns credited to anonymous authors. Samuel Longfellow wrote a letter to Samuel Johnson in which he describes his work in preparing hymns.

> I have six or eight manuscript hymns, some of which you have seen – I think I shall write one or two; won't you? What do you say to this?... Do let us have some more original ones; such as will embody the true ideas, without all the plague of alteration; such as will just suit our sermons. I wish we had done this at first, instead of altering old hymns. Take your sermons, Sam, & write a hymn for each one. This was the way Dodderidge made his book.[13]

In his *Transcendentalism in New England: A History*, their friend Octavius Brooks Frothingham describes how each approached the hymns he wrote and contrasts their approach to Transcendentalist thought. Frothingham was a liberal Unitarian and later President of the Free Religious Association and he also wrote the first historical description of Transcendentalism.

A contemporary and intimate friend of Johnson, a Transcendentalist equally positive, but of more mystical type, is Samuel Longfellow. The two are interestingly contrasted, and by
contrast, blended. Between them they collected and published
a book of hymns – "Hymns of the Spirit" – to which both contributed original pieces, remarkably rich in sentiment, and of
singular poetical merit. Johnson's were the more intellectual,
Longfellow's the more tender; Johnson's the more aspiring,
Longfellow's the more devout; Johnson's the more heroic and
passionate, Longfellow's the more mystical and reflective.[14]

As if doing schoolwork, preparing a hymnbook and writing
sermons at the same time were not enough, Samuel Longfellow
and his friend Thomas Wentworth Higginson came up with the
idea for a small book of poems, which they published in 1853.
The poems were intended for reading during visits to the seaside.
They named the book *Thalatta* and it was considered a collection of poems that rivaled his brother's poetry.

Upon the top of a beautiful cliff crowned with pines and
birches, I planned a little book for people to take with them
to such places, which should contain all the charming bits of
poetry in the language about the sea and seashore.[15]

The "Book of Hymns" unquestionably marked a great advance upon its predecessors in poetical and spiritual quality,
and it was in these respects that it was especially distinguished
from them. While the tendencies of thought in the young men
who prepared it, especially in Johnson, were radical and progressive, how moderate were their conscious departures from
the Unitarianism of their day appears by the structure of this
hymnbook and its particular contents.[16]

As would be expected, the two Samuels had focused more
on the content of the hymnbook than on the business aspects of
getting it printed and distributed. Fortunately, they had friends
who provided Longfellow and Johnson with advice about this
aspect of the project. One of these friends was John Owen who

had graduated from the Divinity School in 1829. He settled in Cambridge, Massachusetts as a bookseller in 1833, and he published the early works of his friend and college classmate, Henry Wadsworth Longfellow, as well as those of James Russell Lowell. Mr. Owen failed in business in 1848.

> But Sam, I have never told you the <u>cold water</u> thrown by John Owen on the project. He says the number needed in Frank's Society <u>will not pay the expenses</u>. There is a blow! He asked if there was no other society who would take it now. Think & answer, communicating with Frank. I shall write to Edw. Hale who is to have a new society in Worcester. How is it with Sargent at Somerville – (whose Sermon I see Furness is to preach – would we were there). Owen said, when we had collected our hymns, he would get an estimate of the cost of printing.[17]

The two friends finished their book in just a few months. They prepared the manuscript, edited the text and sent it to the printers. However, they still had not decided on the final title. In a letter to his sister Anne, Sam Longfellow mentions names they considered.

> The Printers are just beginning upon our Hymn book. Edw. Hale will probably adopt it for his new Society in Worcester. He calls it "The Spiritual Songs of our New England Zion, for Cheerful Churches and Happy Homes." I think its title will be simply "A Book of Hymns for Christian Worship, but the title page is the last thing printed. I am more & more convinced that it will be an excellent collection. I have myself just written a hymn for Edw. Hale's ordination, which I will send you; perhaps it will appear in the register.[18]

Once the book was finished it was ready to be distributed to the congregations. Although Longfellow and Johnson had promised to produce the book for their friend Frank Appleton, he was not the first or even second to receive copies. The first person to use it was Edward Everett Hale, who was at the Church of Unity in Worcester. The hymn written by Samuel Longfellow for Hale's ordination at Worcester in 1846 was one of those included in the book.

The Book of Hymns was also quickly accepted for use by Theodore Parker for his services at the Music Hall in Boston in 1846, and contained Parker's hymn "O thou Great Friend to all the sons of men"[19] Parker, who was related by marriage to Samuel Johnson, apparently enjoyed puns and was the one who coined the name "The Book of Sams" for the hymnbook.[20]

Finally, the two Sams fulfilled their promise to Frank Appleton. One day they met at Samuel Johnson's home in Salem and then took Appleton his promised books.

> I will accept your invitation to come to your house. Friday we will go over to Franks – with all sorts of hymnbooks.[21]

As for other Unitarian congregations, acceptance of the book was not rapid and in some instances there were even concerns regarding its use.

> On the whole, while the collection met with some severe criticism, and in few places superseded the well-established "Greenwoods," it received a gratifying welcome. An edition of five hundred copies was taken up in three or four months.[22]

In a letter to Edward Everett Hale in late 1846, Samuel Longfellow describes some of the reasons he thought congregations did not fully accept *The Book of Hymns.*

> I am glad you have spoken a good word for our hymn-book. ...Though the people of New Bedford spoke kindly of its poetry, none of them seem to have seen the real merit of the book in its higher, healthier, more active, love-to-man tone; in short, its more purely Christian tone. Dr. Ephraim Peabody showed some insight into the book and our views. Remorse for sin is not there, and was not meant to be. Nott that it is not a real, sometimes terribly real, state of soul, but surely not a health one; and surely, too, a most private and individual one,

and (even if one should find a sincere and earnest expression of it in verse) out of place in *public* worship. ...Of course, we look for likers of our book rather in new pulpits than in old.[23]

Samuel Longfellow periodically checked on the progress of the sales of the book. In his journal he tells about a visit to William Davis Ticknor, a Boston publisher whose clients included most of the famous Transcendentalists and Unitarians of the period. "At Ticknor's was surprised to find only fifty copies left out of 215 of the Book of Hymns. If we could but get the money, for meek Metcalf. My settlement must secure a new Edition.[24] Longfellow was not certain that that they had chosen the right publisher because of the lack of publicity they had done for the book and in a letter shares his feelings with Sam Johnson.

> I fear Ticknor thinks he has got hold of a poor bargain. In truth Sam, he was not the right person for the book, does not know ministers & I must say hasn't taken pains to get the book known. He seems to have expected us to do the work. He still keeps the old advertisement with useless notices from the daily papers tho' I long since furnished him with extracts from Examiner and Miscellany.[25]

With or without good publicity their sales were sufficient so that within two years a second edition was necessary. The two Sams welcomed this because it gave them a chance to amend some of what they considered as problems with the hymnbook. Longfellow also began to realize how bold the two hymnbook authors had been in taking on the project.

> No sooner had "The Book of Hymns" been published than the compilers discovered to their own amazement that they had incorporated about sixty hymns which for doctrinal reasons they themselves could not sing. We can understand how a few might have been used by some slip or mistake, but sixty! Apparently the number easily might have been a hundred. Johnson proposed immediate and radical exclusion of these hymns. Longfellow was able to agree with him, for he gradually

drifted into the acceptance of a theology which denied the deity of Christ.[26]

> Ticknor told me he was about printing a new Edition of a certain H. B. and I have sent him a long list of corrections. There were some odd blunders remaining. Then Mrs. Gilman's hymn was to be restored to her & to its true reading as requested by her daughter. And I ventured to affix Hedge's name to his & restore the second verse to its pristine form. I wish we could blot out our sins against whither. I begin to feel more sensible of our audacity. Whether Tick. Will consent to the expense involved in amending stereotype plates I know not. How I longed to get out some whole hymns.[27]

The two young editors received some criticism for the changes and modifications they made to existing hymns. Some of the modifications were significant and consequently generated more criticism. Nevertheless there were those who liked the second edition more. One of these was Convers Francis, professor at Harvard Divinity School.

> I am delighted to see this second edition. It is, I think, much enriched by the Supplement, which contains some fine hymns quite new to one, & has supplied whatever of deficiency there might have been in the book before. It seems to me now decidedly the best Hymn Book I know of; & I am sure, the more our Congregations come to be acquainted with it, the more they will feel their obligations to you & Mr. Johnson for giving them such an admirable collection of religious poetry.[28]

Although they "had achieved the success of even a fourth edition," the two Sams still wrote each other with suggestions and, of course, a royalty was sometimes included. In 1850, Longfellow wrote Johnson telling him that

> Ticknor told me he was about printing a new edition of a certain hymn-book, and I have sent him a long list of corrections. ...Sam, of one grand thought I am sorry to find no expression

in our book – God's pure justice, his eternal law of right. I suppose we could find no true expression of it, most hymns so wretchedly pervert it.[29]

Thomas Wentworth Higginson, who is remembered as a prominent abolitionist, commander of the First South Carolina Volunteers, the first regiment recruited from former slaves in the Civil War and mentor of Emily Dickenson, had been an original contributor to the Book of Hymns and told his friends about a satirical poem his sister wrote about the modifications made for the book.

> There once were two Sams of Amerique
> Who belonged to a profession called clerique
> They hunted up hymns and cut off their limbs,
> These truculent Sams of Amerique.[30]

Sam Longfellow enjoyed the tease and went so far as to illustrate the verses with a sketch showing two men cutting up rolls of paper with large shears. Nevertheless, making the decision what to take out and what to leave in must have been difficult for the two editors.

> We cannot conceive of the hypercritical compilers as engaging in the work of excision without having painful experiences. They were undoing their own work. This discovery of their mistake, as they regarded it, is the most curious fact in the history of hymnology. Their revision of "The Book of Hymns" by exclusion is the phenomenal event in the compiling of hymn-books. It is a study in psychology and comparative religions. Those youthful idealists, trusting to their instincts and piety, and forgetful, for the time being, of their theology, had started their denomination singing the very hymns which expressed what Unitarians have always disbelieved. …The compilers substituted about twenty hymns of their own and about forty selected hymns. Their own were not as good as those condemned, than which there were none better in the literature of the subject. Such changes, however

much they met the opinions of the compilers impoverished their hymnal and slackened its sale.[31]

Not long before his death, Samuel Longfellow explained in a letter to his successor in Brooklyn why it had been necessary to make modifications to the hymns. His practical advice probably applies to compilers of church collections in general.

> It is the principle of *adaptation to a special use* which is the only justification of changes in hymns that I can offer. It is a question of using or not using which makes it needful to change (1) some verses originally written not as hymns, yet which one wants to use as such; (2) some hymns written by persons of different beliefs from those who are to use the hymn--book, phrases in which could not be conscientiously said or sung by the latter, yet which from their general value of strength, fervor, or tenderness could ill be spared. ...If I had been making a collection of hymns or religious poetry for private reading, I should not have altered a single word.[32]

During their experience as ministers in different congregations, both Samuels must have looked at their work and considered both its good and bad points. The theological beliefs of many congregations had become more liberal over the years, though not quite as liberal as Longfellow and Johnson who tended toward the radical. This signified to them that it was time to reconsider the contents of the *Book of Hymns*. In a letter to Samuel Longfellow in 1858, Samuel Johnson said,

> I shudder to say that there are almost half a hundred hymns in that book which my tongue refuses to utter. The hymns about Jesus, especially, look weaker and thinner every year.[33]

Their final revision of the hymnbook, which was basically a new book, had to wait until the two friends took a trip to Europe together in 1860. They traveled in Britain passing quickly through Paris and then on to Switzerland where they spent two months.

They went through the south coast of France and into Italy where they traveled to various cities and spent the winter in Florence. They talked about the new book and did some writing, but waited until they were in one place for a while before doing their major work. An example is described by Johnson.

> Going by Nismes and Marseilles to Nice, we spent there a month. There, shut into the house by constant rains, we set to work upon arranging our materials for the *Hymns of the Spirit*, which we thought it was high time should replace the out-grown *Book of Hymns*, and which was published after our return in 1864. There, in a damp chamber of the "Pension Besson," Johnson wrote the hymns, "City of God how broad and far" (637); "The Will divine that woke a waiting time" (657); and, I think, "Life of Ages, richly poured" (633), which last it seems to me must take the place in the new church which Toplady's "Rock of Ages" holds in the old.[34]

They took out many hymns, some of which were liked by the congregations. One of the hymns deleted was "Christ to the young man said," by Henry Wadsworth Longfellow. In addition to the three hymns by Samuel Johnson mentioned in the above letter, the new book contained six more by Johnson, and nineteen new ones by Samuel Longfellow. However, Samuel Longfellow does not mention when or where he wrote these new additions, "the richest contribution, perhaps, made by any recent author to the repository of sacred song."[35]

In the spring of 1861 they completed their joint trip and their new hymnbook had been completed,

> [t]his purely theistic hymn-book, perhaps the only one of its kind, was published in 1864, as "Hymns of the Spirit." Poetically, and in arrangement, it may have been an improvement on the "Book of Hymns." But its doctrinal limitations were, of course, a bar to its adoption in many quarters, and it probably never reached so wide a circulation as the former collection had at length attained.[36]

The collaborators made no further changes in their hymn-books; however, over the years Samuel Longfellow produced other hymnbooks, including some for children's worship. The Sam's hymnbook continued in use, although it was gradually replaced by more modern editions by other authors that reflected the changes in Unitarian theological thought over the years. Nevertheless, the hymnbooks the two Sams produced continued to be remembered for the significant impact they had at the time of their publication.

Notes:

[1] May, Joseph, Ed.. *Samuel Longfellow: Memoir and Letters.* Cambridge: The Riverside Press, 1894. p. 48-49.

[2] Ibid., p. 49.

[3] *The Christian Register*, v. 11, April 18, 1907, p. 435.

[4] Longfellow, Samuel, Ed. *Lectures, Essays and Sermons by Samuel Johnson*, Boston: The Riverside Press, 1883, p. 30.

[5] May, Joseph, Ed.. *Samuel Longfellow: Memoir and Letters.* p. 48-49

[6] Ames, Charles G. "A sermon preached in the Church of the Disciples, Oct. 10, 1892." *Boston Gazette, Sunday Morning edition.* October 15, 1898.

[7] May, Joseph, Ed.. *Samuel Longfellow: Memoir and Letters.* p. 49.

[8] Hale, Edward Everett. *Five Prophets of Today.* Boston, 1892. p. 49.

[9] May, Joseph, Ed.. *Samuel Longfellow: Memoir and Letters.* p. 49.

[10] *The Christian Register*, v. 11, April 18, 1907, p. 435.

[11] Letter, Samuel Longfellow to Samuel Johnson. Feb. 17, 1846. SLP, LNHS.

[12] Letter, Ralph Waldo Emerson to Samuel Longfellow from. May 13, 1846. SLP, LNHS.

[13] Letter, Samuel Longfellow to Samuel Johnson, November 9, 1846. SLP, LNHS.

[14] Frothingham, Octavius Brooks. *Transcendentalism in New England: A History.* New York: Harper & Brothers, 1959 (original 1876). p. 347-348.

[15] May, Joseph, Ed.. *Samuel Longfellow: Memoir and Letters.* p. 69.

[16] Ibid., p. 51.

[17] Letter, Samuel Longfellow to Samuel Johnson, Feb. 17, 1846. SLP, LNHS.

[18] Letter, Samuel Longfellow to Anne Longfellow Pierce, April 27, 1846. SLP, LNHS.

[19] *The Christian Register*, v. 11, April 18, 1907, p. 435.

[20] May, Joseph, Ed.. *Samuel Longfellow: Memoir and Letters.* p. 55.

[21] Letter, Samuel Longfellow to Samuel Johnson, March 3, 1846. SLP, LNHS.

[22] May, Joseph, Ed.. *Samuel Longfellow: Memoir and Letters.* p. 52.

[23] Ibid., p. 74.

[24] Longfellow, Samuel. *Journal, January 1, 1845 to March 24, 1847*, January 22, 1847.

[25] Letter, Samuel Longfellow to Samuel Johnson, January 31, 1849. SLP, LNHS.

[26] *The Christian Register*, v. 11, April 18, 1907, p. 436.

[27] Letter, Samuel Longfellow to Samuel Johnson, December 3, 1850. SLP, LNHS.

[28] Letter, Convers Francis to Samuel Longfellow, June 28, 1848. SLP, LNHS.

[29] Letter, Samuel Longfellow to Samuel Johnson, December 2, 1850. SLP, LNHS.

[30] May, Joseph, Ed.. *Samuel Longfellow: Memoir and Letters.* p. 55.

[31] *The Christian Register*, v. 11, April 18, 1907, p. 437.

[32] May, Joseph, Ed.. *Samuel Longfellow: Memoir and Letters.* p. 54.

[33] Hale, Edward Everett. *Five Prophets of Today.* Boston, 1892. p. 50.

[34] Longfellow, Samuel. *Lectures, Essays and Sermons by Samuel Johnson.* p. 60-62.

[35] Hale, Edward Everett. *Five Prophets of Today.* Boston, 1892. p. 51.

[36] May, Joseph, Ed.. *Samuel Longfellow: Memoir and Letters.* p. 214-215.

CHAPTER 9 – THE CANDIDATE

Samuel Longfellow began working on the *Book of Hymns* with Samuel Johnson in the mid-1840s and they did not finish their joint work on hymnbooks until they completed *Hymns of the Spirit* on their trip to Europe in the early 1860s. However, in the period between Divinity School and the trip, Samuel Longfellow was also occupied with finding a pastorate. The spring of 1846 arrived and Samuel Longfellow's classes were finally over and graduation was approaching. Samuel Longfellow had written a number of sermons while still a student and presented several of them to Unitarian congregations in order to practice his speaking skills.

Now it was time for Samuel and his fellow graduates to get serious about their skills as preachers so they could make a strong impression on a congregation in order to be asked back and possibly become a candidate for a permanent position. They called this period of visiting different congregations "candidating." This process could be quick or it could go on for a long time, either because the candidates did not receive any offers or the candidates received offers which they turned down.

There were both benefits and drawbacks to "candidating", which were primarily related to the non-religious aspects of the position and the expectations of the congregation. Samuel Longfellow wrote a letter to Samuel Johnson describing how he felt about what the people wanted.

> The people, though, are only too attentive, and will have me to dinner, or to ride, or to call, or to tea, or at least to be introduced to them on the meeting-house steps. The young ladies beg me to come to their Sunday-school class, and the school committee will take me into the young ladies' Academy where I shall be called upon for an address. Sam a young minister must keep clear of these girls! Beautiful enthusiasts, in vain will

all the P____s strive to tame their efflorescence! There is a picture of the whole matter in Retsch, – the poet in the hands of the water-nymphs.[1]

In some instances, the church committee had expectations of what the minister should preach and what they expected to receive from the minister's message. Many of the committees made their theological desires clear and supposed the minister would comply with their wishes. For Samuel, this was often not an acceptable situation. He expresses his ideas on what a minister should convey in a letter to Samuel Johnson.

> The committee who came to see me wouldn't allow but what all was in an excellent state, as if only to the righteous was a minister to go. The gentleman with whom I took tea last night said, in the elegant language of Ezekiel, that they wanted a minister would make a "shaking among the dry bones;" that they wanted some one to "preach up sin!" Can I do that, Sam? Wouldn't it be as well to preach it *down*? I can't understand, nor will I yield to, this morbid desire of some people to be made uncomfortable. If they know they are sinners, as they say, why want to be told so by their minister? I can, however, understand how people may desire to be aroused from inaction and indifference. But I don't like this depending on the minister for excitement; this passive waiting to be moved. Some of the people here evidently want evangelical preaching.[2]

Samuel Longfellow took his turn preaching in several pulpits. One church that asked Samuel to preach was his home church in Portland. This was at the invitation of Dr. Nichols, whom he had known since childhood. However, his family did not want him preaching at a service in Portland. He relates how this situation was resolved in a letter to Sam Johnson.

> Sam, I preached for Dr. Nichols – but not on a Sunday. I found my mother & sister did not want me to appear in my own church yet, but the Dr. urged me & so I proposed to satisfy all by preaching the ante-communion lecture on Friday Evening.[3]

One of the early churches Samuel went to was in Fall River. This was a factory town on the coast and was much different in character than the other towns in which Samuel preached. In a letter to Samuel Johnson, Longfellow describes the town, the workers' situation and his feeling that the rich owners should treat the poor workers better.

> Those great Factories are really worth seeing. I went off before day was fairly come and there were the long rows of windows, lighted up, & the terrible wheels roaring and whirring like Fate – and the poor women & children, Sam, had been at work more than an hour then, & Have been ever since. There is no mercy in steam & wheels. This town is dirty & dreary, & has a homeless look, like Lowell. I don't think I should like a factory town, except for the sake of trying to make the millionaires treat the poor people properly.[4]

One of the rich factory owners in Massachusetts was Nathan Appleton, father of Henry's wife Fanny. However, he was recognized as having an interest in his workers' well-being and creating a non-exploitive system in his factories.

Another pulpit Samuel spoke from was the one in West Cambridge, now known as Arlington, where he had also preached as a student. Henry's wife, Fanny Appleton Longfellow, attended one of Samuel's very early services at West Cambridge in June 1846 and provides her viewpoint of his presentation.

> In my brother Sam's first preaching here Sunday before last. It was the first public performance I ever witnessed of any one connected with me, but apart from that, except my marriage and first communion, I cannot recall a ceremony which ever moved me so much, gave me such deep, delicious joy. He prayed and preached like a young apostle with such tenderness and fervor that I could not help shedding tears. He has just the right spirit for a preacher – most firm and courageous and independent, shrinking not from rebuking public, as well as private, sin, and yet with a gentleness which is all subduing. His style is very simple and manly too for a beginner, and his heart makes

it eloquent as well as his imagination. You know this is not exactly like praising my own brother, so I can do it with a better grace. I confess that I am very proud of him and feel as if he were destined to do much good.[5]

The West Cambridge congregation decided they liked him and gave him a "call" to accept a permanent position there. However, he refused it and accepted only a three-month commitment. "Candidating" was not an activity that Samuel enjoyed very much, as he indicates in a letter to Edward Everett Hale, and even this three-month commitment must have been welcome to him.

> It is rather a bleak time to go to so rural a place, but I weary of wandering about and seeing new faces every Sunday, and "getting the hang" of a new pulpit every week.[6]

In a letter to his brother Alex, Samuel seems ready for this change in his life, even if only for three months. At this point in his "candidating" he was aware that there were societies other than West Cambridge that were willing to give him a "call". Now he had to decide between them.

> After eleven years' abode here, with intervals of absence which seemed only to make it more evident that Cambridge was my "destiny," I have made arrangements to set up my household gods elsewhere. My first stopping place is W. Cambridge, of which you have already heard I suppose from Portland. I shall be there till the first of April whether any longer will depend upon future light. By the first of May I hope to be settled in a permanent home & have a pulpit of my own before that.[7]

When Samuel finished his commitment at West Cambridge, the Society approached him with the request to remain as their permanent minister. However, because Samuel had made a decision to have experience in more churches before settling down, he was not yet ready to make a long-term commitment. The reason he gave them was concern for his health, which, as has been noted before, was a recurring situation throughout his life. This time he decided he would try a water-cure, which was very popular at the time.

Sometimes I feel ashamed to say anything about my health, when I think how many much sicker persons than I are faithfully working away in the ministry. But when I think how much better I can take the time now than ever again, and how much more good it will do now, I feel that I have not done wrong, and that in a few months I shall be able to be strongly and satisfactorily at work. It certainly looks more like cool judgment than enthusiastic self devotion to God's work. Alas, Sam, that baptism has not yet come to me![8]

They were disappointed with Samuel's decision, which he had found difficult to make. He told Samuel Johnson that "and I shall not give them any *farewell.*" Nevertheless, members of the Society gave him gifts, but he found it uncomfortable to show his appreciation.

I hate scenes, and am shy of emotion now. When I feel it coming on, I make myself rigid against it. I used to be too sentimental.[9]

The church leaders "pleaded to the last," but Samuel maintained his decision not to accept their offer.

I hated to resist their entreaties, but I did. The W.'s are still desirous that the Society shall await my emergence from the *Wasser-Kur.* But I will not promise them to come, even then.[10]

During the period he was preaching at West Cambridge, he was also asked to preach in other churches. One of the places that invited Samuel to preach was in Newburyport. He preached there once, but expressed concern about his health and turned down their offer to preach more times.

Among the people who were aware of his health problems were the Dabneys of the island of Faial. They were regularly in contact with him and in a letter from Olivia Dabney to Clara Dabney, she mentioned his health in relationship to West Cambridge and Newburyport and the fact that his susceptibility to seasickness kept him from traveling to the Azores.

> Mr. Longfellow has refused the call to Newburyport, and is still undecided about the W. Cambridge call. His health is not so good, and he had serious thoughts of going to Fayal for the winter, but the dread of the voyage deterred him.[11]

Another congregation he visited was at Woburn. He appears to have viewed this congregation differently than the one at West Cambridge. This may be the reason it did not take long to consider the possibility of a long stay there.

> In the aft. Took the cars at Medford for Woburn – Tead at the Tavern then called on Mr. Nelson & with him went to his house to spend the night. An intelligent & agreeable man living with a pleasant wife in a handsome house on the hill – He returned to his office & I talked with Mrs. N. about Emerson whom she knew at Concord, & Wm. Channing who has been preaching for them & whom she loves and & reverences, as I do. The Society here is a new one, yet in the gristle, composed of Unitarians & Unitarian Universalists – The place is an old stronghold of Calvinism; and now I should think there was a grand chance for a free, independent & really liberal church – The railroad from Boston will let in new people & new ideas – & if they will not build up the Society on a denominational basis, it will be all the better – I have really half a mind to go there myself & let W.C. & Newburyport go – They wish to settle a minister for a year, at first – which would suit me exactly.[12]

> In the aft. I walked back to W.C. by a charming road first skirting the Pond & wooded hill sat at last coming out by the shores of Mystic pond. Either from the beauty of the day or the agreeableness of the Nelsons I took a great fancy to Woburn & proposed myself (to myself) as candidate for the new church.[13]

A few days later, Woburn held a parish meeting

> "To see if the parish will invite Mr. Longfellow to become their gospel minister."
> I took tea with Mrs. W. at Miss Chadwick's & came home early to write my sermon. Mr. Whittemore came in from the meeting to announce a unanimous invitation from the Society or its voting members (23 to 0) with a salary of $900; to which 100 will be added by individual subscription.
> So the matter is fairly before me.[14]

About six weeks later he wrote a letter and declined to accept the position due to his concerns about his health, as he had done at West Cambridge and Newburyport. While Mr. Whittemore was driving him home he told Samuel that his "letter had caused much disappointment."[15] Although the pulpit at Woburn was not the first permanent position that Samuel was offered, it appears to be the first in which he had any significant degree of interest.

One other place he preached that bears mentioning is at Plymouth. He was with his friend Briggs from Plymouth and they dined with Edward Everett Hale and then met other friends in downtown Boston. After the conversation during dinner he soon found himself on the train to Plymouth. His description of this visit in a letter to Samuel Johnson provides an interesting view of historical Plymouth, the religious leanings of the population and also mentions his professional skill as an architect, an activity he first took up when he was looking for work after graduating from Harvard in 1839.

> I stayed until Tuesday morning, having a very pleasant time. Finest weather; clearest sky; bluest sea; how it made my heart bound! The church is Gothic, under the loveliest avenue of old elm-trees. Old Dr. Kendall, a kind-hearted liberal man, like Dr. Flint, had me to tea; and a mile out of town, in a sunny valley, I found my pleasant, enthusiastic, transcendental farmer friend, Ben Watson, living in a cottage which I planned for him, and by and by will have a lovely place; as yet, all is to be made; but he is one who can live a good while on ideals...

Plymouth is really an interesting place. You are terribly disappointed in the Rock, which you can scarcely see in the midst of the wharf. But the upper half, which lies now in front of Pilgrim Hall, I looked at with a good deal of emotion. But the burial-hill and the sea! The heads of the people are full of free thought, excited on all reforms. It is a great place for freedom, as it should be with that sea and those recollections. There is even the social freedom of going into each other's houses without knocking. I fear the railroad will do away with much of its primitive character before long.[16]

While Samuel Longfellow was presenting himself as a candidate, his friend Samuel Johnson was doing the same. However, Johnson had more trouble with the reaction of congregations to his theology and the ideas he presented in his sermons. Because of their close friendship, Johnson and Longfellow exchanged letters regarding their experiences and Longfellow provided consolation for the hard time his friend was having.

Johnson was now passing through a trying period of candidature; attracting by his intellectual power, his spiritual fervor, and his brilliant style, but alarming and offending by his frank avowals of theological heresies, and of antislavery and other reform sentiments. Longfellow wrote him again and again, wise, brave, and reassuring letters well calculated to give him that encouragement of which, in his own despondent moments, he often betrayed his need to his "Damon," as he sometimes styled him. No experience was passed over unnoted, no emotion was unshared between these two friends. They found in each other something of that support and comfort which they were not seeking in the marriage state. [*Memoir*, p 123.]

Once again Samuel Longfellow found himself feeling tired and weak from his activities. In his journal he mentions the decision he made about taking care of his health and taking time off from "candidating".

I have determined to give up preaching for the present or the thought of settlement at least; & take a vacation devoting some months to the establishment of my health – I want to feel strong & well & so, cheerful & active, before beginning this work.[17]

As a result, he arranged to go to Brattleboro, Vermont for "hydropathic" treatment, which was the latest thing to do in order to improve your health. However, an invitation from George Abbot to preach a few Sundays in Washington., D.C. led him to postpone his treatment.[18]

This was his first trip to Washington since he had taught in Mr. Daniel Murray's school in Rockburn, MD, despite the fact his uncle Commodore Alexander Scammel Wadsworth still lived in Washington, and he had an invitation to visit him that was made from the first time he was there. Aside from preaching, Samuel did not have a lot to do in D.C. and "was idly busy." He liked Washington "vastly better than from former experience I supposed I should." His first week there he lived near the Capital and made it his stomping grounds. The other couple of weeks he stayed with his uncle on "the other end of the city" and where he "used to walk among the hills which 'stood about' the city and lead you over to Georgetown.[19]

In a letter to Samuel Johnson, Samuel Longfellow provides an interesting description of mid-19th century Washington, D.C. and the types of people who lived there.

It is the strangest place externally, full of huts, hovels, and barren, gullied commons, in the midst of handsome houses and grand public buildings. Under the sky I felt some of the real beauty of the Greek architecture. Morally, the people are rather indolent than anything else, I should think. I mean the permanent society, but there is such a vast floating population that there is no *tone* of general sentiment, and the place is fearfully corrupt. The whole class of *yellow* people, many of the women of which are pretty, are at once victims and cause of one portion of this corruption. I did not get at much about slavery. In the city the colored people are mostly free, generally degraded, but have schools and churches (Methodist generally). Many of them are well to do in the world and on Sundays dress like Broadway exquisites.[20]

An issue that attracted Samuel Longfellow's attention during his visit to Washington, D.C., was slavery. This was unlike his visit to Rockburn, MD, several years earlier when he did not mention the subject at all in his letters or journal.

> As to antislavery sentiments, as far as I could see or hear, it seemed to amount to this, that slavery was a great inconvenience and trouble to the whites and hurtful to the outward prosperity of the State. 'They disliked it as much as any body could; but there it was, without their fault, and they didn't see how they could get rid of it, but supposed by and by it would disappear. They would not have the slaves set free to remain among them, idle and vicious as they were; the North might take them, since it had such a fondness for them; and any rate, if we were sincere in our desire to set them free, we had better put out hands into our pockets and remunerate their master, etc., etc." This was the amount of what I could gather amid the many inconsistent and contradictory views of those with whom I talked about it. The main difficulty is that the *moral* idea is scarcely thought of. Nobody feels that it is wrong, but only an inconvenience and economically a bad system. It may be the business of the Northern abolitionists to give them this moral idea, though they have been slow to take it, and never may.[21]

Samuel Longfellow wanted to express his concern with slavery in the pulpit, but he had a dilemma for him. Since Washington, D.C. was located in a borderline area, there was a wide range of opinions. The majority seemed to be opposed to slavery, but even here there was disagreement on how they thought it should be dealt with. There were those who were opposed to slavery, but were unwilling to go as far as the abolitionists, as was true in the northern states as well. Some felt that each of the states should be able to make its own decision.

Consequently Samuel was left with the decision of how to prepare a sermon on the topic of slavery, or perhaps better stated, antislavery. His comments on what he should preach also give an indication of how he decided to approach the variety of controversial subjects he spoke about in his career and indicates some degree of insecurity in his willingness to present his viewpoints on these subjects.

> While I was coming on, I was much 'exercised' as to whether I should or should not preach about the matter. Feeling sick and nervous and unable to write, I doubted whether I could say anything worth while; then came up doubts of the purity of my motives; whether I shouldn't be doing it from vanity, or a spirit of bravado; then, whether my words would be wise and calm enough, physically out of order as I felt, and so on.

> ...and so it came to the last service, and I had said nothing directly about the matter. Then I said, It will never do; and I sat down before going into church and hastily wrote two pages about the war and two about slavery, such as they were, and went into church, taking the sermon called 'Repent, the cry of the prophet,' read 'Cry aloud, spare not,' etc., from Isaiah, and then preached. What I said about slavery was very calm and not the least in the 'spare not' vein, only urging that if they say this thing to be an evil, as they profess, they ought not to be indifferent or to acquiesce in it; nor to be content with deploring it; but in earnest to do something, or begin to do something, to remove it. That the way of duty was clear; that God would give unexpected help in the way of right, and that the difficulties would vanish before faith and a sincere purpose. That each should do what he could, feel, speak, plan, or execute as God had given power. This was what I said, encouraging rather than denouncing, and all brief and hasty. Sam, they took it beautifully; nobody *went out*, and some stopped to say good-by to me at the door.

The next day I did not learn that anybody was offended except some *Northern* people.[22]

Samuel Longfellow was also staunchly antiwar. In fact, he felt more strongly about the cause of peace than he did about anti-slavery. The issue at this time that brought all this to the forefront was the 1846-1848 Mexican-American War that he, as well as most of his friends, was opposed to. After a sermon he heard in Philadelphia on his way north he reported the following reaction to Samuel Johnson. In it he emphasizes how enduring and strong his antiwar feelings were.

> Think of these horrid people illuminating, as they did here and in Baltimore and Washington! I felt more indignant about that than about slavery. And these miserable Whigs now taking advantage of Taylor's corrupt popularity to ride into power, after all they have said about the war![23]

> I have been reading some facts about the war to-day, and it is lamentable to see how those weak Whigs, all but sixteen in both Houses were panic-stricken, frightened, cajoled into assuming and supporting the war, – a cunning trick of a despotic President, who first assumed a power to which he had no shadow of claim, and then duped Congress into taking the thing off his hands. It seems that they need not have done anything even to rescue Taylor; first, because any assistance from them must necessarily be too late, and secondly, because he already had authority to demand aid, as he did from Louisiana and Texas. Here is a thing to be reached by political action. Mr. Webster says in that weak speech of his: "If the voting for the war-bill stained a man's hands with blood, then is the whole Whig party red with blood up to the chin." True, O Daniel! Think of it! Only sixteen men straightforward enough to cut through a "complicated question" by a simple fidelity to conscience, – not even acute politicians enough to keep out of this trap of their opponents![24]

After his trip to Washington, D.C., Samuel Longfellow finally took time for his "water cure" in Brattleboro, VT, where he stayed approximately three months. Life at Brattleboro was regimented, following the same daily routine. Longfellow describes his life at Brattleboro in a letter to Samuel Johnson.

I am having a very pleasant time here; but between walking and watering have little leisure to write. ...Having been waked, nearly an hour before, but the tramping of people past my door to their baths, I am invaded by a German Heinrich, who takes my bathing-sheet, and swathing myself in a blanket like an Indian chief, I follow him into the bathroom, where I sit down in a long tub and have water poured over me, and am rubbed for a time; then dried on said sheet, bandaged, and dismissed to dress and walk half or three quarters of an hour before breakfast, generally taking the "circle," as it is called, across the brook and round by the D's, where I stop under the trees and drink a couple of tumblers of water. After breakfast, walking again, rambling exploring, stopping alone or in company. Sam, there are the loveliest places you ever saw, to search after and enjoy; ravines, hills, wood-paths, cascades, green meadows. So till eleven o'clock, when I again resort to the bathroom and sit down in a tub of cold water, clothed in the aforesaid blanket; and when we get a number together along the sides of the room, it is wonderfully suggestive of an Indian council or pow-wow. Bandages renewed and then a walk again to "get up a reaction," that is to prevent being chilly. This brings me to dinner with a ravenous appetite. After dinner, lounging, talking music battledore for a while, or reading and writing, perhaps a siesta till four or five; then, after another sitz-bath, a walk of an hour till tea. After tea, walk, stroll, read newspapers, play, sing; perhaps there is dancing in the saloon, or other family amusements. ...So much for my life here.[25]

In June he had finished a month and he still had not noticed any changes in his health. He was not "getting well, stronger and less nervous." He felt that "not one of the baths is so violent or disagreeable as a blister, the commonest resort of allopathy."[26]

In July he felt that his progress was still slow, so he decided to stay for one more month and on his last Sunday he preached in the Church there, with Channing speaking in the afternoon. After leaving Brattleboro, Samuel planned to go to Portland and invited Samuel Johnson to join him there for old-times' sake and to "put in order the new hymnbook (second edition)."[27]

After his stay in Portland, Samuel took up "candidating" once more. One of the churches he visited was "a beautiful rural city of central New England, in which dwelt particularly refined and cultivated society," which attracted him, although the name is not mentioned in the *Memoir.* However, he did not receive an invitation from them until he had accepted the call from the final stop on his "candidating" tour – Fall River.

Notes:

[1] Letter, Samuel Longfellow to Samuel Johnson, January 18, 1847. SLP, LNHS.

[2] Ibid.

[3] Letter, Samuel Longfellow to Samuel Johnson, March 3, 1846. SLP, LNHS.

[4] Letter, Samuel Longfellow to Samuel Johnson, December 21, 1846. SLP, LNHS.

[5] Wagenknecht, Edward, Ed. *Mrs. Longfellow: Selected Letters and Journals of Fanny Appleton Longfellow (1817-1861).* New York: Longmans, Green and Co., 1856. p. 122.

[6] May, Joseph, Ed.. *Samuel Longfellow: Memoir and Letters.* Cambridge: The Riverside Press, 1894. p. 74.

[7] Letter, Samuel Longfellow to Alexander Longfellow, January 5, 1847. SLP, LNHS.

[8] Letter, Samuel Longfellow to Samuel Johnson, March 22, 1847. SLP, LNHS.

[9] May, Joseph, Ed.. *Samuel Longfellow: Memoir and Letters.* p. 80.

[10] Letter, Samuel Longfellow to Samuel Johnson, March 22, 1847. SLP, LNHS.

[11] Letter, Olivia Dabney to Clara Dabney. ADF, p. 565.

[12] Samuel Longfellow. *Journal, January 1, 1845 to March 24, 1847.* February 3, 1847.

[13] Samuel Longfellow. *Journal, January 1, 1845 to March 24, 1847.* February 7, 1847.

[14] Samuel Longfellow. *Journal, January 1, 1845 to March 24, 1847.* February 12, 1847.

[15] Samuel Longfellow. *Journal, January 1, 1845 to March 24, 1847*, March, 21 1847.

[16] Letter, Samuel Longfellow to Samuel Johnson, March 22, 1847. SLP, LNHS.

[17] Samuel Longfellow. *Journal, January 1, 1845 to March 24, 1847.* March 20, 1847.

[18] Samuel Longfellow. *Journal, January 1, 1845 to March 24, 1847.* March 22, 1847.

[19] May, Joseph, Ed.. *Samuel Longfellow: Memoir and Letters.* p. 84.

[20] Letter, Samuel Longfellow to Samuel Johnson, May 2, 1847. SLP, LNHS.

[21] Ibid.

[22] Ibid.

[23] Ibid.

[24] Letter, Samuel Longfellow to Samuel Johnson, November 9, 1846. SLP, LNHS.

[25] Letter, Samuel Longfellow to Samuel Johnson, May 20, 1847. SLP, LNHS.

[26] Letter, Samuel Longfellow to Samuel Johnson, June 12, 1847. SLP, LNHS.

[27] Letter, Samuel Longfellow to Samuel Johnson, July 5, 1847. SLP, LNHS.

CHAPTER 10 – FALL RIVER

Samuel Longfellow loved nature and the company of a scholarly community with whom he could share ideas. He was a regular walker around the Cambridge and Portland areas, thinking, writing, drawing, as well as talking with his companions. The opportunity to be able to do this was one of the characteristics he looked for in the places where he "candidated."

After preaching at a number of churches, mostly in central Massachusetts, which had the characteristics he wanted, the next place he preached was Fall River in southeastern Massachusetts, which was quite different from the other pulpits where he had preached.

The town of Fall River, and several of the other nearby communities, was built on land bought from the Wampanoag Indians by settlers from the Plymouth Colony. Fall River is located on Mount Hope Bay at the mouth of the Taunton River. On a peninsula in the bay was a town called Mt. Hope and today is known as Bristol, RI. The name Fall River comes from the Quequechan River, which is a Wampanoag word meaning "falling waters," and refers to waterfalls that used to be visible on the river.

In 1675 Mount Hope was the site of the first battle of King Philip's War between the Plymouth Bay Colony and the Wampanoag Indians. King Philip was a Wampanoag Indian who was eventually defeated resulting in virtual elimination of the Native Americans in the region and the disappearance of fur trading. Samuel regularly mentions how he enjoyed the view of Mount Hope Bay and made visits to the town.

In 1811 the first cotton mill was built in Fall River. Mill construction continued and the industry steadily grew. By the end of the 19th century Fall River was the hub for cotton textile production in the United States. It was in this relatively new, rapidly growing industrial town that Samuel Longfellow found himself preaching to the local Unitarian Society. The Fall River Unitarian Church was organized in 1832 and Samuel was their fourth minister. As a point of interest, the Fall River Universalist Society was incorporated in 1840 and Samuel kept in contact with them.

Samuel's initial reaction to Fall River was not positive when he was candidating, as was noted in the previous chapter. This was reinforced by the towns he went to in other parts of Massachusetts after his first visit to Fall River. His friend Higginson reports that Samuel wrote him and,

> ...admitted the comparative barrenness of Fall River (at that time a new manufacturing town), and ended, 'But Mount Hope shines fair in the distance, and I am content.' This was a type of his life; for him, Mount Hope always shone in the distance as fair as the actual mountain from Fall River.[1]

In his 1894 article on Samuel Longfellow, Oscar Fay Adams provided a description of the Fall River Samuel knew. Adams also included his opinion of how Samuel reacted to it.

> Fifty years ago Fall River was a raw, crude place, whose kindly, well-meaning people were too deeply absorbed in the business of making a living to have time for the cultivation of the refinements of life; and so far as appreciation and intellectual sympathy were concerned, a man of delicate, scholarly, aesthetic tastes might as well have taken up his residence in an Arabian desert. To a great extent Mr. Longfellow realized this, but he went thither under as strenuous conviction of his duty in the case as ever any missionary went forth to his labor amid tropic heats or Arctic snows.[2] [*Samuel Longfellow*, Oscar Fay Adams, p. 207.]

Samuel wrote his friend Samuel Johnson telling him that he was considering going to Fall River. He points out some of the reasons against it, but also looks at the opportunities he would have in this type of Unitarian society.

> Now of Fall River, I have a little more than half-a-mind to go. Yet I know it shall be forlorn there. John Ware tells me that he

does not think, nor do I, that I could stay there always. But he does not discourage my going & tells me some pleasant things of the place. I was there a week at the hotel: did not get into many houses, but found that it was not generally known that I was there. I must lay aside all aesthetic & romantic dreams – the ideal church & other ideals for a long while at least, if I go there. Must give up things that I am right in valuing. I must be <u>alone</u> there. It avails not against that, that Weiss & Brooks are not very far off. A man <u>must</u> depend upon the people in the town where he lives for his friends and associates. I remember some dreary hours at W. Cambridge & see many such in prospect at F.R. & to go away for relief I know by experience, makes the loneliness only more dreary when you come back. I know I cannot find a soul to take an evening's walk with; unless on Sunday. – On the other hand I see it to be a centre of influence; it is not yet crystallized: is free to be moulded. I think I could do there as I wished so soon as they have become acquainted with me. I saw some kind hearted men & women.[3]

Despite Fall River not being exactly what Samuel was looking for, he did go there to preach. In fact he went with a positive outlook about what he could accomplish in an area relatively untouched by someone with strong religious beliefs. He told Edward Everett Hale that his decision to go there was "a sort of charge" that came to him as the result of a talk with Ephraim Peabody, who was rector at King's Chapel at the time.

He has inspired me to take some great plans or ideas into my head, and sacrificing romance and hopes of sympathy and of the enjoyments of cultivated social intercourse, to go straight to Fall River and make the church over, or build up its growth after my own ideas.[4]

Samuel Longfellow's original commitment to Fall River was for two Sundays in November 1847, but they wanted him for three. His first reaction was that he "spent a dark, lowering Sunday, thinking Fall River the most dismal place, almost I was ever in."[5] However, before he finished his promised course of sermons, the

Fall River Society showed a "strong desire" to give him a call, which surprised Samuel who had wanted to continue "candidating" till spring." Now he found himself indecisive about what he should do about the Fall River offer.

> A week ago, I should have been ready to say, "No" at once; now I am surprised at myself that I do not say it, – but I do not.
> Sam, I believe it is the bay which has charmed me; I know not what else![6]

Decision time finally arrived and in December 1847, Samuel Longfellow accepted the offer by the Fall River Unitarian Society to become their permanent preacher. He was now entering the mainstream of ministerial life.

> The die is cast, the cup taken! Saturday I sent my letter of acceptance to Fall River, resisting the allurements of an invitation to preach in the Church of the Messiah, New York, and an appealing letter from Albany.[7]

On February 16, 1848, Samuel Longfellow was ordained and installed as minister at Fall River Unitarian Church. Joseph May describes the service and Samuel Longfellow sent a letter to Samuel Johnson to express his own reactions to the ordination.

> The ordination and installation took place upon the 16th of February, 1848. Charles H. Brigham of Taunton, offered the introductory prayer. John Weiss, of New Bedford, preached a powerful and striking sermon, on "The Modern Pulpit." Dr. Convers Francis, of the Divinity School, offered the ordaining prayer and gave the charge; George Ware Briggs, a former pastor, then of Plymouth, delivered the address to the people, and John F. W. Ware, more recently pastor of the society, extended to his successor the right hand of fellowship. Edward Everett Hale read from the Scriptures. The first hymn sung was by the new pastor, and Henry W. Longfellow wrote for his brother that altogether perfect one, beginning

*"Christ to the young man said: 'Yet one thing more, if thou
wouldst perfect be.'"*

Of the service, and its effect upon his own feelings, Mr. Longfellow wrote to Mr. Johnson, "I rejoice that the ordination services so much impressed you. The only want I felt was of something more of a devotional tone to meet *my own* feelings at the
time. The prayer was almost the least moving thing to me, of all;
but during the whole of it, that line of Henry Ware's hymn ran
in my mind, 'Sin, sloth, and self abjured before the altar,' which,
indeed, contains all that could be said. The 'right hand' was the
most interesting part to me. I could not give to the sermon the
close attention it needed, but I felt it was an admirable statement
of what so much needed to be said distinctly now.[8]

Samuel Longfellow had now started his first long-term position
as preacher in a Unitarian society. He may have taken a long
time to arrive at this point, but at the age of 29 he had acquired
the abilities he needed and was skillful in using them. Samuel
Longfellow knew that Fall River was a difficult pastorate, but it
was also one which he felt would be a challenge and provide
the opportunity of his having positive results. However, Samuel
was not able to achieve the results he wanted because of his poor
health. His energy was drained, and this led to his excess sensitivity. As a result, he felt he could not give sufficient value to
the work that he did in relation to the congregation.

In his passage through Harvard and then Harvard Divinity
School, Samuel Longfellow's theological beliefs changed from the
conservative Unitarianism of his youth to a liberal version tending toward radical. His opinions had led him to the religious
position which he held in later years, although he still had not
become completely conscious of what it was. In his communication with friends and his sermons, he still used much of the
terminology of standard Christianity. However, like Theodore
Parker, he was considered by many to be a "Theist," a term that
was coming into popular use at the time.

In his religious life, his devout sentiments and aspirations,
he admitted no mediator between himself and the Divine Spirit.

He conducted his religious work under the spiritual leadership of Jesus, crediting his miracles and resurrection, and recognizing in him qualities highly exceptional. Yet he interpreted the endowments of Jesus in accordance with a strictly humanitarian view, on the naturalistic principles which Furness was now urging with so much force and attractiveness. He was poetical rather than mystical in temperament; an institutionalist in his thought of the relation of man to God, to himself, and to the facts of being.[9]

The reference to William Henry Furness indicates that Samuel's theology had a strong link to Transcendentalism. Furness was a leader among the Unitarian ministers who contributed to Transcendentalism and believed that Christianity did not need to appeal to external proof, such as the miracles of Jesus.

His instinct of spontaneity made formality impossible to him, and custom irksome. A growing individualism, which he shared with Weiss, Frothingham, Higginson, and others of the brightest minds of the day, was weakening his sympathy with the majority of the Unitarians and the organized work of the body. A highly aesthetic temperament created wants which were imperious but, in the prosaic life of New England fifty years ago not easily satisfied, his conscience often reproved what was wholly constitutional and a necessity of his being.[10]

One of the most important aspects of the job of a minister was "tending to his flock." Dealing well with people had always been one of Samuel Longfellow's strong points and his involvement with the social situation of his congregation would characterize him throughout his life.. He was gifted with the ability to understand people's personal and spiritual problems and the talent to help them or make them more contented by just paying a little attention to them. People "were drawn to him by a power of which they could hardly explain the charm."[11] As previously stated, he maintained a special love for children and they were attracted to him even more strongly than their parents, and this assisted in his providing care for those considered the neediest.

At first, Samuel did not find working with his parishioners easy because he was dealing with people in a mill town whose ways of dealing with life were different from those in the other communities he was familiar with. Nevertheless, as mentioned above, he started with positive expectations, but not without doubts in his own abilities.

> But when the excitement of installation in his new post had subsided; before he had formed organic relations with the life of the community, or had become acquainted with his people; condemned to live at a wretched country hotel, to eat his solitary meals in a bustling dining-room; scarcely meeting his parishioners except at church, and expected to produce two discourses each week, our young minister, at first found the situation dreary. He discovered a few congenial women; among men, the only one who supplied to him that near companion-ship which was so needful to him was a "transcendental music--teacher, who has some good ideas and a deep, true feeling for his are." The poverty of suggestion in his conditions, out of which sermons could not flow and could with difficulty be squeezed, his conscientious mind too willingly interpreted as "spiritual deadness" in himself. He needed philanthropic acti-vities, the sphere of which he could not immediately find amid a prosperous, self-sufficient, busy population. To the pres-criptive duties of his post he gave himself faithfully, already characteristically trying to make all religious occasions genuine and freshly significant.[12]

In general, Samuel was able to provide what his parishio-ners sought from their preacher and he often went beyond the basics to provide the emotional and spiritual support he saw they needed.

> The absolute truthfulness of his character took from all his ministrations among his people the professional air, and made them the affectionate expressions of trusty friendship. Old obser-vances became instinct with fresh reality and significance. He could not be restricted in his sympathies or services to the limits

of his parish, but much more a man and citizen than a minister, he overflowed in good works to all about him whom in any way he could reach.[13]

Among the standard functions of a preacher for his parishioners was the performance of funerals, some for people he really did not know. He liked the rural funeral custom where the coffin was carried on the shoulders of friends in the familiar surroundings of the deceased better than "the long procession of carriages and an entombment in a public graveyard... It is always hard to keep one's calmness and serene faith amid so many tears, and at the same time sympathize with the sorrow..."[14]

Another important function of a minister is performing marriages. Samuel describes his first wedding ceremony to his sister Anne.

> I have just come from performing for the first time the marriage ceremony, an occasion to me of much & serious interest. It troubles me to think with what little of thoughtfulness, with how faint an idea of its real meaning & purpose & the true consecration & self-devotion it requires, many enter into this relation. Another thing pains me – that marriage & the love that leads to marriage should be the constant theme of the most trifling jests, should be spoken of almost always in sport.[15]

Illness was a common reason for Samuel Longfellow to visit the homes of his congregation. He explains the way that he believed the ill should be approached by their minister in dealing with his ill parishioners.

> I visit daily a young girl, patiently sinking in consumption. Only now and then do I find what to say to her upon spiritual things. I find a prayer the best expression. I feel, Sam, that in visiting the sick, the minister should be able to carry with him an atmosphere of *physical health* which would be as reviving as a breath of fresh air. Spiritually, I feel that he needs to reach

that height which shall make him equally calm in the presence of the joyous and of the suffering; which shall practically reconcile those apparent contrasts and discords that are always side by side in life, and from one to another of which he may be constantly passing in his intercourse with his people. If he can look upon all as serenely as God's light shines at once upon the festival and the sick-chamber, the prison-cell and the workshop, then he will be welcome and helpful everywhere; will be a true divine presence. But what self-conquest, and baptism of the spirit, before that height of spiritual health can be reached![16]

Both illness and early death were frequently the result of poverty. Because Fall River was a new factory town it had a higher level of poverty than other towns. Samuel was concerned with taking care of the poor and responded

> ...to the call made upon a Christian church by the suffering and evil that existed in the narrow dirty streets and miserable houses where the Fall River poor live in want and sin. I have felt ever since I came here that I ought to do something for these children of wretchedness and neglect; but haven't known how to get at them. Now, I have found one kind-hearted woman who visits them, and I mean to put myself under her guidance, and I hope soon to engage a little band of Christians in this work. I feel that a common object of this kind will do more than anything to bring about that union of interests of which there seems to be so little in my society.[17]

A man approached Samuel one day and asked for help in finding work, but Samuel was unsuccessful in his task and "it made [him] sad, feeling, moreover, that here was one of but so many." Samuel felt "a growing interest" in the problems of unemployment, poverty and other social problems.

> Certainly one cannot look at the poverty, wretchedness, ignorance and inevitable sin which exist as a permanent element in our fairest communities, without a shudder at the terribleness

of the evils of whose depth most of us have but faint conception; and without feeling that it cannot be God's will that
it should continue; that it ought not by man's allowance and
aid to continue. But – not to dwell in dreams of future and far
off renovation – to discover what is to be done now, – *hic labor!*
The evil is so vast, the problem so complicated that appalled
we ask where to begin, and he is a wise man who can answer.
Plainly, the evil will not grow less or the problem clearer.
Almsgiving, it is plain is but superficial alleviation. Free education doing so much does not reach those most in need, – the
lowest, and that an increasing class – since of that the children
are too useful at home to be sparred for school. Our factories
make the law a dead letter.[18]

Given his feelings toward children and his experience as a
teacher, he provided books for the children to use in his home
or in the Sunday school. However, as with the older hymnbooks,
Samuel was unhappy about the content and theological concepts
presented in a number of the books. He wrote to Edward Everett
Hale describing his feelings toward the books that had been made
available.

I have occasion to keep a store of little books for little
children who come to my study, or to distribute in my Sunday
school, and I am compelled for the most part to resort to the
Sunday-school Union, which furnishes an abundant supply of
such books of every size, very neatly printed and prettily illustrated. But those books are not safe; they come in packages
and of every package several have to be burned; others will
do with pen-alteration of a word or two, and others again are
very good. But I wish *we* could be as well furnished with books
of the same style, built after our ways of thinking; which would
impress the lesson of truthfulness without allusions to the "lake
of fire," and teach the presence of God in some other character
than that of spy; and warn against evil without the exhibition
of an angry God who holds" a rod to send young sinners swift
to hell;" and tell of Jesus without stating the object of his life to
be "to save us from going to hell;" and inculcate the importance

of time without the stimulus of reference to the terror of death and the gloom of grave.[19]

In keeping with this effort for children, the city of Fall River showed its esteem for Samuel Longfellow by appointing him as Chairman of the School Committee, the perfect job for someone who was so concerned with children's education. He tells Edward Everett Hale a little about his new position.

> I write in an interval of official labors (!), with an official steel pen and official blue ink. ...The exclamation point is not an ironical tone-mark, but an embodied sigh of weariness. Monday, yesterday, and to-day, I have been incessantly engaged, morning, afternoon, and evening, examining scholars and teachers, and a vista of work opens itself through the rest of the week which convinces me that I repose in no sinecure, for a time at least.[20]

After working on the school board for a period, Samuel began to develop opinions about the need for education. In a letter to his sister-in-law Fanny, Samuel talks about education and its importance for future generations.

> I have been much in the Public School of late attending the examinations & have felt more than ever before how much depends upon these and such as these. They are to be the next circle in the great tree of Society, to carry forward its growth; through these the fresh and living currents are to circulate. They are to build life & build on where we leave off. And the coming time shall be what they make it – what they are. May it not be that when Christ looked upon those young children & said "Of such is the kingdom of heaven," he meant something more than that the child-like spirit was needed for the reception of his gospel.[21]

Not long after taking charge of his congregation, Samuel held his first communion service, an event that was momentous for him. In a letter to Edward Everett Hale he said that he wanted

"to have it open to all, and if possible to have the whole congregation remain, even if they do not all partake of the bread and
wine."[22]

After the communion service he wrote a letter to his mother
describing it and how he felt about it. Although the letter quota-
tion is long, Samuel's complete explanation of his very different
approach to one of the basic sacraments deserves to be presented.

> I think you will be interested to hear of my first communion;
> so I shall delay my pastoral visits this afternoon till I have
> written you a brief account of Sunday's service.
>
> I learned that the number of communicants was small,
> though the invitation had been always extended to all. The
> service was appointed for the afternoon, as there is always
> the largest attendance in that part of the day. In the morning
> I preached a sermon, giving my views upon the communion;
> that it was one of the ministrations of religion which should
> be open to all with entire freedom; and that all should *feel* at
> liberty to unite in it; that it should be a simple, cheerful comme-
> moration of Christ, from which all feeling of dread should be
> banished; that no one need shrink from coming to the table
> of him whose love was toward all men, and who ate with
> publicans and sinners, any more than he need shrink from
> approaching in prayer the All Holy Father. I dwelt somewhat
> upon these points, endeavoring to remove the unfounded and
> injurious feeling of awe and mystery which, to many minds,
> veils this rite, and I closed by saying that I should invite *all* to
> unite with us, who should feel at the time a desire to do so,
> whether they had ever before or not, and whether they would
> ever again or not; that some might find satisfaction in partaking
> of the bread and wine, and others be best helped by joining
> in spirit in the prayers, the meditations, the associations of the
> time. I wished first and most of all to impress a sense of *perfect
> freedom;* thinking this essential to open the way to a spiritual
> understanding and reception of the rite. In the afternoon, the
> whole service – hymns, scripture and prayer – was made a
> remembrance of Jesus. I preached my sermon on the sufferings
> of Christ, closing it with a reference to the communion and a

repetition of my desire that all should feel at liberty and welcome to unite with us. Then I gave a benediction, and after a pause of a few minutes, than any might have an opportunity to retire who wished I came down to the table. Not a person left the house. I made a short extempore address, applying more particularly the sentiment of the sermon and then a prayer. Then breaking the bread, with the usual words, I took it from the table and carried it myself to each pew, offering it to all, and the same with the wine, repeating at intervals appropriate sentences from the Scriptures. Only a few partook of the elements, perhaps none who had not been accustomed to do so. We then united in a silent prayer, followed by the Lord's Prayer and the benediction.

The only thing that was not entirely pleasant to me was the feeling that those who did not partake of the elements might feel an embarrassment at refusing what yet they did not feel quite prepared to receive, and it would have been pleasanter, certainly to me, if all or nearly all had partaken of the bread and wine. I think that if they continue to remain, more and more will gradually do so.

I liked very much the distributing the elements myself rather than by deacons; it is simpler and less sacerdotal and official. It brought me nearer to my people. It seems, too, to be carrying out the spirit of the chapter which I had read where Jesus washes his disciples' feet, and says that he came not to be ministered unto but to minister. It was suggested to me by Mr. Ware. I felt the more encouraged to hope that all would remain from Edward Hale's having told me that they did so from the first in his church. I have been glad to find from several who have since spoken to me that the service was generally felt to be very interesting. I suspect the only way to induce all the congregation to remain is to make the communion a part of the service of the day, and not a separate service, as is usual.[23]

From his comments it is apparent that he was greatly interested "in giving new life, and especially the spirit of freedom, to the ancient rite."[24] Shortly after the communion service Sam

Longfellow wrote to Sam Johnson about a misgiving that he had. As his theology matured, this misgiving became the controlling direction for his religious beliefs. He told Johnson: "I begin to have something of Higginson's feeling about the word 'Christian.'"[25]

Three years later, he wrote another letter to his mother with a very detailed description of the communion service he performed. He also included some problems he had with the communion service and how he resolved one of them.

> I do not get over the feeling I have had from the first that the material elements of the bread eaten & the wine tasted are in the way & I do not always partake of them. Another thing that I have felt the want of is of more of the sense of a communion, a social feeling among those who join in the service they seem isolated & sundered; & it was partly to get over this that I invited them to come up together to the table instead of carrying the bread & cup to the pews as I used to do.[26]

This is an indication of Samuel Longfellow's move to the more radical faction of the Unitarians. His friend Thomas Wentworth Higginson was quite a radical in a number of areas. In religion, his radical ideas took him toward the idea that there was no one right church. In later life he was involved with the Free Religious Association, as was Samuel Longfellow.

> For us, the door out of superstition and sin may be called Christianity; that is an historical name only, the accident of a birthplace. But other nations find other outlets; they must pass through their own doors, not through our's; and all will come at last upon the broad ground of God's providing, which bears no man's name. The reign of heaven on earth will not be called the Kingdom of Christ nor of Buddha, – it will be called the Church of Good, or the Commonwealth of Man. I do not wish to belong to a religion only, but to the religion; it must not include less than the piety of the world. If one insists on being exclusive, where shall he find a home? What hold has any Protestant sect among us on a thoughtful mind? They are too little, too new, too inconsistent, too feeble.[27]

Approximately six months after he began at Fall River, Samuel was returning home after a trip and ran into Mr. Battelle, whom he had first met before he had accepted the Fall River society's offer. Battelle had told him that he wanted to study Christ's life and had decided "to devote five hundred dollars in the course of three or five years, to the purchase of books,"[28] that Samuel could select if he came to Fall River. Battelle was the "lay monitor" of the society and spent the whole evening on the trip expressing dissatisfaction with Samuel's performance. Samuel was greatly depressed because Battelle said,

> the most disheartening things about the need of a minister's recognizing the division of labor, and confining himself to the elucidation of the gospel, leaving slavery and intemperance to be discussed by those who had had time and opportunity to examine these subjects thoroughly, – as the minister could not if he attended to his proper work. He said I was invited here, "not to be a minister of religion, but a minister of the gospel," etc. The answers were obvious, but I was too weary to contend with him it chilled and discouraged me, though, to be met thus on my return, and the next day I felt both unwell and homesick, and did not write any Sermon.[29]

While the comments expressed clearly distressed Samuel, he was able to write a sermon on Saturday and apparently did not make an issue of the conversation in his letters to his friends and family.

Approximately five months earlier Battelle had sent a letter to Samuel expressing both his congratulations and criticism of Samuel's preaching, probably relative to Samuel's approach to the communion service.

> I called twice this evening to see and congratulate you upon the success of your method of this day – although I supposed that the audience supposed that the intention was to dismiss them before your arrangements had intended. The reasons for the course followed, and method, will have to be repeatedly explained, before the people will all understand so great a

departure from the customs of other denominations and for the most part of our own, but if continued until it is understood and appreciated, it must be productive of happy results.[30]

During the time that Samuel preached at Fall River, Battelle appears to have continued to be somewhat discontent with Samuel's preaching. He even got to the point of walking out during a sermon, as Samuel describes to Samuel Johnson.

Battelle called Sunday evening & said he really had some doubts whether he could conscientiously aid in supporting a preaching which he conscientiously felt was so positively erroneous in its method & topics as that of our Unitarian pulpits – tho' I don't think he finds anything elsewhere that suits him better. Last Sunday, he went out of our church & went into the Universalist house where a "Bible class" is held in the A.M. He is very sincere about it, poor man, & always frank with me & personally friendly & I can't help feeling that it is hard for him to sit [?] & pay largely for what feeds him not & what he thinks feeds not others or feeds them amiss. But what a dreadful state of spiritual dyspepsia to get into, isn't it.[31]

A few months after Battelle's comments, Samuel celebrated his first anniversary at Fall River. His description of what he believed some of his congregation felt about him may relate to Battelle's comments.

The 16th [of February] was the anniversary of my ordination. I gathered my people under my wing, in the evening, in a social meeting at the parsonage. Some fifty came, and it was very pleasant to me, and, I believe, to them. The Sunday after, I preached a brief anniversary sermon to a handful of people in a snowstorm. I could not congratulate them upon an increase of numbers. But I never had any extravagant hopes as to numerical growth. I have neither the bustling energy to bring people in, nor the popular oratory to attract. I should be satisfied with our numbers if there were more life. I know that some are interested in my preaching, and do not let myself doubt that it has done good, nor am I discouraged. But I feel a lukewarmness and passivity in the society which communicates itself to me. At least, I have not spiritual life to outweigh it. However, my temperament indicates gradual operation to be my method, and I hope I am gaining power for more impressive action by and by.

With place and people personally, I am well content. But I do not find myself as yet taking deep root here.[32]

Regardless of his feeling that the congregation may not have accepted him 100%, he put his congregation to a simple test to see if they would willingly accept what he did.

The Universalist minister came to see me yesterday and I liked him; is from the West, having lived in Kentucky and Illinois. He has stentorian lungs – I heard him as I passed his church last Sunday. It will make my people stare to see him in our pulpit, but't will do them good. And I shall not, like ___, ask them beforehand if they are willing to hear a Universalist, but take it for granted they have too much sense to object.[33]

Samuel tried to preach what he believed was best for the society members, but he was not able to please them all, even some of the board members who had selected him. This lack of full acceptance by the Society must have been discouraging and may have been one of the principal reasons, Samuel gave for resigning from the Fall River Pastorate three years later.

During his second year, Samuel Longfellow started preaching on Sunday afternoons in an area near Fall River called Stone Bridge, which was a mission station. The people were poor and did not have a church or minister and had to rely on the missionary work of other ministers of various denominations in the area, including Samuel. He describes one experience there in a letter to Samuel Johnson.

Last Sunday I was at home in the morning; in the afternoon went to the Stone Bridge, and discoursed to quite a numerous auditory, for an hour, upon man the child of God, made in his image. "Little lower than the angels" was my text; and the greatness and worth of the human soul, its divine capacities and destiny, my theme. Needful words to them too seldom heard there before, I fear. To-day they have a Baptist elder from Newport, and the Sunday after I go again. It was beautiful, as I stood in the pulpit, to look through the windows or the open door upon the waters of the bay, which come up within a short stone's throw of the house.[34]

A year later, he wrote to Johnson describing his missionary activities in Stone Bridge.

I have been and am going again, a missionary, to the Stone Bridge, about six miles from here, where I preach in a quaint old meeting house right on the water's edge. I go down Sunday afternoon after my service. Isn't that brave?[35]

For the next two years Samuel continued his work with the Fall River Unitarian Society.

He carried out his duties "with diligence and sympathy, and with that unfailing sincerity which made all his ministrations so fresh and real."[36] He was interested in the city and its people and worked energetically with charitable and moral improvement groups, but "a certain congeniality between himself and his position, which was indispensable to his happiness and sense of fitness, seems to have remained wanting,"[37]

He gave his best efforts, but Samuel never felt that he fit into the Fall River church or community. He also must have felt disheartened at not being able to attract new members to increase the size of the congregation, and he did not receive positive feedback from the existing congregation for his work and ministrations.

Samuel's reaction to the above along with criticism from Mr. Batelle and possibly others led him to consider whether he should continue as minister in Fall River. These were likely reasons for him to decide to leave Fall River. Additionally, his sorrow as the result of his parent's deaths could have put him in a psychological state in which his ability to deal with what was going on in Fall River was limited. Furthermore, Samuel's health had gotten worse since he had arrived in Fall River, which usually resulted in him desiring to take a break from what he was doing.

In late May of 1851, Samuel Longfellow submitted his resignation to the Fall River Society.

> I have spoken plainly and strongly, and I know there are some in the Society who do not want to hear or have such preaching. But I must do them the credit to say that they have manifested no disposition to interfere or oppose, and I believe the majority of my Society would not be satisfied with a minister who should be wavering or wanting in this matter. So that we have had no trouble on this point, and, so far as I know, the "lukewarmness" has not come of it.
>
> After considerable delay occasioned by some legal difficulties, the Society voted last Tuesday evening to request me to withdraw my resignation, and to raise eighteen hundred dollars by tax on the pews for repairing and putting in order the house. And they have got enough subscribed to pay all the annual expenses. The crisis called the people out, and quite a strong personal interest has been manifested toward me. One man, who does not go to church and whom I never spoke to, said he would give *"five dollars!"* rather than have me go out of town.[38]

Around the time that Samuel submitted his resignation letter, Fanny Longfellow sent him a note proposing a trip to Europe as a tutor. If he were interested, she would inform William Appleton, her father Nathan Appleton's cousin.

> Fanny's note unfolded an idea, which, though it may never be realized, I will communicate to your. She wrote that Mr. William Appleton wished to send his son Charles (an amiable youth of 18) abroad for a year & was looking out a companion for him, and she wished to know if I should like to visit Europe under such a relation. I wrote her that I should like it very much, if it could be brought about, but I thought there would be a

theological or ecclesiastical difficulty in the way. Mr. Appleton
being an Episcopalian.[39]

Samuel's leaving Fall River was not as simple as he would have
liked. At a meeting of the board, they did not accept his resignation as he tells his sister Anne.

> It was not till last night that I was informed of the result
> of the meeting of Tuesday Evening. That result was, as far as
> concerned my resignation, a vote not to accept it – 26 to 3.
> A further and quite important question was whether they could
> raise money for my salary, and a committee was appointed to
> report on this subject at an adjourned meeting next Tuesday.
> For myself I am not decided what to do. At times I feel inclined
> to leave them to their fate & at others to stay awhile at least &
> see if I can do anything for them. I wait further developments.[40]

As the letter to Anne indicates, despite his positive response
to Fanny about the trip to Europe, he still was not sure what to do.
In another letter to Anne, he mentions some of his latest plans
that might be acceptable to the Board.

> My present idea is to stay for a year at least (if I don't go
> abroad & see if I cannot do more for them than I have done
> & if they will not do more for themselves.[41]

Regardless of the various ideas occupying his thoughts and the
Board's refusal to accept his resignation, Samuel finally decided
to leave Fall River and take up the offer from Mr. Appleton. Samuel
Longfellow began his preparations for the trip to Europe and he
left for England with Charles Appleton a couple of months after
resigning.

Nevertheless, he did not leave Fall River without some feelings
of remorse. In a letter to Samuel Johnson he mentions his feelings
and also describes some things he learned at Fall River.

> I felt very sorry to leave Fall River, in the depressed condition
> of the Society; but it could not be postponed, and I trust to their

finding some stirring person who will really 'build them up' outwardly without failing of true spiritual ministration. I found quite a regret at my departure on account of my connection with the schools, where it seems my services were esteemed, though I did not know it. One thing I shall have more faith in now, – in the influence that may be exerted, and recognized, from a very quiet person. I thought that, in a community like that of Fall River, a man must take an active part in public affairs, be able to speak in public meetings, and take the lead in movements.

I have never regretted that I went there. It has been a good thing for me and I was very independent there. I should have been glad if it had proved the place for me, for I do not like transplanting, and with each year one gains power to do more in those which shall follow.[42]

The Fall River Society was looking for another minister and asked Samuel Longfellow for suggestions. The Society then expressed their interest in Samuel Johnson. Sam Longfellow contacted Samuel Johnson and told him that Fall River would like him to preach there for an extended period, but he did not take up the offer. Although Fall River wanted to have continuous preaching, they did not have enough money for a permanent preacher and it took them time to find someone to fill their pulpit. The year after Samuel Longfellow left Fall River, the congregation chose Josiah K. Waite as their next minister.

Notes:

[1] May, Joseph, Ed.. *Samuel Longfellow: Memoir and Letters.* Cambridge: The Riverside Press, 1894. p. 97.

[2] Adams, Oscar Fay. "Samuel Longfellow." *The New England Magazine,* October 1894, v. 17, n.° 2, p. 205-213. Boston., p. 207.

[3] Letter, Samuel Longfellow to Samuel Johnson, December 11, 1847. SLP, LNHS.

[4] Letter, Samuel Longfellow to Edward Everett Hale, November 21, 1847. SLP, LNHS.

[5] Letter, Samuel Longfellow to Samuel Johnson, November 20, 1847. SLP, LNHS.

[6] Ibid.

[7] Letter, Samuel Longfellow to Samuel Johnson, December 1847. SLP, LNHS.

[8] May, Joseph, Ed.. *Samuel Longfellow: Memoir and Letters.* p. 104-105.

[9] Ibid., p. 108-109.

[10] Ibid., p. 111.

[11] Ibid., p. 110.

[12] Ibid., p. 112-113.

[13] Ibid., p. 110-111.

[14] Ibid., 126.

[15] Letter, Samuel Longfellow to Anne Longfellow Pierce, September 21, 1848. SLP, LNHS.

[16] May, Joseph, Ed.. *Samuel Longfellow: Memoir and Letters.* p. 125-126.

[17] Letter, Samuel Longfellow to Samuel Johnson, September, 5, 1848. SLP, LNHS.

[18] Letter, Samuel Longfellow to Edward Everett Hale, January 6, 1849. SLP, LNHS.

[19] Ibid., no date.

[20] Letter, Samuel Longfellow to Samuel Johnson, May 17, 1849. SLP, LNHS.

[21] Letter, Samuel Longfellow to Frances (Fanny) Appleton Longfellow, December 24, 1849. SLP, LNHS.

[22] Letter, Samuel Longfellow to Edward Everett Hale, March 1, 1848. SLP, LNHS.

[23] Letter, Samuel Longfellow to Zilpah Longfellow, March 7, 1848. SLP, LNHS.

[24] May, Joseph, Ed.. *Samuel Longfellow: Memoir and Letters.* p. 119.

[25] Ibid.

[26] Letter, Samuel Longfellow to Zilpah Longfellow, March 21, 1851. SLP, LNHS.

[27] Higginson, Thomas Wentworth. "The sympathy of religions." An address delivered at Horticultural Hall. Boston: February 6, 1870.

[28] Letter, Samuel Longfellow to Samuel Johnson, December 11, 1847. SLP, LNHS.

[29] May, Joseph, Ed.. *Samuel Longfellow: Memoir and Letters.* p. 128-129.

[30] Letter, Mr. Battelle to Samuel Longfellow, March 5, 1948. SLP, LNHS.

[31] Letter, Samuel Longfellow to Samuel Johnson, December 3, 1850. SLP, LNHS.

[32] Letter, Samuel Longfellow to Samuel Johnson, February 27, 1849. SLP, LNHS.

[33] May, Joseph, Ed.. *Samuel Longfellow: Memoir and Letters.* p. 137.

[34] May, Joseph, Ed.. *Samuel Longfellow: Memoir and Letters.* p. 138.

[35] Letter, Samuel Longfellow to Samuel Johnson, June 21, 1849. SLP, LNHS.

[36] May, Joseph, Ed.. *Samuel Longfellow: Memoir and Letters.* p. 150-151.

[37] May, Joseph, Ed.. *Samuel Longfellow: Memoir and Letters.* p. 151.

[38] Letter, Samuel Longfellow to Samuel Johnson, June 26, 1851. SLP, LNHS.

[39] Letter, Samuel Longfellow to Anne Longfellow Pierce, June 10, 1851. SLP, LNHS.

[40] Ibid.

[41] Ibid.

[42] Letter, Samuel Longfellow to Samuel Johnson, July 30, 1851. SLP, LNHS.

CHAPTER 11 – BEYOND FALL RIVER

While he was minister at the Fall River Unitarian Church, Samuel Longfellow maintained contact with his friends and family elsewhere. Sometimes he took a trip to Cambridge or Portland to visit family or into the Boston area to visit friends or enjoy cultural events not available in Fall River. Most of these visits were during the week or they could be on a weekend if he paid for a substitute in the pulpit. Unfortunately, not all of Samuel's communications or visits involved enjoyable activities.

Six months after Samuel went to Fall River, there was a sad event within the Longfellow family with the death of Henry and Fanny's youngest child, Frances, known as Little Fanny. This was the first death in Henry Wadsworth Longfellow's family and was sure to have saddened Samuel. In August 1848 the almost $1^{1/2}$-year old girl became sick and gradually worsened over the weeks until she died on September 11. In her journal Fanny describes her daughter's last hours.

> Sinking, sinking away from us. Felt a terrible desire to seize her in my arms and warm her to life again at my breast. Oh for one look of love, one word or smile! Mary was with us all day. Painlessly, in a deep trance, she breathed, Held her hand and heard the breathing shorten, then cease, without a flutter. A most holy and beautiful thing she lay and at night of look angelic and so happy.[1]

Being in Fall River during little Fanny's life, Samuel did not really know his niece well. With his great love of children, the loss of one was painful to him. He responded to Fanny's letter about her daughter's death with an expression of profound sorrow.

> What can I say to reach a sorrow such as I have never known and cannot know a mother's sorrow! Yet I do wish that you

may feel my heart near yours now. The intelligence that your note brought me last night, I was so entirely unprepared for, that I cannot think of our little Fanny except as I have seen her still making bright the home with her soft eyes & sweet smile. She has left me that beautiful remembrance. And to you, too, that, and now much more. Yet your feeling now must be only of something gone. The thoughts tune involuntarily to what has been filling them almost wholly and are startled and find themselves arrested only by a sense of loss. The heart goes forth in search of its wonted rest and finds its object no longer where it has never failed to be. It is hard to assume the new relation to the dear one, whom we have known through the bodily form, when at once that form is stopped for a spiritual garment. Yet before long the spiritual shape glides in & is a felt presence in all the old places, at times almost "quivering into visible being" before our eyes.[2]

Death had not finished with the Longfellow family and starting in August 1849, Samuel went through a 1?-year period during which he lost three members of his family. The first person to die was his father who was very important to him. Stephen, Sr., died on August 3, 1849.

You have heard of my father's death, in the early morning of the day I reached home. It is a great comfort to me to have been with him [previously] in his sickness, to render those little attentions which are so great a satisfaction to our hearts. I felt nearer to him than I have ever done before. And we all had the strongest sense of his presence with us after he had left the body, a joyful presence, as of one from whom a cloud had passed and a burden fallen, and who now stood among us in health and new life, giving us his happy benediction. I am sure that sickness has often drawn a thicker veil between him and us while he dwelt in the flesh than death has now done, which seemed rather the lifting of a veil.[3]

Stephen Longfellow, Sr. had suffered from a disability that made him an invalid for the last third of his life. In his journal, Henry Wadsworth Longfellow talks about his father's death.

This morning at three o'clock my father died very quietly, a gentle release from a world in which for twenty-seven years he has borne the burden of invalidism and despondency. In the midst of his career, at the age of forty-five, he was smitten with this disease which now terminates fatally at the age of seventy--three.[4]

The basis for Stephen, Sr.'s invalidism is not certain, but "he suffered from debilitating ailments, including what were diagnosed as epileptic attacks, and in mid-career he seems to have suffered a major failure of confidence in himself."[5] Charles C. Calhoun also mentions the possible influence of the death of 21-year old Elizabeth, his first child to die. "The family circle had been broken and the mother and father were never quite to recover."[6]

Fanny Longfellow describes her visit to Portland with Henry just before Stephen, Sr's. death. She also comments on other members of the family and the condition of Stephen, Sr.

You will be surprised to see Portland instead of Newport at the head of this note. It was a very sudden change of plan, caused by the illness of Henry's father. He has been very feeble all winter, and within the last ten days has seemed to be failing so rapidly that Henry was twice summoned here by telegraphy, and finding he was likely to linger in this state some time, or drop away at any moment, we decided to give up Newport and take up our abode here for the present. I am very glad we did so, for even if he should rally from this apparent giving way of the vital powers it will probably be his last summer on earth.[7]

His father has happily no pain, and lies perfectly tranquil, dozing nearly all the time and rarely recognizing anyone. He has been an invalid many years having ruined his constitution by too close application to his profession, and has been so depressed by his loss of activity that it will be no pain to him to leave his weary body. He has the dignity and courtesy of the old school, added to a gentleness and sweetness of disposition all his own. He has now the comfort of seeing all his children about him, Mary having fortunately arrived within a few days from New Orleans, and Alex within a few weeks from southern bays where he has been all winter surveying. Annie is therefore relieved from her great responsibility and care, and mother, though at first brought to her own bed by the sudden trial of her feeble strength is now cheerful and composed, and prepared to meet her loss with a Christian confidence.

***

Our painful anxieties and long watching here are now over. Henry's father is at last at rest, after many years of suffering and depression which made life almost a burden to him. He died on the third at three o'clock in the morning, most peacefully. The day before I was with him all day. He was evidently dying, and no longer recognized any one, but it was a great comfort to see so gentle and natural a departure: he met death as a friend and not as an enemy. If he could have recovered sufficient consciousness to have spoken a few words to us, it would have been an additional consolation, for during this last illness he has not spoken at all beyond a greeting, but we rejoice his spirit is peacefully released from the "body of death" it has carried so many years. He was a most pious, excellent man, beloved and respected by all, and it is touching to see the general interest of all the citizens here. I shall never forget his affectionate greeting to me as his daughter the first time I ever came here, and his tenderness ever since. It has been a great satisfaction to me to help him, and his memory is very dear to me.[8]

A little over a year later, on September 19, 1850, Samuel's oldest brother Stephen, Jr., died at the age of 45. His health had been destroyed by his excessive alcohol consumption that began during his teenage years. Despite efforts by his parents and his brother Henry, Stephen was never able to overcome his problems. After Henry had received a letter from his brother Alex, Fanny Longfellow wrote Anne Longfellow Pierce and talks about Stephen's health.

How soon again all these sad offices have been renewed to you, but poor Stephen's health was so shattered, and so little happiness seemed in store for him in this life, that we can hardly regret rest is at hand and an existence where his warm affections can meet with due reward. Pray give my truest love to him if he is still able to remember me.[9]

Samuel also received a letter about Stephen, Jr.'s failing health, probably also from his brother Alex. Samuel wrote to Samuel Johnson telling him about his brother's health and then continues into a general discussion of health, life and death that tied in with his religious beliefs. From the text of the letter it seems possible that Samuel did not go to visit his brother on his deathbed.

I found that my brother had revived after they wrote me; but he was very sick, and is daily growing weaker. It seems impossible that he can continue more than a very a very few days. How strangely the vital powers resides the attacks of disease! Like the defenders of a besieged city, driven from outpost after outpost, rallying and retreating, till, shut up in the citadel, they stand at bay and hold out still. So powerful is life, so hard to conquer; anon, a slight obstruction, a pin's prick, and it is gone at once! Shall we ever so know and obey the physical laws that this bountiful energy shall have its full course? And then will there still be a limit, as we are wont to say, or will the thought of some prove true, that "death shall itself be abolished"? Why may not the healthy process of renewal endlessly repair the daily and hourly waste? We say the soul would choose not to be confined forever in these fetters of the flesh that its wings cannot expand here. But how has ever reached the possibilities of an earthly expansion? If, from year to year of man's physical prime his mind enlarges in power and attainments, who can place the limit to this enlargement, supposing the body to be continually renewed? Who that dies oldest, most vigorous, having accomplished most of acquaintance with what this world has to teach, has yet done more than begin a knowledge of even the natural world?[10]

The last death during this period, and probably the saddest for Samuel, was that of his mother. Zilpah Longfellow died on March 12, 1851 at the age of 73. Like her husband, Zilpah had been an invalid a large portion of her life. In a letter to Samuel Johnson, Samuel Longfellow describes his recollection of his mother's life more than focusing on her death.

I came down here last Thursday on receiving a telegraphic note communicating the sudden death of my mother; sudden, but gentle and placid; such a death as I have often heard her wish might be hers, and a fitting close to a life serene, quiet, loving, and holy.

I did not think I should ever weep again, at such a time; but when I went at night to the chamber where through my childhood, I slept next to my mother's, the remembrance of all the loving care which had embosomed those years came over me and forced tears that would not be stayed at once. Now I have only the most peaceful and happy thoughts, and sweetest sense of the presence through all the house of a meek and tranquil spirit, a spirit calm and gentle and full of love.

My mother had long been an invalid. I do not remember her as other than such. We had not supposed that she would stay here to number seventy-three years. But I know not how to be thankful enough for the guidance and influence of such a character and heart and life. She was remarkable for her piety, – the simplest, most unobtrusive, most childlike, most pervasive and controlling trust in God; not very often spoken of in words, I think, but always speaking in the life; in her daily patience, cheerfulness, calmness and active goodness; in the devout book she love to have in her hand; in her love for all things beautiful in nature, whether in commonest flower or the thunderstorm which I first learned not to fear by seeing her always sit at the window to watch its glory.

She had remarkable calmness and self possession, – the fruit, I believe, of her piety. It did not falter under many and frequent trials and sorrows. I shall not forget how, years ago, after the death of my almost twin sister, she stood with me beside the body and simply, by the cheerful calmness of her tones, took from me the dread of death. Sand severer trials than the death of children I have seen her bear with equal serenity.[11]

Samuel wrote a letter to his sister Mary Longfellow Greenleaf concerning his feelings about his mother's death. Henry's wife Fanny also wrote Mary expressing how she felt about Zilpah Longfellow.

As suddenly to me as to you the telegraph brought its brief announcement of our dear mother's death. I had not even heard of her sickness. But I could come home the next day to look again on the sweet, calm face, which you have, indeed, in your remembrance. I had always thought that I should be with mother at the hour of her death, perhaps to supply to her the words of prayer, leaning on which she might pass through the veil. But the Father led her so gently & and so without warning through, that there was no time & surely no need for any other prayer than that constant prayer of her trusting, serene and waiting spirit. Her hand had been in His for many a year & needed not to be placed there by aid of any.

Death came as swiftly as gently. No one knew it was so near, not even herself. But we have heard her wish that her departure might be so & her desire was granted. And it is pleasant to remember & think of her last hours as so comfortable & cheerful & her release so untouched by a pang. It was a fitting close to a life so serene and gentle, so calm, so holy and prepared as hers. We wish that we could have been with her, but we know that tenderest care was watching her, & the thoughtful affection which for so many years has been devoted to her, without ceasing.

I did not know that I should ever weep again; I have sometimes feared lest my feelings might have become deadened through the necessity I have felt in approaching the afflictions of others to be myself very calm. But when I came at night to go to the chamber where I had slept when a child went to mother's own room, the whole remembrances of childhood & the motherly love of her who had guarded it came rushing over me & with them tears I could not resist.[12]

How truly do I sympathize in the sudden shock the news of dear mother's departure must have given you and Alex. ...It came likewise to us without a warning, but I can hardly call it a surprise. She seemed to me ever lowering upon the brink of that better land, and I have hoped she would thus gently leave us when God willed to release her from her weary body. In what harmony with her life was such a transition-- this continuance rather than change of being already clothed upon with immortality and assumed its natural place without effort or suffering. I trust Annie feels reconciled, and that you all will, to such a removal, without the prostration of prolonged illness, so painful to witness in so feeble a body; without a cloud upon her mind she fitly closes a long life. There is something very beautiful and touching to me in her death, and it brings the next life nearer and nearer to us. Ah, if we could all be as fine and gentle in soul as she was, as free from passion and selfishness, as fine and cheerful in doing and enduring, it would never seem afar off, and so quietly might we all be led to it.

I shall greatly miss the motherly tenderness with which she always greeted me, but am deeply grateful I have been allowed to enjoy it so long.[13]

Some of Samuel's trips were to areas not far from Fall River. One of his early trips was with some friends to visit Mount Hope, the bay just south of the city. Samuel described it as "a friend of many years" recalling an India ink sketch on the walls of his childhood bedroom. While they were there, the Hutchinson Family Singers were also present and provided some entertainment. This male quartet was very popular with Samuel and his friends. Not only were they entertaining singers, but they were also very radical in their politics, especially in regard to Abolitionism.

While not a strongly aggressive Abolitionist like his friend Higginson, Samuel was a strong opponent to slavery. Nevertheless, in a letter to Samuel Johnson just after his visit to Mount Hope he expressed his doubts about the ability of the government to do anything about it.

I hope little from political action against slavery. But so far as the government acts at all upon the matter, I wish it to be against rather than for slavery; and if men opposed to slavery can conscientiously go to Congress, I am glad to have them there, and in the President's chair, too![14]

One other place he visited in the area around Fall River was Newport.

"It happened to be the day of the great Yearly Meeting of the Quakers. After our service I went into their vast meeting-house, but I got no seat, for the press, and so I soon came out, leaving a man lifelessly calling us through his nose to "go into the vineyard of the Lord." How I longed for somebody to speak a living word to that great concourse from a *real* "moving of the spirit."[15]

Samuel also traveled to more distant places to hear lectures or concerts or to visit friends. If he were in the Boston-Cambridge area, Samuel could stay at the Craigie House with Henry and his family. However, the Town and Country Club was created and one of its purposes was to provide places to stay for out of town visitors.

In late spring 1849, Samuel was invited to participate in the Town and Country Club in Boston. This group was established primarily at the suggestion of A. Bronson Alcott and the name was chosen by Ralph Waldo Emerson. It had a spectacular list of 104 members on its roster, including Samuel Longfellow.

Alcott has sent me a summons to the first meeting of the Town & Country Club. If well managed, I think it will be a pleasant thing, especially for those who live out of town & when visiting the city will like to have a place where they can meet people they will like to see. I find that Alcott's prominence in it repels many. It originated with Emerson, you know, whose visit to England developed the social element in him. Hurlburt seems rather shy of it.[16]

In addition to Emerson and Alcott, the members included Henry Wadsworth Longfellow, Thomas Wentworth Higginson, William Lloyd Garrison James Freeman Clarke, Theodore Parker, Thomas Starr King, James Russell Lowell, Charles Sumner, Octavius Brooks Frothingham, Edward Everett Hale, William Channing, William D. Ticknor, James T. Fields, Nathaniel Hawthorne and a number of others. In his book *Cheerful Yesterdays*, Thomas W. Higginson said that the Town and Country Club was "rather short-lived". He later carried on the Club in a more permanent situation in Newport. A number of members gathered in the Boston Club for various reasons, however the Town and Country Club in Boston did not serve meals.

> In fact, it erred on the side of asceticism, being formed, as Emerson declared, largely to afford a local habitation and dignified occupation to Mr. Alcott.[17]

The question of allowing women members into the Town and Country Club was a distressing subject from the beginning. Higginson forced the issue by putting the names of Elizabeth Peabody and Mary Lowell Putnam (Lowell's sister) in the nomination book.

> Emerson himself, with one of those serene and lofty coups d'etat of which only the saints are capable, took a pen and erased these names, although the question had not yet come up for decision, but was still pending when the erasure was made.[18]

The same problem arose over the nomination of "colored" nominees Frederick Douglas and Charles Lenox Remond.

> This Lowell strongly favored, but wrote to me that he thought Emerson would vote against it; indeed, Emerson, as he himself admitted to me, was one of that minority of anti-slavery men who confessed to a mild natural colorphobia, controlled only by moral conviction. These names were afterwards withdrawn, but the Town and Country Club died a natural death before the question of admitting women was finally settled.[19]

Given the Club's activities and the attitudes of some of its members, it is not surprising that Samuel Johnson had a negative opinion of the Club. To a lesser degree, Samuel Longfellow had his own problems with it.

> I thought your remarks on the club showed you slightly rabid. Short of complete isolation, I can hardly imagine anything that would less limit or label anybody than paying five dollars for a share of a room where you might meet the all-sided, motley, unlabelable set of people who have got together in this club, from Fields and Whipple to Garrison, Parker, and Dwight. So don't bristle and put out your quills (or your pen) against this harmless chimaera. ...At the club meeting Hurlbut came out gallantly in favor of asking in the women. Emerson and Dwight opposed, which I should think quite un-Fourieritish. Wentworth [Higginson] spoke also in favor of the fair.[20]

As already mentioned, Samuel did not particularly like participating in groups. Nevertheless, he was willing to speak at conventions and meetings of groups whose principles he supported. He also expressed his opinion in articles he submitted to some of the magazines of the era.

In the book *Cheerful Yesterdays*, by Samuel's friend Thomas Wentworth Higginson, the section called "the birth of a literature" describes the development of American Literature with an emphasis on the writers and poets from the 1840s on. He mentions several magazines to which Samuel submitted articles or was mentioned in an article. Also contributing to this set of magazines were several of Samuel's friends, as well as his brother Henry.

Among these magazines were *The Dial*, a magazine that existed from 1840-1844 and highlighted the Transcendental movement; *The North American Review* and, in the 1850s, *The Atlantic Monthly*, both literary magazines; *The Massachusetts Quarterly*; and, *The New Englander*. Aside from these regional and literary magazines, Samuel regularly read Unitarian-oriented magazines. One was the *Christian Register*, which was published by the American Unitarian Association, and the *Christian Examiner*, which was more important to Samuel because of its support of the liberal wing of the church. The National Anti--Slavery Bazaar published an annual volume of anti-slavery poetry, to which both Samuel (1851 and 1856) and Henry (1845 and 1846) contributed.

Sometimes Samuel read something in a publication that he disagreed with. On these occasions he sometimes wrote his feelings to his friends, wrote to the publication or spoke about it at a convention or gathering, or a combination of the actions. As an example, Samuel wrote a letter to Samuel Johnson and describes his speech at the "Unitarian Festival" against the opinion he read in a Fall River newspaper.

> Speaking of associationists, did I tell you of my gallantly coming to the rescue of the Fourierites against an occasion of a foolish & ignorant article about them in the Fall River News, confounding them with the communist & the advocates of "All Property is Robbery" – & taking as their exponent a certain radical Mr. West. …I good naturedly put them right in a brief way as to the ideas of the Fourierites about property. They pointed my note & appended remarks to the effect that they didn't know anything about the matter & doubted whether the Fourierites themselves knew any more.[21]

Samuel Longfellow was involved in a number of efforts to improve human rights. Samuel's comments in his letters about the lack of rights of the factory workers in Fall River show his sensitivity to social problems and his desire to do something that would help advance equality. His greatest interests appear to have been in the areas of anti-slavery, peace, equal economic rights and woman's rights. While not leading the movements, he was there when his presence was needed.

In 1848, the first Woman's Rights Convention was held in Seneca, New York, through of the efforts of Elizabeth Cady Stanton, wife of an antislavery agent, and Lucretia Mott, a Quaker preacher. Their decision to hold the convention came as the result of the six women from America not being allowed to sit as delegates at the World Anti-Slavery Convention in London in 1840, although Mott was allowed to speak.

The Seneca Falls Convention was held on July 19 and 20 at the Wesleyan Methodist Church. However, since "No woman felt capable of presiding... Lucretia's husband James Mott" ran the meeting.[22]

Using the design of the Declaration of Independence, Elizabeth Stanton drew up the Declaration of Sentiments to be considered. She listed 18 "injuries and usurpations on the part of man toward woman," and proposed eleven resolutions. The only resolution that created problems, even shocking Lucretia Mott, was a woman's right to vote. All the other resolutions passed unanimously and only a persuasive speech by the former slave Frederick Douglass, then editor of the *Rochester North Star*, convinced the attendees to agree to the right to vote.

Newspapers ridiculed the conference and its resolutions. James Gordon Bennett of the *New York Herald*, whose son funded Stanley's search for Livingston, wanted to show how ridiculous the Declaration of Sentiments was and printed them. Elizabeth Cady Stanton said

> Just what I wanted. Imagine the publicity given to our ideas by thus appearing in a widely circulated sheet like the Herald. It will start women thinking, and men too; and when men and women think about a new question, the first step in progress is taken.[23]

Samuel was acquainted with both Stanton and Mott and spoke at the 10th National Woman's Rights Convention in 1860. While he was in his next pulpit at Brooklyn he had Mott preach one Sunday, in spite of her being a Quaker.

In 1861 Elizabeth Stanton was involved in women's rights in marriage and divorce and spoke on the subject at a meeting in New York and proposed several resolutions. There were speakers against her, but one particularly upset her when he spoke and called the whole discussion irrelevant and asked that it and the resolutions not be recorded. However, Samuel gave her words of encouragement.

As I greatly admired Wendell Phillips, and appreciated his good opinion, I was surprised and humiliated to find myself under the ban of his disapprobation. My face was scarlet, and I trembled with mingled feelings of doubt and fear-doubt as to the wisdom of my position and fear lest the convention should repudiate the whole discussion. My emotion was so apparent that Rev. Samuel Longfellow, a brother of the poet, who sat beside me, whispered in my ear, "Nevertheless you are right, and the convention will sustain you."[24]

On November 23, 1849, in Cambridge, Massachusetts, the wife and daughters of Dr. John Webster, a Harvard chemistry professor, were preparing to go to a party and waiting for the doctor to come home from Boston Medical College. At the same time, Dr. George Parkman, a physician, was on his way to Professor Webster's laboratory to collect a long-overdue debt. Apparently the two men began to argue and Dr. Webster finally lost control and hit Dr. Parkman over the head, killing him. According to trial testimony, the body was dismembered and the clothes and skull burned in a furnace. The rest of the pieces were hidden under a privy and in a tea chest. Ephraim Littlefield, the janitor, searched for Parkman's body because he was sure Webster had killed him. He eventually discovered body parts and called the police.

With the evidence pointing towards Dr. Webster, he was arrested on November 30. His twelve-day trial ended in conviction on April 1, 1850, and he was hanged at the Leverett Street Jail on August 30, 1850.

Virtually every text that deals with this trial calls it "the most celebrated murder trial during the 19th century". It involved two Harvard professors embroiled in a dispute that "gentlemen" should not have had and that had an especially vile result even less in keeping with their social status.

The friends of both the Websters and Parkmans included a large portion of the Cambridge-Boston academic and literary community, including Samuel Longfellow, Henry Wadsworth Longfellow and his wife Fanny and Dr. Parkman's brother, the Rev. Parkman, who had baptized the Webster daughters. The entire community was greatly shaken by the events that transcended the social code that governed the behavior of their class, although there had always been rumors that Dr. Webster had a checkered past and was considered financially irresponsible.[25]

With the indictment and trial, the Boston Brahmins behaved according to their rules, which considered that even among family members, the less said about negative events the better.[26]

> As the trial progressed, the community emerged like the Greek chorus who commented on the unfolding tragedy. Henry Wadsworth Longfellow's wife, Fanny, witnessed the community's retreat into a social dumb show: "All gaiety in Boston is stopped by this tragedy – the community is stunned, and cannot easily recover, nor should it..." Other community members were equally as incredulous.[27]

> Henry Longfellow wrote to Richard Henry Dana: "I do not dare to touch upon the dreadful Cambridge Tragedy which pollutes the very air around us." The sordid murder turned his world upside down and destroyed those values and traditions that the poet prized.[28]

The trial judge was Lemuel Shaw, Chief Justice of the Supreme Judicial Court of Massachusetts (1830-1860) and was also Herman Melville's father-in-law. Witnesses testifying as to Webster's character included Dr. Oliver Wendall Holmes who worked in the hospital with Parkman and Jared Sparks, president of Harvard at the time.

The prosecution used a very graphic strategy displaying a three-dimensional model of the school, maps of the various locations important to the trial and even placed pieces of a life-size drawing of a skeleton on the positions where they were found. However, there were some who felt that there were other suspects who should be considered, such as Littlefield, who was a

> ...perfect scapegoat. After all, the janitor, a working class bloke, allegedly gambled in Dr. Webster's laboratory and trafficked in corpses. This certainly described the profile of a

murderer better than the cherubic faced, intellectual Harvard professor who socialized with Charles Dickens and Henry Wadsworth Longfellow.[29]

In his charge to the jury, Judge Shaw had to address the fact that the legal grounds were shaky since no clear evidence of a single body had been found. This was also a trial that included the first use of forensic dentistry. He was later criticized because of his "treatment of burden of proof concerning *corpus delicti*, his presentation of the law of circumstantial evidence and the extreme bias of his summation of evidence in his charge to the jury."[30]

Samuel Longfellow was affected by the trial because the Websters were good friends with the Longfellow family in Cambridge. Samuel gave his opinions on the trial and what was going in a letter to his sister Anne.

> Dr. Webster's trial fills the newspapers and the thoughts of the people. The examination of witnesses so far elicits little or nothing that is new, only presents the facts in a more definite shape. There is certainly much for him to explain. But I see no proof yet against him. The most important witness is yet to be questioned – Littlefield. It is said that two ladies are ready to testify to having seen Dr. Parkman Friday afternoon. Dr. W. is known to have been in Cambridge up to midnight of Friday. But why speculate?[31]

Samuel also knew it was a traumatic experience for the Dabney family in Faial, where Samuel went to tutor in 1843. Besides being friends with the Webster family, their son John Pomeroy Dabney was married to Webster's daughter Sarah and Samuel Wyllys Dabney, lifelong friend of Samuel Longfellow, married Harriet Wainwright Webster on April 2, 1851, a year and a day after her father's death.

After Webster had been convicted and sentenced to death, he wrote a confession saying that he had killed Parkman in a fit of anger, without premeditation. Thus, he was guilty of manslaughter and not first-degree murder. Despite numerous protestations to the Governor from his friends and people around the country, he was hanged on August 30, 1850.

The murder and trial had effects that extended far beyond those it had on the community of Webster's friends and colleagues. One important legal outcome is that Justice Shaw's charge to the jury is still cited as a precedent on circumstantial evidence (see *Commonwealth v. Webster*, 59 Mass. (5 Cush.) 295 at 303 (1850)).

Herman Melville appears to have used the charge to the jury by his father-in-law Justice Shaw as a basis for statements by Captain Vere in the trial of Billy Budd in his book *Billy Budd*. Similar to the real life event, Billy Budd was convicted and hanged.

Samuel Longfellow was a great lover of music and went to concerts when he could find the time, most of the concerts being in Boston. Among the singers he heard was Jenny Lind, "The Swedish Nightingale." She drew large crowds wherever she went because of her voice, whose quality was touted by the master of publicity P.T. Barnum.

In 1850, Phineas Taylor Barnum brought Jenny Lind, one of the attractions that made him famous, from Europe. Jenny began her American tour of some 90 concerts for P.T. Barnum beginning September 11, 1850 at the Castle Garden Theater in New York City, where she also sang her final performance on May 24, 1852. In his publicity for Jenny Lind, Barnum said:

> A visit from such a woman who regards her artistic power as a gift from Heaven and who helps the afflicted and distressed will be a blessing to America. ...It is her intrinsic worth of heart and delicacy of mind that produces Jenny's vocal potency.[32]

P.T. Barnum is generally associated with unusual spectacles, circuses and a museum, but he also was a dedicated member of the Universalist Church who had a number of Unitarian and Universalist ministers as friends. He was liberal with his financial gifts to the church and was also involved with other social causes such as the Woman's Movement, in which he participated.

Jenny Lind earned a large amount of money from her concerts and. like Barnum, she was liberal with financial donations and gave some free concerts for charity. While she donated money to churches, she also gave personal gifts and a good part of her philanthropic activities were directed toward schools, hospitals and clinics for children. These latter would surely have met with Samuel Longfellow's endorsement.

Samuel describes the concert where he heard Jenny Lind and the "Swedish Nightingale" herself in a letter to his mother.

> On Thursday I went to hear the Nightingale in the crowded Tremont Temple. My three dollar ticket gave me a seat on a settee in the aisle under the gallery and not far from the door. I am confident that I could not hear her to advantage, but I had an excellent view. So with the singing I was not carried away, but with her appearance I was much charmed. Her manner is simple, sincere & suffused with feeling, tender and earnest. Henry says she appears to much greater advantage in public than in private where you see her face to be rather coarse.[33]

As indicated in the letter above, Henry had Jenny Lind as a guest in his house accompanied by Mr. Goldschmidt, who married her before they returned to Europe. Henry briefly describes the visit in his journal of June 26, 1851.

> Jenny Lind called this morning with Mr. Goldschmidt – a young pianist from Hamburg. We had a pleasant half-hour's chat. There is something very fascinating about her; a kind of soft wildness of manner, and sudden pauses in her speaking and floating shadows over her face. Goldschmidt we like extremely.[34]

On July 3, 1851, Emily Dickinson heard Jenny Lind sing. Apparently this made an impression on the young writer. Another person who had a significant effect on Emily Dickinson was Thomas Wentworth Higginson who was her mentor during much of her life, and also a good friend of Samuel Longfellow. An article on the Lind-Dickinson connection mentions the effect of both Jenny Lind and Thomas Higginson on the up and coming writer.

Surprisingly little attention has been paid to an event in Dickinson's life that rivals her famous encounter with Thomas Higginson in importance and suggestiveness. Given the fascination with Lind that Dickinson expresses in her letters and the fact that Dickinson witnessed the singer just as she was on the brink of her own poetic career, I am certain Lind made a decided impression on this singular member of her listening audience. Jenny Lind, as the most public of public women, served for Dickinson as both an intriguing and troubling example of the female artist in the marketplace.[35]

Notes:

[1] Wagenknecht, Edward, Ed. *Mrs. Longfellow: Selected Letters and Journals of Fanny Appleton Longfellow (1817-1861)*. New York: Longmans, Green and Co., 1856. p. 141.

[2] Letter, Samuel Longfellow to Frances (Fanny) Appleton Longfellow, September 14, 1848. SLP, LNHS.

[3] Letter, Samuel Longfellow to Samuel Johnson, August 26, 1849. SLP, LNHS.

[4] Samuel Longfellow, Ed. *Henry Wadsworth Longfellow, Vol. I*. Boston: Ticknor and Company, 1886. p. 145.

[5] Calhoun, Charles C. *Longfellow, A Rediscovered Life*. Boston: Beacon Press, 2004. p. 20. Ibid., p. 68.

[6] Wagenknecht, Edward. Mrs. Longfellow... p. 153.

[7] Ibid., p. 154.

[8] Ibid.

[9] Letter, Samuel Longfellow to Samuel Johnson, September 12, 1850. SLP, LNHS.

[10] Letter, Samuel Longfellow to Samuel Johnson, March 17, 1851. SLP, LNHS.

[11] Letter, Samuel Longfellow to Mary Longfellow Greenleaf, March 18, 1851. SLP, LNHS.

[12] Wagenknecht, Edward. Mrs. Longfellow... p. 176.177.

[13] Letter, Samuel Longfellow to Samuel Johnson, June 29, 1948. SLP, LNHS.

[14] Letter, Samuel Longfellow to Samuel Johnson, June 1848. SLP, LNHS.

[15] Letter, Samuel Longfellow to Samuel Johnson, April 25, 1849. SLP, LNHS.

[16] Higginson, Thomas Wentworth *Cheerful Yesterdays*. Boston: Houghton, Mifflin and Company, 1898. p. 174.

[17] Ibid.

[18] Ibid., p. 175.

[19] Letter, Samuel Longfellow to Samuel Johnson, May 17, 1849. SLP, LNHS.

[20] Letter, Samuel Longfellow to Samuel Johnson, 6 July 1849. SLP, LNHS.

[21] "The Seneca Falls Convention." Washington, DC. National Portrait Gallery Collection Description, www.npg.si.edu/col/seneca/senfalls1.htm.

[22] Ibid.

[23] Ibid.

[24] Chaney, Karen Elizabeth. *The Cambridge Tragedy: The George Parkman Murder Case and a Community in Crisis in Mid-Nineteenth Century.* Boston, Personal Communication.

[25] p. 13-14.

[26] Ibid., p. 13.

[27] Ibid., p. 18.

[28] Ibid., p. 19.

[29] Ibid., p. 18.

[30] Halttunen, Karen. "Divine Providence and Dr. Parkman's Jawbone: The Cultural Construction of Murder as Mystery." *Ideas, vol.4, N.° 1.* National Humanities Center. Research Triangle Park, North Carolina. 1996.

[31] Letter, Samuel Longfellow to sister Anne Longfellow Pierce, March 22, 1850. SLP, LNHS.

[32] "Jenny Lind." *Wikipedia, The Free Encyclopedia.* 17 Nov 2007, 07:38 UTC. Wikimedia Foundation, Inc. 17 Nov 2007 <http://en.wikipedia.org/w/index.php?title=Jenny_Lind&oldid==172051727>.

[33] Letter, Samuel Longfellow to Zilpah Longfellow, October 19, 1850. SLP, LNHS.

[34] Samuel Longfellow, Ed., *Henry Wadsworth Longfellow, Vol.II.* Boston: Ticknor and Company, 1886. p. 197.

[35] Pascoe, Judith. "'The House Encore Me So': Emily Dickinson and Jenny Lind." *The Emily Dickinson Journal.* 1992, 1.1,. p. 1-18. Baltimore. Emily Dickinson International Society. John Hopkins University Press.

CHAPTER 12 – TUTOR IN A REVOLUTION

Samuel's first European trip was accompanying Charles Hook Appleton as a tutor on a trip planned for two-years. Charles was the son of Mary Ann Cutler and William Appleton, the latter being a cousin of Nathan Appleton, who was the father of Fanny Longfellow.

A possible reason for the timing of Charles Hook Appleton's trip was that his father William Appleton had been elected as a Whig in 1850 to the U.S. House of Representatives from Massachusetts' 1st District. As a result he would be spending a significant amount of time away from home and from his son in order to attend Congressional meetings in Washington, D.C. Then in 1852 he was elected to the Massachusetts 5th District, which he served from 1853-55, but lost the elections in 1854 and 1856. His cousin Nathan had also been elected to the U.S. House of Representatives, serving the Massachusetts 1st District from 1831-33.

In May 1851, Fanny sent Samuel Longfellow a note saying that William Appleton was looking for a tutor to accompany his 18-year old son to Europe. Among the various options Samuel was considering, including staying in Fall River, he decided to take the offer to travel and teach and informed Fanny of his decision. Samuel made contact with Mr. Appleton and met with Charles Appleton. In a letter to Anne, Samuel mentions his first meeting with Charles.

> I saw Charles, who is a good looking amiable youth, is backward in his studies, & has never been away from home.[1]

Even after meeting both Charles and Mr. Appleton, Samuel still had some doubts about accepting the proposal. However, his hesitation had nothing to do with what Mr. Appleton had put forward, but was based on his personal desires.

If I go, it will not be exactly as I shd. Choose, for I should
like a companion of my own age; & I shall be confined by the
daily studies. Still, I really prefer the plan of making a considerable stay in places, to a constant traveling, & making the stay
it will not be amiss to have some occupation.[2]

Once Mr. Appleton had decided on Samuel as the tutor for his
son, and Samuel had decided to accept the offer, Mr. Appleton
wrote a letter telling Samuel how he expected the tutoring to
proceed. In addition, he advised Samuel how he should monitor
Charles' studies to ensure he was working. He also told Samuel
that after they had spent time in England and France, they should
go on to Germany and Italy and that Samuel was in charge of
the travel arrangements.

My wish is that he should continue his studies in English
history, mathematics, and the essential branches of English education. My impressions are, that on your arrival in France, you
will locate yourselves in private lodgings, that you will engage
for my son a French teacher who should instruct him under your
directions, a portion of each day, and at other periods, you
would instruct him yourself in the branches before named.
That you would be his friend, tutor, and companion feeling
that had the responsibility of a parent as to his morals, and in
all cases to see that others you may employ do their duty and
that he fulfills his part by such application as you deem expe-
dient. As to the number of hours that would be proper to apply
to study, you would be the judge.[3]

Samuel and Charles departed in 1851 shortly after Samuel left
his position in Fall River and arrived in Liverpool at the beginning of September. They stayed there a couple of days and then
went to London in a comfortable carriage on the express train
that took them $6^{1/2}$ hours to make the trip. Along the way Samuel
took pleasure in looking out the window at the beautiful scenery.

Green fields crossed by lines of dark green hedge & hedge
row trees, under road bridges arched of solid masonry always,

by harvest fields spotted with stacks of grain, by old red farm houses with thatched roofs nestling under the trees, by Elizabethan station houses, by old & rather shabby & straggling little villages of red brick, by grey stone churches.

***

As we neared London the country grew more finely cultured, the golden green meadows smoother, the park-like trees more frequent, the villages more elegant. Harrow spire pointed upward from the Hills, as when Byron was a boy there. Then we shot through a long tunnel & by house-gardens & suburban houses & were in the spacious glass-roofed Terminus of Euston Square.

Student and tutor had arrived in London and went to their hotel located on Cavendish Square. Their accommodations had been arranged by Mr. Lawrence, who Mr. Appleton had asked to handle the details of the trip. The hotel was a converted mansion and most of the 30 guests were American.

In London a young man about the age of Charles joined them. The new addition was "John Coolidge who, as I believe I wrote you is to be with us till a new tutor comes out for him proves a very pleasant addition to our party. I like him very much & should be glad to have him stay with me if it might be." [*letter to Anne*, September 12, 1851.] A couple of months later he got to know the boys better and described them better to Anne.

[John] is a fine boy, frank & simple hearted, very truthful, considerate & kind: full of generous impulses, which need only to be fined into principles to make a fine manly Character. Charley is less interesting & more conventional, but he is good natured & pleasant. They have, neither of them any inclination to go astray, so that I have no anxieties on that scene. The only reprehensible tendencies I have discovered are an inability to resist the temptations of the pastry cooks & confectioners, a propensity to purchase new waistcoats, and a hallucination on the part of Charles in respect to spending his evenings in the "passages" or covered streets of shops.[5]

In addition to the daily lessons, Samuel and the two boys went around London to see the sights, which were pretty much the same as tourists see today. They visited several museums and galleries, the Houses of Parliament, Westminster Abbey (including the Poets Corner where a bust of Henry was placed in 1884), St. Paul's, the Tower of London, Buckingham Palace and Madame Tussaud's, as well as other sights on the tourist itinerary. Samuel enjoyed going into shops, and was impressed by the number of bookshops, where he purchased gifts and books.

Of particular interest to the group was the Great Exhibition of 1851. It took place in the newly constructed Crystal Palace, which was then located in Hyde Park. The purpose of the Exhibition was to show the industrial, military and economic strength of a number of countries, with a special focus on Great Britain. Samuel found the exhibition interesting and in the American section there was a "reaping machine which is already getting in for itself a harvest of reputation & a precision," the "wounded Indian of Stevenson did not detain me," and "the freed slave a little farther on interested me as it had never done before."[6]

At some point during the visit, Charles and John "got separated" from Samuel. However, he never worried about them because had had confidence in their ability to take care of themselves and not get into trouble. When he got to the hotel at the end of the day, they were there. This happened several times during the trip, sometimes because they found something more interesting to a boy's taste. At night Samuel and either one or both of the boys went to dinner or to visit people to whom they had letters of introduction, and even at these times they would sometimes go off on their own. "I have no fear in letting them go out together at any time quite sure that they will not go where I should not approve, and that when they return, however late at night I shall know what they have been doing.[7]

Mr. Lawrence suggested to Samuel that he and the boys take a trip through northern England and Scotland before going on to Paris. He wrote Mr. Appleton and Mr. Coolidge, and took responsibility for the trip. As a result they got to see some places that they had not expected on their trip. They stopped in several places on the way that interested them such as Windsor Castle, Eton, Stratford and Shakespeare's house, the Universities at Oxford and Cambridge, Coventry and Melrose Abby. They crossed into Scotland passing through Edinburgh and Glasgow and a few other places in the country.

One of the highpoints of their trip was a stop in the Lake District to visit Rydal Mount, the home of William Wordsworth from 1813 till his death. Wordsworth had died almost a year and a half before Samuel visited the poet's house, where his wife still lived. Samuel and Charles had trouble finding the house and wandered around till they ended up at the back door. The maid led them to the front door and let them into the house.

They went through the poet's rooms and Samuel saw the man's presence as much as the contents. Samuel was taken by the view that Wordsworth had of the "landscape which His eyes had so often rested on & whose hues & forms had entered into his soul,"[8] and asked permission to sketch it. He saw a table on which there was an inkstand and pens and he wondered, "had any one of them written an undying line."[9] As their tour through the house came to an end, Samuel writes in his journal,

> Oh how I longed for a visible presence of him who having lived there had made the spot sacred & my visit to it a pilgrimage. The spiritual presence was there & made that humble homely house grander than the princely palaces.[10]

From the north of England, Samuel and the two boys returned directly to London. They had four more days in London and then their visit to Great Britain came to an end. They started on the next stage of their trip traveling from London to Dover and crossing the English Channel to Calais and then took the train to Paris, where they arrived October 7.

Samuel and the two boys moved into apartments on the first floor at 13 rue de la Victoire owned by Monsieur and Madame Grozier. The apartment was just off the Rue la Lafayette in the area of the Grands Boulevards. Samuel and Charley shared a 15 ft. by 18 ft. furnished apartment with several rooms and John had his own room on the same floor at the top of the stairs.

After breakfast at 8:00
Charley looks over his French lesson & at nine Mon. Donville
comes and stays with him for an hour, during which I am generally present. At ten he goes to John, & Charley & I take a
short walk & attend to little matters till eleven when we go down
to "dejeuner," breakfast or luncheon as you may choose to call
it, with Mons. & Madame Grozier.[11]

Samuel believed that it was important to learn to speak French
well. He had learned it in school in America, but was quick to
notice the difference in his classroom French and what was spoken in the country. He listened to Charles' lessons and sometimes
had individual help

to learn French, which we always speak at table, & I am
far from loquacious, as you will suppose. It is a vastly different
thing to read a language & to speak it, apart from the embarrassment which makes you forget even what you know.
It gives one a singular feeling this ignorance of the language
of the people you live among. It is like being in prison and
struggling with your fetters, or like one of those nightmare
dreams where under the most aggravating circumstances
you cannot for your life articulate a syllable. One has a realiz-
ing sympathy with the deaf & dumb. But I find myself com-
prehending much of the conversation at table & occasionally
launching forth into a long sentence, tho' mostly for the present I confine myself within the safe commonplaces of the
table.[12]

In the afternoons, they walked around the city sightseeing,
shopping or visiting someone. Samuel also occasionally stopped
in a church to see a service or listen to music. Sometimes the
boys went off by themselves and Samuel enjoyed the peace of
being alone to write or read. Although he was raised in a large
family, after he left home, with the exception of Craigie House,
there was usually no more than one other person in the house,
and they did not depend on him. During his recent years in Fall
River he lived alone except when he went to visit other places.

I get along poorly with letter writing here. I have been to long used to solitude that the presence of another person in the room rather disturbs me, & Charley, writing at the same time, is continually putting in words for me to spell, which however appropriate to his sentences have no place in mine.[13]

Among the places they visited were the Louvre, the Tuileries, the Place de la Concorde, the Champs Elysée, the Arc de Triomphe, the Hotel des Invalides, and the cemetery Père la Chaise. The also visited a lot of churches and went to shops to buy personal items and gifts.

One afternoon shortly before they left Paris, Samuel was invited to the atelier of the artist Ary Scheffer, which Sam tells Anne about.

A week ago I enjoyed a great pleasure in visiting the atelier of Ary Scheffer where I saw some wonderfully beautiful pictures & heard some music of Beethoven and at the end found my friend William Tiffany who has come out to Paris again to paint.[14]

A respected artist, Scheffer had been born in Holland and studied in Paris. The end of his studies occurred at the beginning of the Romantic period, but he painted in the Classical style. Scheffer also had political problems in France since he had ties with the royal family at the beginning of the Second Republic in 1848. William Tiffany was a Harvard classmate of Samuel who studied art for several years in Europe.

Samuel liked Paris because
Its aspect is extremely pleasant, much more cheerful than London, as it is more picturesque. The style of the buildings has something to do with this; the trees in the streets something; the bright sunshine more; that is when the sun does shine, which is not every day, at this season.[15]

The hour before dinner was dedicated to reading French History. In the evening after dinner, they sometimes stayed in the apartment and other nights they went to see a show, an opera or a play. One night they "went to see Houdin a marvellous magician." Jean Eugène Robert-Houdin, who died in 1871, was considered one of the greatest magicians of the era and the father of modern-day magic performance. The magician Harry Houdini took his name to honor Houdin.

Another night Samuel went to the play *Adrienne Lecoureur* and saw the famous actress Rachel. He was not impressed with the play, but was greatly taken by the actress. "I was never so entirely carried away. The excitement of feeling was intense & concentrated, too much so for speech."[16]

Some Friday evenings, Samuel and Charles went to the weekly reception held by Mrs. Goodrich, wife of Peter Pauley, the U.S. Consul. They met a number of people there and one time the publisher Fields from Boston took Samuel to meet poets he knew that were staying in Paris.

> We met a good many Americans, among them Fields of Boston who asked me to go with him the next morning to see Robert Browning, the English poet & his wife Elizabeth Barrett, whom I thought to be in Florence, but who are passing the winter in Paris. We found them in a sunny chamber looking on the Champs Elysées. Browning was extremely cordial, genial & animated, looking not unlike brother Alex. But alas for dreams, his wife is a most unpoetical & unspiritual looking personage; instead of a dreamy, moonlit face with a fire only in the deep dark eyes, as the writer of the "Duchess May," & the "Cry of the Children," & "He giveth his beloved sleep" should have – a red complexion & should I say it – a red nose! But it was a comfort to know that she was no longer the wretched invalid she has been.[17]

On Monday, December 2, the visit to Paris took a startling turn. John came into the room, eyes wide, and announced to Samuel and Charles, "There is a revolution," and he was right. President Louis Napoleon had illegally dissolved the National Assembly, becoming the supreme ruler of France. He also reinstated national suffrage and scheduled a vote for December 21 in order to ratify the changes he had effected. The date that had been chosen for the revolution to begin was the anniversary of Napoleon's coronation in 1804 and the victory of Austerlitz in 1805. In a letter to Anne, Samuel gives the details of the events as he saw them.

> By an audacious movement of Louis Napoleon, the National Assembly is dissolved and Paris is under martial law. Troops to the amount of a hundred thousand men are assembled in the city. The shops are closed, the streets filled with crowds of expectant people and paraded by soldiers. Some barricades have been build & removed: two or three men have been killed. But so far there is no dangerous disturbance, & I trust there will be none. One is strangely divided between the desire to see the whole matter & the fear of getting hurt. But you know that guns & powder have no fascination for me, & you need not have any anxiety for my personal safety. Our street – you will say fortunately – is too retired to be the scene of operations.
>
> ***
>
> Of course, it is quite exciting to be really in the midst of such proceedings, as heretofore one has known of only in books or newspapers.[18]

Samuel wasn't quite as safe as he told Anne, but this was because "it was exciting" to go out into the streets to see what was going on. Several extracts from Samuel's journal give his picture of the revolution and what was going on around him.

> I went up to the Place de la Concorde & found all its avenues "defendeues" by soldiers & its centre filled with troops. The Elysée also guarded, along the Quay a line of cuirassiers. By the bridge de la Concorde I met, of all persons in the world, Pons just up from a sick-bed & forbidden by his physician to go home this winter. The crowd was immense & expectant. The bridge was occupied by troops & the opposite Quay, where after a while was a commotion & shouts just audible. It was the

President making a detour near us the cry was "vive le Republique" but I heard none for the President.

***

The shops were shut, little groups with eager faces were
gathered as the doors – everything had a silent fearful & serious
aspect. Now & then a man would gesticulate to our driver. At last
he stopped. John put out his head & heard a shot. The driver
said they were firing in the next street & we though it best to
retrace our steps.

***

The papers speak of barricades & men killed.

I went out after breakfast upon the Boulevard. Cafes & shops
all closed the sidewalks crowded. A body of soldiers came down
from a cross street & passed along the boulevard. The people
shouted vive la Republique continually. All at once a shot was
heard. I ran with others into a shop where the door was shut
upon us. After a while I went out into a court in the rear, but
the gate was shut & I could not get back into the shop. At last
they let us out & turned homeward, but could not resist the
desire to go up on the Boulevard again. The crowd was great,
but nothing occurred & I came home. After a time John came
back. He had really been in danger, being on the Boulevard
while there was firing. Some men had foolishly fired on the
troops from the windows & the incensed soldiers had returned
the fire.

***

After dinner I left the boys in Mrs. Grozier's parlor & went
out toward the Boulevard, but half up the Rue LaFitte I heard
a discharge of musketry behind me & men came running up
the street. They said it was near the Lorrette Church & fearing
my return might be cut off I hastened home by Rue Chauchat.

***

Nothing of importance has occurred today. People say
"it is finished," but do not seem to be quite sure of it. The
shops are still closed & the streets occupied by soldiers. I saw
some dead bodies carried by on the Boulevard & the pools of
water on the sidewalks were in some places bloody. In the
evening I walked on the Boulevards Montmartre & Poissonniére.

The houses on the right are terribly shattered & marred by the balls & bullets of the troops.[19]

By the evening of December 4, the city was returning to normal. Samuel wrote to Anne to assure her that he was fine and describe the aftereffects of the revolution.

> I am safe &, if we may believe the newspapers, that France is saved. At any rate, the city is quiet again; barricades are no more, paving stones are restored to their innocent & legitimate functions; shops & cafés are reopened, the streets mostly vacated of soldiers & the current of Paris life returned to its wonted channels. The workmen are fast repairing the shattered windows & battered fronts of the houses on the Boulevards. The rains have washed off the blood from the pavements; the crowd no longer pauses to lift its hat while murdered men are carried through. The dead are buried in the ground; the wounded are healing in the hospitals. Perhaps desolated homes are not so easily rebuilded & embittered spirits nor aching hearts so soon cured. But still it is as if a weight were lifted off the spirits, & I cannot but hope that there will be no more such trouble.
>
> Thursday was the darkest day. One could not go out without hearing the report of musketry, or sit at home without hearing the cannon. The streets had a fearful aspect. The shops shut as they never are even on Sunday, the cafes & alarmed groups gathered at the doors or at the corner, the sight of men & women flying from the shots of the soldiers – "the shadow of a fear" hanging over all – the knowledge that men were desperately dying near at hand. It was awfully & solemnly exciting – But by Saturday morning it was entirely over & one could traverse the city in entire tranquility & find it hard to realize that any such terrible thing had occurred.[20]

The excitement over and life was returning to normal, but Samuel wondered if the situation would get better. The election was coming up and he was not sure that this would resolve anything more than just going along with what Louis Napoleon wanted. Samuel had one further comment on the effects of the revolution on him.

> It seems as if a weight were lifted off. But that gay street of Boulevards will never be to me as it has been. I shall always see blood upon its pavement & the phantom of soldiers & dead bodies among its crowds.[21]

Life for Samuel and the two boys returned to its routine of morning studies, afternoon wandering and evening pleasure. Sometimes they had specific plans and other times they sought out things and places they had not experienced. Although life for the Parisians had returned to normal, Samuel was curious about the opinions of those on the Republican side since "the papers are all muzzled or won over to the side of the Strongest."

On December 21, Samuel and the boys were out walking and stopped by the Mairie. The vote promised by Louis Napoleon was underway, but when they tried to enter and observe they were not allowed to enter. In his journal, Samuel said that he "tried in vain to find a 'non' vote coming home." Bearing out his inability to find a negative vote was the final total of 7,145,000 for and 600,000 against, thus the people approved Louis Napoleon's proposals and he was elected for 10 years as what the people called him the Prince-President.

Despite Louis Napoleon's enormous victory, Samuel considered him a despot because of all the "enormities committed by the soldiery."[23] The problems were not the only ones having problems. The Goodrich's, Americans whose receptions Samuel had attended, told him that conversations in their salon were being reported to the police and they knew who the spy was but could do nothing about it because the government was in control of the espionage.[24] Despite his negative feelings about the President, Samuel was invited to a Ball given by Louis Napoleon in the Palace of the Tuileries in February.

One Sunday in February, Samuel went to a chapel close to their apartment. It had a simple "Quaker like quiet" and he enjoyed being there. By coincidence, Robert Browning was also at the service and at its end they saw each other and shook hands.

> As we went out I asked him if he often came to worship there so far from his home. He said yes, it was the simplest service in Paris & therefore most agreeable to him. I asked him to walk home with me which he did & sat awhile talking mainly about Margaret Fuller (d'Ossoli). He was anxious to see Emerson & Channing's Memories but feared it would hardly do justice to all her character. She must have grown so much during her Italian life, especially in the affections. He found all Americans speaking of her as purely intellectual, they, in Florence, had loved her as a warm hearted woman. He spoke of her husband as refined, gentle of generous tendencies, but uneducated. They met in St. Peters first, where he rendered her some service in a crowd & so opened to her a new life.[25]

Margaret Fuller had died in 1850 in a shipwreck off the coast of Fire Island, New York. Also killed were her child and the father of the child, the Marchese d'Ossoli (their marital status was never clarified). The Brownings had been asked by Emerson and Channing for reminiscences so they could prepare a memoir of her life. She was a Unitarian and Transcendentalist and associated with a number of Samuel's friends. She was considered to have an exceptional mind and abilities and the New York Herald Tribune took the extraordinary step of making her their foreign correspondent in Europe. She wrote *Women in the Nineteenth Century* in 1845, three years before the First Woman's Rights Convention was held in 1848 at Seneca Falls, New York.

Taking a break from Paris, in May they took a five-day trip to England. They went to visit Charles' aunt and uncle who lived about 40 miles outside London. They spent two days and a night there and were welcome to stay longer, but Charles "found the country dull and was restless."[26] After the visit they returned to Paris, which Samuel compared to London in a letter to Anne.

We went & staid but five days; the weather was cold and Charles was homesick for Paris. It was the first of May that we went & the 7th that we came back. I was astonished to find how differently London looked after Paris, dark, dingy & meager in architecture. I wondered how I had even thought it so fine.[27]

Charles had started feeling ill around the middle of April and after they returned to Paris Charles began to feel worse. Samuel took him to the doctors and they told him it was a heart problem and gave some suggestions. Samuel wrote Charles' father about the situation, and he also let Anne know because it would likely affect the rest of his trip.

The truth is the physicians discovered an organic trouble in the heart. It is not dangerous & can be prevented from becoming so by remedies and precautions. It necessitates, however, a quiet life & the avoidance of excitement. Charles is now forbidden to travel for the present. This will keep us I suppose at least two months longer at Paris. What will be our movements afterwards I can not say. It will take him a long time to get well; and he may prefer to return home. At present he does not wish to.[28]

Mr. Appleton wrote back to Samuel and informed him that he had decided that Charles should return home as soon as possible. Although the trip had been planned for two years, Charles' health would not permit it and they had to skip their planned visits to Italy and Germany. Samuel did not want to send Charles home alone and tried to find someone among their friends in Europe. Samuel also wanted to travel more in Europe, however he did not want to travel alone. Since John was going to travel, he thought of him, but he ended up traveling with his French teacher. However, Samuel could not work out his plans, and considered the year wasted except for the improvement in his health. However, Charles Appleton must have gotten something out of the trip because he later traveled to France with John Coolidge and was also accompanied to Paris by his brother--in-law Copley Green. He studied in Geneva for a year and then traveled. Many years later, Charles Hook Appleton returned to France and he died in Nice in 1874.

> I am pretty much decided to return home with Charley in the steamer of the 7th August in which I have written to engage a state room. Even if we should find some one going at that time who could be a companion to Charles.

***

> It is certainly a disappointment not to see the Rhine & Switzerland & Venice & Rome, the very writing of the names whereof is enough to awaken one's longings and to have spent nine months of my year in Paris, which I cared for least of all, second a lamentable mistake in the programme. Nevertheless, there is always at least the possibility of another opportunity & under better auspices.[29]

Returning to America brought Samuel back to the same question he had before he left – what should he do next? This is a dilemma that seemed to follow him throughout his life. However, the decisions he made show he took the opportunity to obtain a variety of experiences that he considered positive. In a letter to Anne the month before returning to America, Samuel acknowledged his need to make a decision, but seemed in no hurry.

> But what shall I do, if I come home now. I would gladly live with you in Portland, always excepting your cold winters. But now? The colleagueship you speak of there are serious objections to in my mind and a new church if it were possible might not be fair toward the others. This need not be settled now, however.[30]

Notes:

[1] Letter, Samuel Longfellow to Anne Longfellow Pierce, June 25, 1851. SLP, LNHS.

[2] Ibid.

[3] Letter, Mr. William Appleton to Samuel Longfellow, June 24, 1851. SLP, LNHS.

[4] Letter, Samuel Longfellow to Anne Longfellow Pierce, September 12, 1851. SLP, LNHS.

[5] Letter, Samuel Longfellow to Anne Longfellow Pierce, October, 21, 1851. SLP, LNHS.

[6] Samuel Longfellow. *Journal, 1851-1852*, September 4, 1851.

[7] Letter, Samuel Longfellow to Anne Longfellow Pierce, November 10, 1851. SLP, LNHS.

[8] Samuel Longfellow. *Journal, 1851-1852*, September 30, 1851.

[9] Ibid.

[10] Ibid.

[11] Letter, Samuel Longfellow to Anne Longfellow Pierce, October 21, 1851. SLP, LNHS.

[12] Ibid.

[13] Letter, Samuel Longfellow to Anne Longfellow Pierce, November 27, 1851. SLP, LNHS.

[14] Letter, Samuel Longfellow to Anne Longfellow Pierce, May 27, 1852. SLP, LNHS.

[15] Letter, Samuel Longfellow to Anne Longfellow Pierce, October 21, 1851. SLP, LNHS.

[16] Samuel Longfellow. *Journal, 1851-1852*, December 23, 1851.

[17] Letter, Samuel Longfellow to Anne Longfellow Pierce, November 19, 1851. SLP, LNHS.

[18] Letter, Samuel Longfellow to Anne Longfellow Pierce, November 27, 1851. SLP, LNHS.

[19] Samuel Longfellow. *Journal, 1851-1852*, December 2-5, 1851.

[20] Letter, Samuel Longfellow to Anne Longfellow Pierce, December 8, 1851. SLP, LNHS.

[21] Samuel Longfellow. *Journal, 1851-1852*, December 6, 1851.

[22] Ibid., December 17, 1851.

[23] Ibid., January 1, 1852.

[24] Ibid., January 23, 1852.

[25] Ibid., February 1, 1852.

[26] Letter, Samuel Longfellow to Anne Longfellow Pierce, May 27, 1852. SLP, LNHS.

[27] Ibid.

[28] Ibid.

[29] Letter, Samuel Longfellow to Anne Longfellow Pierce, July 1852. SLP, LNHS.

[30] Ibid.

CHAPTER 13 – BROOKLYN

Samuel was in better health when he returned to Cambridge from his trip to Europe with Charles Hook Appleton. He needed to find a job so once again he began "candidating." Nevertheless, Samuel also thought about doing other things, as he says in a letter to Samuel Johnson a few months after he returned.

> I find myself very much unsettled, both as to plans for the future and doings for the present. The idea flits before me that I may go abroad again in the spring, to complete my tour. Sometimes I think of a free church somewhere. And then of a regular settlement in some pleasant town, with a gothic church and a parsonage. Sometimes I want to make a tour through our own country, visiting prisons and reform-schools, and sometimes dream of getting myself made chaplain in one of the latter, thus combining satisfaction of my philanthropic and philo-paedian propensities.
>
> Meanwhile nothing is accomplished save stray Sunday preachings.[1]

While he was considering his options, he continued as a candidate for a preaching position. When he went to Bridgewater he took a side trip to Fall River where he received a warm welcome and was invited to stay and preach in addition to being invited to several dinners and teas. As a result he stayed almost a week. Samuel also visited the church at Woburn, which had been the first to offer him a permanent position, but which he had refused, and in addition went to New Bedford.

> To the former place I wended on the Monday morning & so warmly was I welcomed & so urged to stay & so invited to

dinner & to tea that I did not get away to N.B. till Saturday morning, being obliged to with stand manfully all entreaties to stay & preach.[2]

Among his non-sectarian activities, he had the chance in 1852 to hear William Makepeace Thackeray, on his first lecture tour in America. The lecture Samuel heard was about the playwright (not the inventor) William Congreve and the writer Joseph Addison.

A pleasant piece of literary criticism, touching lightly and brightly along the surface, but not sounding any depths; with a pleasant voice and quiet, gestureless delivery.[3]

Samuel Longfellow was still seeking a pulpit and thinking about other options, two months after his January letter to Samuel Johnson when an invitation to preach in Brooklyn arrived. The Brooklyn Unitarian Church split in 1851 and formed two churches: the First and Second Unitarian Churches. The split came about because of a divergence in beliefs resulting in liberal and orthodox factions. The new first church practiced a more orthodox Unitarianism, while the Second Church was more progressive. Nevertheless, many families were divided in their sympathies toward the two churches and had a difficult decision to make.

The Second Unitarian Church had its first service with a visiting minister on April 20, 1851, although the church was not legally organized until June 1852. Their next step was invite ministers to preach in order to find a permanent minister.[4]

The Second Brooklyn Unitarian Church invited Samuel to preach twice during the month of February, 1853. They must have liked him the first time he preached there not long after returning from his trip to Europe the previous year. Samuel considered preaching in Brooklyn as just another stop during his visits to various churches, and he wrote and thanked Samuel Johnson for suggesting him to the congregation. He also urged Johnson to go to Brooklyn if they offered him a position.

A month later, Samuel Longfellow told Johnson that the Brooklyn committee had invited him to take the pulpit during a six-month period. However, as was his pattern, Longfellow had some doubts that he could meet their religious and social expectations of him. "I don't see how they are to be satisfied with my preaching after yours."[5]

Probably the most important task he had was bringing the conservative and liberal factions of the congregation together, although he was pleased that the liberals were in the majority. However, he also was not sure about a "permanent settlement" in Brooklyn because it was "so decidedly a *city* place." Given that Brooklyn was the third largest city in America and Samuel had lived most of his life in smaller cities, his reaction to living in a much larger, more densely populated area was not surprising. However, he told Henry, "I was enough pleased with Brooklyn & the people I saw to desire a further acquaintance. It is in many respects an excellent position."[6]

Samuel had another concern. Even though he was secure in his religious beliefs, Samuel lacked confidence in his ability to convince the congregation to accept his ideas. He mentions this to Samuel Johnson at the beginning of his six-month stay.

> I am so quiet a person, have so little of the 'popular' quali-
> ties; am so little calculated to lead a 'movement,' – to make
> any *éclat*. Starr King [an earlier candidate] seemed rather to be
> their ideal, and I am far enough from that type. But I though
> it might be good for me to be thrown into a position making
> greater demands upon me. I may develop some new phases; at
> any rate, I shall test myself. An arrangement for a few months
> was, therefore what I wanted.
>
> Brooklyn is certainly a handsome city, and in the summer
> its neighborhood must be charming.[7]

Aside from his general reticence to push his beliefs on others, another reason for his lack of confidence was the feeling of inadequacy that had carried over from Fall River, and emphasized by the run-in with Mr. Battelle, the "lay monitor" mentioned in chapter 10. This was that some of the congregation may not have fully agreed with his liberal beliefs, and that had gradually become more liberal over the years.

In his *Memoir* of Samuel Longfellow, Joseph May provided a short background of the changes in Unitarianism over the years and summarizes how Samuel Longfellow's own religious philosophy had changed from childhood to the present.

> Samuel Longfellow parted very gradually with the forms of thought and the pietistic associations which he brought with him from his home. In the Divinity School, he says, his views were more conservative than those of Johnson. It was chiefly that the cast of his mind was more sentimental and idealistic; that of his friend more purely intellectual. His growth was slower than that of many of his companions, and, as Colonel Higginson has said, more steady, without reactions. It was less conscious, because it was less by the intellectual and formal recognition of truth, with consequent conviction, and more an assimilation of it which made it a part of himself.[8]

Regardless of the possibility that his sermons may not please all the listeners, he did not overly concern himself with the congregation's reaction. He felt that being honest with them and expressing his own religious and social beliefs was very important. "Longfellow felt that no human concern was inappropriate to the pulpit."[9]

> I don't try to 'please both sides' you *know*. I suppose my natural position is a *mesothesis*. I sometimes wish I had more 'excess of direction,' as Emerson calls it, and more enthusiasm. But I will not leave people in doubt on which side my sympathies are.[10]

Samuel heard ideas such as the one mentioned by Emerson when he was at get-togethers in Cambridge that included a number of the religious, transcendentalist and social leaders of the time. Many of these gatherings were at his brother Henry's house.

> At Cambridge was a pleasant dinner where Emerson, Hawthorne, Lowell, Clough and Charles Norton were guests.[11]

A couple of months into his temporary stay at Brooklyn, Samuel Longfellow preached two controversial sermons showing he could overcome his concerns about the congregation not agreeing with him.

> I preached a sermon upon the true position of the pulpit, especially in respect to free inquiry in theology and to reforms in society; and another upon the true Unity to be sought not in form or creed, but in the Spirit urging the society to take its position distinctly on the ground of absolute freedom; and I was glad to find they were willing to take this platform. At least, they wanted to print the sermons, and one gentleman who had been considered most conservative was most strenuous in this behalf.[12]

In the sermon mentioned in the letter, Samuel presented his long-term aspiration for the Unitarian Church as a whole. He did not consider himself part of the Unitarian Church, which he makes very clear in a letter to Samuel Johnson about the American Unitarian Association. This group was established in 1825 by a group of Harvard Divinity School graduates as a body to represent Unitarian ministers. They promoted Unitarianism, published documents and helped provide temporary ministers (including Samuel Longfellow) for churches that needed one when theirs was sick, had another commitment or was on a trip.

> I did not get a sight of the celebrated A. U. A. Report; I fancy it was but a statement of the basis upon which the Association will carry on its operations, and of no bearing upon those out of the Association, – not even a creed of the denomination. My own connection with the Unitarian body is so slight as hardly to be worth the breaking. But, as you know, my real affinities are with the free men and churches. I want it to be so with my Society, and therefore wish they had not the name Unitarian. I shall ask them to change it, if I remain; but it is not a point upon which I could insist.[13]

The Second Society of Brooklyn very naturally did not ascent to their pastor's suggestion that they should drop the Unitarian name and connection.[14]

In a letter to Fanny, Samuel expresses the direction of his own theological ideas and indicates that he would like his congregation to be open in their choice of direction.

> I confess my sympathies are all with free enquiry nor am I afraid of the company into which it may bring me, though I may not accept all their conclusions. I want that our church here should found itself not upon uniformity of belief among its members, but upon a common aspiration after truth & life, & a common purpose to establish a practical Christianity in the world: the kingdom of God upon earth.[15]

Despite his controversial sermons and opinion about the official Unitarian organization, Samuel was able to impress the congregation with his preaching and they welcomed his pastoral activities. He also had the honor to speak for the first time just one week before the Second Church moved from "the old lecture room" of the Brooklyn institute to their new quarters in the Brooklyn Athenaeum.

> When Mr. Longfellow began his temporary engagement, the Society was worshiping in a small and rather dismal hall. Its numbers also were small, but there were warmth and hope, and the new minister won his way rapidly to the hearts of his people. His preaching attracted much attention by its originality and vigor, directness and simplicity, and especially by its spiritual quality and its moral elevation.[16]

In the summer of 1853 the Brooklyn society asked him to accept the position as their first permanent minister. The offer came while he was on a trip to Cambridge and may have been something of a surprise.

> While everything about the position of the society is attractive and encouraging, I feel a strange want of energy and enthusiasm

for the undertaking. I have been physically out of sorts since I have been here... so, personally, I don't feel a great desire to stay.[17]

Samuel may not have known that their offer had been made to several others before him. However, these ministers, many his friends, had disappointed the society by turning down the position. If he had known, he may have wondered why so many people had turned down the position.

> For a permanent minister, members of the Second Church chose Andrew Preston Peabody, but he declined. Although their second choice, James Freeman Clarke, agreed to come for six months, he reneged when his wife fell ill. Their third choice, Horatio Stebbins, accepted "and not until a house had been provided for him and a sum of money raised to furnish it did he discover that his duty lay else where.
>
> Stebbin's rejection was followed by a rejection from Thomas Starr King. Members of the congregation then considered Henry Giles and Samuel Johnson. When Johnson preached for them, some heard him "with boundless satisfaction, others with incredulity and alarm." Aware of his mixed reception, Johnson suggested his Harvard Divinity School classmate Samuel Longfellow.
>
> Longfellow preached on 16 April 1853, the Sunday before the congregation moved to the Brooklyn Athenaeum. After many disappointments, the Second Church had a new home and a new minister – a minister who with his two immediate successors would make this Brooklyn church one of the most liberal and progressive churches in America.[18]

Samuel discusses his thoughts about accepting the position in a letter to Anne. The increase in the attendance must have pleased him since this did not occur with the Fall River congregation. His biggest problem seems to be lack of a social life. Since he mentions only two other candidates who turned them down, it is apparent he did not know there were six others who were offered the job before him.

Everything about the position & prospects of the Society is encouraging. There have been continued accessions to our numbers since I came & they appear interested in the preaching. The call was unanimous, everybody voting who was present at the meeting – though it was only a business meeting of twenty four men.

I wish therefore that I felt more enthusiasm & more desire to remain than I do. The truth is I have not been very happy here, partly because I have not been well, having had a general biliousness which has rather taken down my spirits and energies ever since I have been here, and partly because I do not find the social life that I sigh for. I am afraid they are not more hospitable than the Fall River people. I have called on about half of the families, but very few of the gentlemen have called upon me nor have I had many invitations even to tea which is the clergyman's privilege. Not that I feel this as a neglect but it gives me a sense of loneliness sometimes rather forlorn. If I stay I shall have perhaps to take the matter of sociability in my own hands & do more than my half.

And I think I shall stay the other day when I was perplexed about this matter & feelings that I could not be happy to remain here, I thought – why should I not ask guidance from the Father. And immediately with a sense of peace there came to me the thought, as if an answer, "Do what is your duty & do not think of your happiness. And it does seem to me that I ought not to leave this society now. It has been twice disappointed in respect to a minister & it might be a discouragement to them to be again deserted. That is my feeling to-day at least.[19]

Samuel Longfellow finally accepted the offer to be the Second Church's first full-time minister and began his second full-time pastorate. His installation was celebrated at an evening service on October 26, 1853. The installation service was more conventional than Samuel would have liked. He always preferred a simple service rather than the usual more formal one most churches favored, however, the Society was not quite prepared for his type of service. Another disappointment for Longfellow was that Samuel Johnson could not attend and did not even send the hymn that Longfellow had asked him to write.

> It was in the usual order of things that in this first important occasion of their history the neighboring Unitarian churches and ministers should chiefly share. Mr. Johnson was unable to accept the invitation of the Society to attend, nor did he send the hymn which had been so earnestly besought by his friend from his reluctant muse. Another friend of Divinity School days, William Henry Hurlbut, who had recently relinquished the pulpit through the changes of sentiment prevalent at this time, was represented in a hymn; but among those who took part in the services, only Rev. Dr. Furness the preacher of the evening, and, probably Rev. John Parkman, of Staten Island, who read Scripture selections, were peculiarly in sympathy with Mr. Long-fellow's characteristic views. The other clergymen participating were Rev. Samuel Osgood, of New York; Rev. Frederick A. Farley, D. D., of Brooklyn, who offered respectively the introductory prayer and that of installation; Rev. W. Bellows, of New York, who gave the right hand of fellowship; Rev. E. H. Chapin, of the Universalist Church of New York, who addressed the people; and Rev. William Hall of Ireland, who closed the services with prayer. Mr. Longfellow composed for this service his beautiful hymn "In the beginning was the Word."[20]

From the beginning he preached a radical theology. "He preach-ed a pure theism, in which the associations of Christianity held their place only as illustrative of universal religion."[21] As a Theist Samuel believed that God created everything and continues to maintain an active role in the universe, including individual lives. This is the contrary to Deism which believes that God ended his work with the universe after creation.

The first sermon Samuel gave after his installation was entitled, "A Spiritual and Working Church." With it he set the theme of his pastorate in Brooklyn.

> It defined and luminously portrayed a particular church as a "society of men, women and children associated by a religious

spirit for a religious work." That in his definition he should have included *children* token of one of his warmest sentiments, but it also intimated the breadth and completeness of his conception.[22]

In his sermons, Samuel generally spoke "of the personal and inner life, of domestic and social relations of faith and conscience and mutual love and service." Nevertheless, "No subject of human welfare was foreign to his pulpit. On political and social questions he never failed to speak, as occasion arose with frankness and fervor."[24] However, all his sermon topics, even if on non-sectarian topics, had a religious basis.

Always he preached *religion*; whatever his particular topic, its interpretation was a *religious* one. The sense of divine things, of the presence of God in human affairs and with the private soul, was constant and vivid with him.[25]

One of the members of the Brooklyn congregation gives her reaction to Samuel Longfellow.

> One of those gravitating to him was Arethusa Hall, who had recently arrived in Brooklyn. She found everything in the modest chapel "arranged with great taste, the platform with its background of crimson drapery and its soft blue canopy seemed to form a fit setting for the golden hair and gentle form of its minister. His services were particularly harmonious, the whole – music, prayer, scripture readings, and sermon – having the beauty and Completeness of a poem. ...I often went away from the little chapel," she remembered, "feeling that it was... the very gate of heaven."

Even after taking the position, Samuel felt lonely in Brooklyn, as he stated in the letter to Anne about taking the job or not. In a later letter to Anne he says that he wants "something nearer & closer than the friendliness of acquaintances and parishioners, even the most kind."[27] During his stay in Brooklyn, Samuel had visits from some of his friends from Cambridge, in addition to others he knew, or got to know, in New York City. At one point, Ralph Waldo Emerson had Samuel Longfellow make contact with Walt Whitman through one of their mutual friends. Samuel was surprised that Whitman showed up unannounced, "wearing his usual knockabout clothes." He kept his hat on while he was sitting in Samuel's parlor, but he was "not in the least boisterous in manner."[28]

> He talked freely about growing up on Long Island, his experiences as printer, newspaper editor, and now publisher of his own book. He was preparing a second edition, which Fowler and Wells were still willing to distribute for him, and meanwhile writing a series of articles – about the opera and Dr. Abbott's Egyptian Museum – for the firm's *Life Illustrated*. Longfellow was charmed, yet found him "not so handsome a person as his verses are handsome." "Isn't it a quite wonderful book [*Leaves of Grass*]?" he wrote to Hale, whose review he had just read. "Such quick and live senses, such love of men, boys, women, babies, trees – all things that are. So keen to see, so vigorous to touch with right words, Such marvelous little pictures in tow or five words. Such human tenderness at times.[29]

In addition to individual visitors, Samuel had gatherings in his house in Brooklyn. They included a number of the literary figures in the New York area.

> Walt [Whitman] inevitably became a Topic – like William Lloyd Garrison, Fanny Kemble, and Henry Ward Beecher-at Brooklyn soirées in 1856. "I was not their kind," he [Whitman] said about Samuel Longfellow's circle, "so preferred not to push myself in, or, if in, to stay in." But Longfellow managed to recruit him from time to time, and although Walt had little to say at these gatherings he was nonetheless the center of attention, according to Bronson Alcott, father of Louisa May, then a fledgling author of thrillers. Survivor of high-principled experiments in living, of Pythagorean diets of squash, turnips and cold water, Alcott had responded to *Leaves of Grass* when

he first read it as if twenty years were suddenly subtracted from his age and he had broken his life-long vows about alcohol – his empyreal prose took on a Whitman bluster.

***

Walt was a guest at Longfellow's house a few days after Christmas [1856], when Alcott, itinerant transcendentalist sage, conducted one of his celebrated "Conversations," Orphic and metaphysical rites of sometimes stupefyingly elevated discourse, chiefly monologue.[30]

As at Fall River, Samuel provided pastoral care for the Society members. He carried out these functions in a simple, straight-forward manner, spreading truth and "religious spirit." In this way he provided the personal assistance needed and influenced their religious beliefs. "He was a sunny, refining presence amidst their joys, and made himself as a member of each particular household by the ease and delicacy with which he entered into its interests and happinesses."[31] As with everything else that Samuel Longfellow did, he had his own distinctive way of seeing it through.

Another aspect of Samuel's work was the performance of the sacraments. He followed his parishioners through the different stages of their lives, from baptism to marriage and finally death. His approach to these is described in Samuel May's *Memoir* and the book published by the present day First Unitarian Church of Brooklyn.

> The happy home in which Samuel Longfellow had been brought up left on his mind a deep impression of the sacredness of all the family ties. For the marriage relation he cherished peculiar reverence, and, though he never entered into it, he seemed to apprehend by intuition its deepest meanings. The ceremony of marriage he always conducted in a manner original to himself, seeking to adapt its impressions to the particular occasion, that it might not fail of full significance. Of the other religious rites, he especially loved that of baptism, celebrating it in the broadest spirit, as a service of gratitude to God

for the precious gift of a child, as still more a child of God and of self-dedication, on the part of the parents, to the sacred task of rearing it religiously and morally.[32]

When Longfellow baptized children, "the service was a tender jubilee," and when he married people the ceremony was "a sacred inspiration." "No ministering to the sorrowful was ever less formal or more comforting." During an era when many young people died, his words and actions at funerals helped children in his congregation overcome their fear of death.[33]

Samuel continued to hold communion services in the manner he had during the years in Fall River. However, he eventually decided to stop performing communion in the way he thought most appropriate in order to avoid controversy.

He at length discontinued the [communion service] custom, however; not from any change of feeling towards it, still less towards its object, on his own part; nor apparently from an impression that it tended to become a formality; but rather it would seem, because he had come to feel that its effect was too intense, – possibly, that it was difficult to prevent its influence from being of too mystical a character.[34]

In a radical departure from common practice, he administered the Lord's Supper to the entire congregation. This communion service seemed both "human and divine, as he moved among the people, carrying the elements in his own hands and breathing fragmentary words out of the Bible or from his own spiritual deep."[35]

As was his custom, Samuel was especially interested in the needs of the younger people in his congregation. Joseph May describes some of the activities with youngsters and even older youth and adults.

Naturally, Mr. Longfellow interested himself especially in the religious culture of the children and youth of his Society. He early prepared with much care a manual of devotional services adapted to Sunday-school use. He superintended the conduct of the school, taking part in its exercises of worship, teaching a class of adults or older youth, and making himself well known and dear to the children of all ages. He had a happy tact in composing for them little addresses, half sermon, half story, some of which remain, and are very graceful and suggestive. He joined in their amusements with full zest, enjoying and promoting picnics and the winter festivals, which he was full of expedients to make entertaining. He possessed, in a singular degree, the art of conveying useful thoughts to the young, almost without stating them. "He attracted all boys," writes one of his young friends of this period. "We felt a curious confidence in his interest in us, which boys always appreciate and repay in affection to their elders."[36]

In addition to the pastoral and religious duties performed by all ministers, Samuel created a new addition to the Sunday services. He had previously mentioned this idea to some of his friends and finally chose to put it into practice in Brooklyn after the congregation had agreed to it after a period of deliberation. The idea was to replace the afternoon service with an evening service he named "Vespers."

The order of the vesper service was different and "music was the leading mode of expression."[37] He used highly trained musicians and a choir. In addition, the congregation allowed him to preach on any topic, "and this he reduced to a meditative address." In order for this service to be successful, it needed "the influence of a leader with whom worship was an habitual mental attitude, and who combined the instinct of religion the art of the poet and of a musician."[38]

The music portion of the vesper service was very important to Samuel and he was very particular about what was presented. Samuel wrote hymns for his vesper services and some of these became popular in other churches. He wanted his words and music to carry his beliefs to the hearts of those in the congregation.

Like his brother, Samuel Longfellow was a poet. His pleased parishioners claimed that while Henry Wadsworth Longfellow became a poet, their Longfellow was born one, as attested by his many beautiful hymns. In these hymns his ministry achieved universality and immortality, for they appear in many hymnals and are cherished around the globe.[39]

The vesper service also included responsive readings, something that was "almost unknown" at the time in Unitarian and Congregational churches. With the addition of the vesper service, Samuel Longfellow produced a richer service that was a "pleasing relief" to a regular afternoon or evening service that was not much more than a repeat of the morning service. This service was well liked by the congregation, and "became common at the suggestion given by these services of the Brooklyn Society," and spread to a number of other congregations.[40]

Notes:

[1] Letter, Samuel Longfellow to Samuel Johnson, January, 1853. SLP, LNHS.

[2] Letter, Samuel Longfellow to Samuel Johnson, December 26, 1852. SLP, LNHS.

[3] Ibid.

[4] Hoogenboom, Olive. *The First Unitarian Church of Brooklyn, One Hundred Fifty Years.* New York: The First Unitarian Church of Brooklyn, 1987. p. 45-46.

[5] Letter, Samuel Longfellow to Samuel Johnson, March 7, 1853. SLP, LNHS.

[6] Letter, Samuel Longfellow to Henry W. Longfellow, March 30, 1853. LP.

[7] Letter, Samuel Longfellow to Samuel Johnson, March 7, 1853. SLP, LNHS.

[8] May, Joseph, Ed.. *Samuel Longfellow.* Cambridge: The Riverside Press, 1894. p. 164-165.

[9] Hoogenboom, Olive. *The First Unitarian Church of Brooklyn.* p. 48.

[10] Letter, Samuel Longfellow to Samuel Johnson, May 18, 1853. SLP, LNHS.

[11] Letter, Samuel Longfellow to Samuel Johnson, June 16, 1853. SLP, LNHS.

[12] Letter, Samuel Longfellow to Samuel Johnson, May 18, 1853. SLP, LNHS.

[13] Letter, Samuel Longfellow to Samuel Johnson, June 16, 1853. SLP, LNHS.

[14] May, Joseph, Ed.. *Samuel Longfellow: Memoir and Letters.* p. 178.

[15] Letter, Samuel Longfellow to Frances (Fanny) Appleton Longfellow, June 4, 1853. SLP, LNHS.

[16] May, Joseph, Ed.. *Samuel Longfellow: Memoir and Letters.* p. 176.

[17] Letter, Samuel Johnson to Samuel Longfellow, June 29, 1853. SLP, LNHS.

[18] Hoogenboom, Olive. *The First Unitarian Church of Brooklyn.* p. 46-47.

[19] Letter, Samuel Longfellow to Anne Longfellow Pierce, June 30, 1853. SLP, LNHS.

[20] May, Joseph, Ed.. *Samuel Longfellow: Memoir and Letters.* p. 174-175.

[21] Ibid., p. 176.

[22] Ibid., p. 179.

[23] Ibid., p. 187-188.

[24] Ibid., p. 187.

[25] Ibid.

[26] Hoogenboom, Olive. *The First Unitarian Church of Brooklyn.* p. 48.

[27] Letter, Samuel Longfellow to Anne Longfellow Pierce, January 18, 1854. SLP, LNHS.

[28] Kaplan, Justin. *Walt Whitman: A Life.* New York: A Bantam Book, 1982. p. 213.

[29] Ibid.

[30] Ibid., 217-218.

[31] May, Joseph, Ed.. *Samuel Longfellow: Memoir and Letters.* p. 189.

[32] Ibid., 190-191.

[33] Hoogenboom, Olive. *The First Unitarian Church of Brooklyn.* p. 47-48.

[34] May, Joseph, Ed.. *Samuel Longfellow: Memoir and Letters.* p. 191-192.

[35] Hoogenboom, Olive. *The First Unitarian Church of Brooklyn.* p. 48.

[36] May, Joseph, Ed.. *Samuel Longfellow: Memoir and Letters.* p. 191-192.

[37] Ibid., p. 193.

[38] Ibid., p. 193-194.

[39] Hoogenboom, Olive. *The First Unitarian Church of Brooklyn.* p. 47.

[40] May, Joseph, Ed.. *Samuel Longfellow: Memoir and Letters.* p. 193-194.

CHAPTER 14 – BROOKLYN – THE NEW CHURCH

In 1857, the Second Society of Brooklyn began a project that was of interest to Samuel. The church set about raising money to build "an inexpensive chapel"[1] at the corner of Clinton and Congress streets on leased land belonging to the Catholic Church. Samuel always referred to this new building as a chapel, even though 600 people would fit in the Norman-style, brick and stone building.

The cost of the project exceeded its early estimates and steps were taken to cut costs. They began to use wood in the structure and the roof was made lower than planned. This latter modification affected the internal beauty and external appearance resulting in the nickname "The Church of the Holy Turtle."[2] The final cost of the project was $25,360. The church, or "chapel," was completed in the early spring of 1858. The dedication of the newly constructed building was held on March 2, 1858. The service, for which Samuel asked Henry and Samuel Johnson to write hymns, was simple since Samuel had been successful during his four years getting the congregation to give up the formalities that they had been holding on to and which had been used in his installation. The sermon was entitled "The Doctrine and the Spirit."

> It was at once transcendental, yet intensely practical, – if it be practical to exhibit the most elevated truths as applicable to the whole tenor of men's actual lives.[4]

During his tenure in Brooklyn Samuel invited some interesting persons to take the pulpit in the new Chapel. In January 1858 Samuel invited Lucretia Mott to preach at the Brooklyn church. She was a Quaker minister and active in the abolitionist and women's rights movements. Along with Elizabeth Cady Stanton, she set up the Seneca Falls Convention – the first American women's rights meeting. Samuel told his friend Samuel Johnson that when she spoke

> the Hall was filled to overflowing. Our friend Leaver was diligent in sending notices. Beecher reading the notice said whatever opinion they might have about women's speaking in public, nobody could doubt but what Lucretia Mott was a truly ordained minister of God.[5]

In March of 1858, Thomas Starr King, who was a respected Boston Unitarian preacher recognized for his skills as a speaker, wrote to Samuel asking him what sermon he would use if they exchanged pulpits.[6] This exchange did not take place, but in late 1858 Samuel was suffering from a bad cold and King was his substitute in the pulpit. In 1860, King went to San Francisco where his congregation grew greatly because of preaching. California was in a crisis over whether to side with the free or slave states, but was leaning toward the side of the slave states. King spoke adamantly before large crowds and almost single handedly kept California on the side of the Union. He was so well respected for his accomplishments that California selected him in 1913 as one of the state's two greatest heroes and a statue of him was placed in the United States Capitol.

Also in 1858, Samuel's friend Thomas Wentworth Higginson spoke to the congregation on spirits and spiritualism. At this time there was much interest in spiritualism and there were presentations of spirit activities, such as the poltergeist-like Rochester knockings which attracted large numbers of people. Higginson considered the communication of spirits as a positive effect for those who had lost a loved one. Samuel describes Higginson's ideas in a letter to Anne.

> His position is this and seems a just one – The things which he has observed & experienced can only – or can best – be explained on the theory of communication from disembodied spirits. That communication being not impossible or improbable he accepts as established by the facts. He does not think

that any truths of much value have been communicated: he thinks there is much room for delusion. But, it is of great value that to multitudes the simple fact of the reality of this intercourse with the spirit world has been established & so the anguish been removed from death and separation.[7]

After the construction of the new Second Church in Brooklyn was completed, Samuel would stay only two more years. He felt that he needed to take his leave for a "change and rest."

> Even at the date of the dedication he was physically weary and unwell. He wrote afterwards to Mr. Johnson that he would gladly have laid down his service even earlier, but could not leave his people while they were struggling with the problem of permanently establishing the society and securing their new building. But he was longing for change and rest, and when the congregation was well housed and at home in the new "chapel," he felt that he must take a long period of repose from work.[8]

Samuel felt that the Second Church was well established, financially secure and was in a position where the Society should search for a new minister. However, much of the congregation had no interest in replacing Samuel and believed they would have a hard time finding someone they liked as well. As at Fall River, there was a sentiment for him to stay. Therefore, he decided to stay another two years.

Samuel would make use of his two remaining years to present his "truths" to the congregation. As during the previous four years, the reaction of the congregation to his sermons would be mixed.

> Even among his own progressive and thoughtful people there were some who had been disturbed and even angered by the bold assertions from their pulpit of the "higher law," which politicians were then flouting; its earnest protests against the sin of slavery, and warnings of the evils to arise from complicity with its wickedness.[9]

The members of the congregation he referred to were not "the corrupt and reckless of our Northern communities," but rather "from some of the best people, so blinded was that generation."[10]

He ran into his greatest problem when he gave a sermon in January 1860 that was a "hearty tribute" to the fanatic abolitionist John Brown, who was known for his violent actions. In general, northerners adopted a peaceful approach to eliminate slavery, and did not accept Brown's methods, or those of outspoken abolitionists in general. Although Samuel had a long history of being against slavery, his actions were basically limited to the pulpit where he made his beliefs known, but did not draw much attention. His brother Henry published antislavery poems and supported escaped slaves for which he and his friend Senator Charles Sumner received honorary degrees from Harvard.[11] Samuel reports on the reaction to this sermon in a letter to Samuel Johnson.

> You will be surprised to hear – as I certainly was & disappointed – that a sermon which I preached after my return, upon John Brown gave offense to a number of my congregation. I believe three families have left!… I was charged with doing all I could to break up the society, with destroying my influence, etc. O ye of little faith. The truth is, we got lifted out at the Athenaeum, but since we came into the Chapel a number of new families have joined us & the process must, I suppose, be repeated. Certainly the truth must be preached, but the more thoroughly. "What is the chaff to the wheat saith the lord!"[12]

Miss. B., a woman in his congregation requested a copy of the sermon. In his letter of response to her, Samuel described the reasons for his support of John Brown. He also strongly states his position supporting peace and against the use of weapons.

> My sermon on John Brown was not written out; and the manuscript would be of no avail to you.
> It was a hearty tribute to the noble qualities and aims of the man; a man of qualities rare in these days and therefore

needing to be honored in pulpits, especially while men of mere talent are eulogized.

I spoke of him as a man brave, honest, truth-telling, God-reverencing, humane, – a lover of liberty.

In the presence of such genuine virtues, one would hardly have the heart to blame the methods, even. So I simply said that his method did not seem to me to be wise, or the best. As an *ultra* peace man I deprecate the use of destructive force even to secure great rights. But the *world* believes in the weapons of war, and they who honor the heroes of the American Revolution have no right to blame John Brown because he used weapons of war in the last necessity.

Before the earnestness of such a martyr spirit, I feel how little most of us are doing and suffering in behalf of the slave.

My sermon, I am sorry to say, was not cordially received by my people. I was suffering under physical depression, and did not do justice to my own feelings. Yet there was not a word which I wish to take back, – but only to say more strongly.

I feel that most momentous times are opening upon us. It seems to me like the time before the breaking out of the Revolution. I do not doubt the result. God give us heart to be faithful.[13]

Samuel's expression of admiration of the "grand old fanatic's" actions antagonized a number of people in the congregation. However, "he had the support, in his antislavery views, of a large proportion – perhaps the majority – of his congregation, and the respect and affection of all."[14] In 1854 Samuel already had strong views against slavery as he writes to Samuel Johnson.

But what a Nemesis is Slavery, that it should be putting away with its own hands the foundations of its own strength, and destroying that "sacredness of compromises" which has stood in the way of moral insight and practical fidelity ever since the Constitution was made.[15]

Another person who was strong in his anti-slavery beliefs and who liked John Brown was Samuel Johnson. He had met John

Brown six months before Samuel Longfellow's sermon on Brown and describes the meeting in a letter to Longfellow.

> Whom do you think appeared on Saturday night at Lynn, and whom do you suppose you would have had to introduce, as I did, to a meeting in Sagamore Hall, had you been in my place, – but old Osawatomie Brown of Kansas, who was there to tell his story of that noble exodus of slaves which he carried through in triumph last winter. He is a genuine old Revolutionist, and believes with all his soul and all his *life* that slavery has no rights upon the earth. There seems to be not a tinge of revenge, and anything but a disposition to shed blood, in this old warrior, though he has terribly suffered from slavery, one son being murdered by the border-ruffians and another driven mad from cruelties inflicted by them. He says he has *a call* to kindle a fire in their rear in Missouri itself; and the terror he inspires may be judged from the fact that a price of three thousand dollars is set on his head by Missouri, and two hundred and fifty dollars by Buchanan. Methods differ, but such self--sacrifice and practical devotion to the slave is exceedingly refreshing in these days. He is after aid in carrying on his plans of delivering the slaves.[16]

Samuel Longfellow submitted his resignation not very long after the John Brown sermon, partially due to pressure from the congregation about this sermon. However, this in itself probably would not have been sufficient for Samuel to resign. Joseph May supports this idea by remarking that there were also some personal reasons behind the decision. His health was a regular problem for which he wanted time away from working. In addition he was considering a trip abroad with Samuel Johnson, and, in fact, this was likely to be the main reason for resigning from the Brooklyn pastorate. This is supported by a letter Longfellow wrote to Johnson.

> I do not see how I can go before the end of June. Feeling that the time has come for me to make my visit to Europe, I see no way so clear as to withdraw from the Brooklyn pulpit. I have

some private reasons for thinking this will be best. I wished to do so two or three years ago, but then the depressed condition of the society prevented me. I did not like to leave them in that state, with a virtual confession of failure. Now they are tolerably prosperous & well established with the Chapel, etc. and ought to be able to go on by themselves & find a minister they will like as well & better than me.[17]

The first week in May the Society held a meeting where they voted to accept his resignation. They sent a letter relating this action and their first two resolutions address the refusal, but show their gratitude for his work. There were three other resolutions, one relating to the Society's religious beliefs, another expressing their regret on his leaving and the last asked for publication of the resolutions in the *Christian Inquirer.* The first two resolutions are:

> 1st Resolved that Mr. Longfellow's resignation be now accepted.
> 2nd Resolved that we recognize, now and at all times, the service which Mr. Longfellow has rendered to us, in his ministrations, both in and out of the pulpit; in the admirable ordering of the services of this beautiful Christian home, which he has helped us to build; in the entire self-forgetfulness with which he has devoted himself to our highest good; and in the noble stand which he has always made for freedom and for truth.[18]

During the 1850s Samuel Longfellow became a strong supporter of the women's movement, but was never in the forefront of the action. A lot of the people he knew who were Abolitionists or active with the temperance or peace movements were also active with the women's movement. Elizabeth Cady Stanton, one of the leaders of the women's movement, said in the *History of Woman Suffrage* that Samuel believed that women have the "right to stand side by side with man in all departments of life, and to add her feminine influence and fiber tuned in with man's influence and fiber" and hoped men would become aware "that in the sphere of politics, as well as in the sphere of literature and art, woman's influence is needed."[19]

At a convention in New York one of the male speakers made a negative comment about the content of the convention. Elizabeth Cady Stanton took this as a personal affront and reacted strongly. Samuel However, sitting next to her was Samuel Longfellow, who whispered in her ear, "Nevertheless you are right, and the convention will sustain you."[20]

Samuel's major contribution to the women's movement was when he participated in the National Women's Convention on May 10, 1860 in New York. The "Tenth National Woman's Rights Convention" was held in New York on May 10th and 11th 1860 while Samuel Longfellow was minister at Brooklyn Second Unitarian. The admission fee was ten cents, which some felt was high, "but this did not prevent the gathering"[21] of six to eight hundred people. Susan B. Anthony called the meeting to order and read the list of officers. After the President, Martha Wright of Auburn, N.Y. spoke, the Secretary, Susan B. Anthony, read her report. In her account she indicated that the movement was making progress.

> Each year we hail with pleasure new accessions of numbers to our faith and works. Strong words of cheer have come to us on every breeze. Brave men and true from the higher walks of literature and art, from the bar, the bench, the pulpit, and Legislative Halls, are ready now to help the woman up wherever she claims to stand.[22]

Samuel was the second speaker on the second day of the convention. Some of the points he advocated regarding women having equality with men in the work place were somewhat before their time.

> But if home be the sphere of woman – as none of us deny or doubt for a moment – if it be a sphere for woman high and noble, and to some altogether sufficient to bound their capacities and bound their desires, it is also a sphere for man – a sphere which he altogether too much neglects, not knowing how high and noble it is, and that his duty lies at home, however much he ignores it, with his wife and with his children.

But when it is said that home is woman's *only* sphere, – and that is what is meant, – it is simply a mistake; it is simply a narrow statement.

Let the wide sphere of work be opened to woman, that she may select from it, just as man does, whatever her strength and skill are sufficient for her to accomplish. She is not to be shut up, it is claimed, and justly, to a few poor, small, and wretchedly paid employments, by which she can, with her own hands and skill, gain a living, but is to be allowed and encouraged to open to herself every variety of employment wherein she shall be paid an equal sum with that which man is paid for doing the same work; a claim which has been too long ignored and set aside, but which will press itself until its manifest justice shall compel its admission.[23]

Samuel also provided a comment about the women's right to vote

If the right to vote was granted to woman, – from which I do not see how we can escape, – I do not suppose that all women would go to the polls, for I know that many men do not, although they have much to say about the great privilege which every man enjoys, of having a voice in the government, and the responsibility of a voter. Things would remain much as now if to-morrow every obstacle were removed from woman's path.[24]

On June 24, 1860, Samuel Longfellow preached his final sermon at the Second Unitarian Church of Brooklyn. It was most appropriately based on Deuteronomy 15:1 – "At the end of seven years, thou shalt make a release." The central theme of Samuel's seven years at the Brooklyn Society was, "the intimate nearness of the living God, the Universal Spirit."[25] The sermon mentioned how the congregation should pursue both religious and national righteousness and contained a full description of how Samuel felt about Slavery on the eve of the Civil War. He also presented his opinion of how slavery affected the nation.

And I have not failed to urge upon you the claims of national Righteousness, without which no people can be free, can be strong, can be truly prosperous. Against the great immorality of our nation, its great disobedience to the divine law, Slavery, I have not failed to utter my protest. I have urged upon you the critical character of this question among us; how the liberties and moral life of our land are involved in it; yes, and the personal manhood of every one of us. Of its barbarism and its despotism I have not failed to speak; of its frequent and frightful cruelties, and its essential and perpetual injustice; that I might engage your heart and your conscience to work for the righting of this great wrong, the removal of which would ennoble and aggrandize every part of our country, and let it breathe its first full, free breath. Of the duty of the pulpit in this regard I have never felt a moment's doubt.[26]

In a closing summary to his sermon and seven-year pastorate, Samuel said:

I wish to say today that you have fully respected the freedom of this pulpit; that through all, no persuasion or inducement has been addressed to me to do anything else than preach my full conviction of this matter. I am glad , and you are glad, today, that I can say this.[27]

Samuel Longfellow's tenure at the Second Unitarian Church in Brooklyn was influential on his congregation and to some degree on other Unitarian churches. He likewise enjoyed and benefited from his seven-year stay.

He had loved his congregation, had been much at home among them, and parted from them affectionately and regretfully, yet amidst the happiness of most tender expressions of their regard and their sorrow at his retirement. He was to meet them often again, and always to find assurance that his memory was kept green and remained dear.[28]

Notes:

[1] May, Joseph, Ed.. *Samuel Longfellow*. Cambridge: The Riverside Press, 1894. p. 196.

[2] Hoogenboom, Olive. *The First Unitarian Church of Brooklyn, One Hundred Fifty Years.* New York: The First Unitarian Church of Brooklyn, 1987. p. 50.

[3] Ibid., p. 48.

[4] May, Joseph, Ed.. *Samuel Longfellow: Memoir and Letters.* p. 197.

[5] Letter, Samuel Longfellow to Samuel Johnson, February 1858. SLP, LNHS.

[6] Letter, Thomas Starr King to Samuel Longfellow, March 15, 1858. SLP, LNHS.

[7] Letter, Samuel Longfellow to Anne Longfellow Pierce, December 8, 1858. SLP, LNHS.

[8] May, Joseph, Ed.. *Samuel Longfellow: Memoir and Letters.* p. 202.

[9] Ibid., p. 203.

[10] Ibid

[11] Bosco, Carla "Harvard University and the Fugitive Slave Act." *The New England Quarterly,* June 2006. p. 227-247. Boston. The New England Quarterly, Inc., p. 247.

[12] Letter, Samuel Longfellow to Samuel Johnson, January 1860. SLP, LNHS.

[13] Letter, Samuel Longfellow to Miss B., January 11, 1860. SLP, LNHS.

[14] May, Joseph, Ed.. *Samuel Longfellow: Memoir and Letters.* p. 205.

[15] Letter, Samuel Longfellow to Samuel Johnson, March 1854. SLP, LNHS.

[16] Letter, Samuel Johnson to Samuel Longfellow, June 1, 1859. SLP, LNHS.

[17] Letter, Samuel Longfellow to Samuel Johnson, March 29, 1860. SLP, LNHS.

[18] Letter, Brooklyn Unitarian Society to Samuel Longfellow, May 8, 1860. SLP, LNHS.

[19] Stanton, Elizabeth Cady, Susan B. Anthony, Matilda Joslyn Gage and Ida Husted Harper, Eds. *History of Woman Suffrage, 6 vols.* New York: Fowler and Wells, 1881-1922. Vol. I, p. 712.

[20] Stanton, Elizabeth Cady. *Eighty Years and More: Reminiscences 1815-1897.* New York: European Publishing Co., 1898. Ch. XIV.

[21] Yerrington, I.M.W., Ed. *Proceedings of the Tenth National Woman's Rights Convention, Held at the Cooper Institute, New York City, May 10th and 11th, 1860.* Boston Yerrinton and Garrison, 1860. p. 3.

[22] Ibid., p. 4.

[23] Ibid., p. 62-63.

[24] Ibid., p. 63.

[25] May, Joseph, Ed.. *Samuel Longfellow: Memoir and Letters.* p. 206.

[26] Ibid., p. 209-210.

[27] Ibid., p. 210.

[28] Ibid., p. 211.

CHAPTER 15 – THE SAMS ABROAD

After Samuel left his congregation at Brooklyn Second Unitarian Church, he departed on a trip to Europe with Samuel Johnson. The two Samuels embarked on June 30, 1860 and traveled through several countries, sometimes traveling together, sometimes separately. The high point of the trip was their collaboration on a new hymnbook during a rainy month in Nice where, "shut into the house by constant rains, we set to work upon arranging our materials for the *Hymns of the Spirit*."[1] Their work on the new hymnal is described in Chapter 8, but the rest of their trip is described here.

In the early summer of 1860, we took passage for Liverpool. After a few days in that city and in London we ran over to the Isle of Wight, spending a week walking through that charming epitome of English rural scenery. Then hastening through Paris to Switzerland, we spent two months there, half in foot-travel. We got out first exciting vision of the snow mountains, after two or three days' waiting, from the Enge, just outside of Bern. There, beyond the nearer hills and against the far sky, as the reluctant mists lifted, we saw the marvelous reach of the Bernese Alps; peak after peak moulded, as it seemed, of some celestial substance of dazzling glory and soft blue shadow; in the centre the Jungfrau, lifted like the "great white throne" of the Apocalypse. Toward those hills we set out in the morning and at evening saw them flush into a passionate glow and then fade into a pallor "beyond death" my companion said. A month's foot-travel followed through the changing grandeur and beauty, whiteness and verdure, of that wonderful land, where all possible charms of nature are concentrated. We walked, I remember, with easy independence, now one far ahead and now the other, as we stopped, now to sketch – Johnson's sketches, though unskilled, always caught the characteristic forms – now to ask "how far" of some short brown-coated peasant, or to return the greeting of some brown-faced boy lifting his hat, or to buy berries or Alp-roses of some sweet demure-faced little girl; or to throw ourselves tired upon the turf, till roused by the organ-like-echoes of an Alp-horn. The month of October we spent at Glion, high up above Montreux, on the shores of the Lake of Geneva, – so pleasantly pictured in Mathew Arnold's *Obermann Once More*. There we stayed, – intercalating a trip to Chamounix, where I had the delight, waking early one morning, to see from my window, in the gray half dawn, the morning-star lingering above the "awful front" of Mont Blanc – till the maples turned to gold, and the grapes to purple, and the autumn mists began to warn us toward Italy. Going by Nismes and Marseilles to Nice, we spent there a month.[2]

The traveling companions spent the winter in Florence, taking rooms in the Casa Pini. In addition to the places mentioned in the text above, they spent many hours in the galleries of the Uffizii, the Pitti and Academia, becoming familiar with and enjoying their art treasures. They also visited Dante's birthplace, Galileo's tower, the Cathedral and the Arno River bridges. They also met three American sculptors who were living in Florence: Hart, Jackson and Hiram Powers. The last produced the sculpture "Greek Slave," which Samuel was sure to have seen at the Great Exhibition of 1851 in the Crystal Palace in London on his previous trip with Charles Appleton. This piece was one of the most famous sculptures of the second half of the 19th century and inspired a sonnet by Elizabeth Barrett Browning, a fellow Florence resident and who Samuel Longfellow met in London on the earlier trip.

One other place of special interest to Longfellow and Johnson was the grave of Theodore Parker, who had died in Florence in May 1860, the month before the companions set off on their trip. As a tribute to their dear friend, they gathered ivy in the Boboli garden and planted it on his grave in the Protestant cemetery.[3] In a letter to his sister, whom he refers to as K, Samuel Johnson describes the cemetery visit and gives a short eulogy to Parker (which extends beyond the section quoted).

Theodore Parker's grave is in sight of all this divine beauty
of the Val d'Arno. The little Swiss cemetery stands just outside
the Pinti gate, its paths set with tall cypresses, and its soft slope
gently inclined from the city wall, which is clothed with ivy,
towards the mountains. Green Fiesole is in view, with its double summit, and the tall tower of its old church between, and
the undulating hills, deepening, as they recede from amber
and warm gray into blue, and then into that mystery of color,
for which there is no name; and beyond, the Apennines, with
their grand white crowns, ever softened in winter as in summer
by the tender haze, that so steadfastly abides brooding like a
heavenly presence, over the Val d'Arno, and making those stern
snows and their ideal purity preachers of the Infinite Love.
The cemetery is small and rather crowded, but nothing could
be more simple and serene more free from every form of pride
or vain show. The noble brain and heart that worked so faithfully and fearlessly to the last, that were, in fact the widest
passage opened in all this century for theological and moral
truth and practical liberty and justice, to the popular conscience,
rest in the shadow of a plain gray stone, marked with his name,
and with the place and date of his birth and of his death.
A few violets and periwinkles are growing from the earth above
them. We shall plant a vine of this brave warm Tuscan ivy
beside the stone. My thoughts of him would not stay by the
grave.[4]

Accompanying the two travelers in Florence was the 17-year
old American Marshall Oliver, who was studying art in Europe.
None of the documents available describe much about the young
man and the information included here comes from letters
between the two Sams.

From Florence the two friends went in different directions.
Samuel Longfellow headed south to Rome and Naples, and Samuel Johnson headed north accompanied by Marshall Oliver.
In Turin someone stole 20 Napoleons from his trunk, which was
almost all his funds. As a result he had to limit how much he
could travel and headed home through Germany and England
arriving back home in Salem in the fall of 1861.

Samuel Longfellow visited the major sights of Rome and visited some people that he knew. He also took a trip down to Naples and Vesuvius. However, what interested him greatly was the political turmoil in Italy, primarily between the Republicans with Garibaldi, King Victor Emmanuel, the French, some of the independent cities and the Vatican. He describes what was happening in his letters to Fanny and Anne and makes some comparison with the American Civil War, which had begun in the spring of 1861.

In Rome he learned that Fanny Longfellow had died on July 10, 1861. However, instead of hearing it in a personal letter, he read about it in an English newspaper in Rome. Samuel's description of the terrible event is included in his biography of Henry.

> On the ninth of July his wife was sitting in the library, with her two little girls, engaged in sealing up some small packages of their curls which she had just cut off. From a match fallen upon the floor, her light summer dress caught fire. The shock was too great, and she died the next morning. Three days later, her burial took place at Mount Auburn. It was the anniversary of her marriage-day; and on her beautiful head, lovely and unmarred in death, some had placed a wreath of orange blossoms. Her Husband was not there, – confined to his chamber by the severe burns which he had himself received.
>
> These wounds healed with time. Time could only assuage, never heal, the deeper wounds that burned within. This terrible bereavement, made more terrible by the shock of the suddenness and the manner of it, well-nigh crushed him.[5]

Samuel was shocked and in grief over his sister-in-law's death. They had been very close and Samuel saw her as a sister. He wrote a letter to Henry sharing his grief and providing words of condolence.

> The news of your bereavement came to me in the most startling way, in an English newspaper which I took up at the hotel here. My letters I shall not get for several days, as I have ordered them to be sent before me.

You will know how much I feel with you in this heavy grief which in so painful a way has come upon your heart & home. Yet I cannot but hope that light is in the cloud also. We know that such sorrow & pain would not be permitted by our Father, if there were not good hidden in them made to spring from them – a good that belongs among the eternal things of our being & stays with us after the anguish, which at longest is but for time, shall have passed. "I looked" said George Fox "and beheld an ocean of Darkness: but I saw also that around it flowed an infinite ocean of Light." And our own experience shows us that in the rendings of a great bereavement there are openings into depths of unexpected Peace; and upliftings of the spirit into divine heights and revelations of the nearness of God & the presence of his angels. And though the veil is drawn again & the opening heavens closed, yet the Light will have given us strength to bear & wait till the perfect consummation in that world where she has gone to walk hand in hand with her mother & her child

***

I have thought much of the children in this their great loss. We know what the blessing is to have a mother stay with us to our full years. Perhaps the next blessing is the sainted memory of a mother early taken to Heaven – the heart's secret worship of a Heavenly Mother. That she will watch over them from above I cannot doubt. My earnest hope is that they will sacredly cherish her memory; will love the things she loved; strive to be in disposition, character & conduct all that she would wish them to be, avoiding everything that would give her pain, as feeling that she is watchful of them: and in their increased love & thoughtfulness for their father & for each other, try in some degree to make up for the loss that has fallen upon you all.

May God comfort you & bless the home which he has consecrated by his death-angel![6]

Samuel was confronted with another death at this time. On June 29, 1861, Elizabeth Barrett Browning died in Florence.

Samuel had become acquainted with Robert and Elizabeth Browning when he was in Paris in 1851. He tells Henry of her death and Robert's grief.

> In my last letter to Fanny – I know not that she ever received it [She didn't; it was written July 12] – I spoke of my visit to Mrs. Browning and knew not then that she had since passed into that world from which she so desired communications. Browning, too, is heavy with a sorrow like yours. So does one after another enter into the waters of this great baptism, which seems an overwhelming and is a consecration.[7]

From Italy Samuel headed north and stopped in Saint Gilgen in Austria. He was making a pilgrimage to see the reality of the place described in his brother Henry's prose romance *Hyperion*.

> But I want most to tell you of my beautiful Sunday at St. Gilgen: to which I went as on a pilgrimage. I left the golden ship at Salzburg Saturday afternoon and with toiling up the long hills it was already dark when I reached Hof. "On the brow of the breezy hill" it still stands & the inn & the church are still opposite each other with the churchyard crosses between: but inn & church are both new & enlarged, a fire having burned those which you saw. Only faintly could I see through the night mists the lake of St. Wolfgang as we descended the hill at 10 o'clock & stopped at Franz Schöndorfers gasthaus. The next morning I was greatly disappointed to find the whole landscape covered with a thick chilly fog, & when I went, which I did first of all, to the little chapel to read the inscription.
>
> ***
>
> I walked up on the hill above the village. Already the sun had come out warm & cheerful & the mists rose & melted from off the lake – leaving only a tender softness on the near hills and a dreamy faintness upon those beyond. ~~the water.~~ The village lay stilly in its nest only the church bells sounding

from the bulbous steeple that rose darkly against the clear water: and the trouble was all over. I went into a little summer house to sit & enjoy the beauty & the peace. And then it was that there came to me a holy Presence: Fanny's Spirit was with me. I had not felt it before much as I had thought of her. And now she was near to my spirit, calm, pure & elevated, & lifting me into calmness, purity & strength. She seemed to know all & to promise to help me. The words of the inscription came to me with new meaning and I went down to the little chapel again.

***

The lake lay lovely & peaceful, a mirror under the hills reflecting tremulously the woods & the high cliff: nearer it was softly rippled & shot with every lovely color of purple & blue & green & rose & amber & white, as if troops of angels were moving unseen across its surface first touching the waters with their passing feet & casting the reflection of their airy wings. The hours passed by in this sweet Sabbath of the heart where every restlessness was stilled & it was mid-afternoon before I returned to the inn. My dinner was set in the large sunny front chamber, perhaps the one in which you slept – there were flowers in the windows, geranium & cactus, but the old fashioned lattice had given place to modern square panes. At sunset, after a parting visit to the chapel, I was rowed over to St. Wolfgang by the boatman & his wife.[8]

The inscription from *Hyperion* on the Chapel that Samuel mentions is:

> Look not mournfully into the Past. It comes not back again. Wisely improve the Present. It is thine. Go forth to meet the shadowy Future, without fear, and with a manly heart.[9]

While in Austria, Samuel also visited Vienna, where Beethoven, his favorite composer, had lived. He went to several places recalling the composer including Beethoven's grave "in the pretty little churchyard not far from town," where Haydn, Schubert and Mozart were remembered in death.

With a deeper interest I walked through the little valley, an hour's walk out of town, where he composed the Pastoral symphony. A tiny trickling book, at the foot of the vine-hills, green with shrubs & overhung by trees – pretty, but commonplace enough to the outward eye. But under those trees he used to love to sit & write, & the music of that very brook he had woven into that delicious symphony; & consecrated it forever by his genius.[10]

Between his visit to Austria and that to Germany, Samuel received a letter from Marshall Oliver, who was working in an atelier in Paris. The letter indicates that Samuel had written him a number of letters providing advice and support in his work and life. Marshall expresses his feelings about Samuel in a letter and asks him to visit Paris.

Scarcely a day passes that I do not think of you & long to see you here at Paris and late at night I have sat before my fire, as much with you as if we really stood face to face & hand in hand. It seemed impossible that you could not have been thinking of me, so strongly was I impressed with your presence.[11]

On his way home in February, 1862, Samuel passed through Paris. He saw Marshall and wrote about him to Samuel Johnson.

I find Marshall well as usual working steadily, but very often, he says, discouraged. We dine & spend the evening together, these few days of my transit & it is good you may be with him again. He sends his love & says he has not received any answer to the letters he wrote you in England. Pray write him (care of J. Munroe & Ce.). Isn't it too bad that he can't go to Spain with me?[12]

Samuel Longfellow kept track of Marshall over the years and in 1874 he received a letter from him saying he was to be married

A letter from Marshall Oliver announces his impending marriage. He says "I have not his address (yours) and wish you would tell him for auld lang syne." The lady's name he does not mention. I have heard & forgotten it.[13]

In Germany, Samuel went to Berlin where he went with a letter of introduction from Emerson to visit Hermann Grimm, son of the fairy-tale Grimm brother Wilhelm, and his wife Gisela von Arnim, daughter of Bettina von Arnim, who wrote *Goethe's Correspondence With a Child*. Among the topics Samuel and Hermann Grimm discussed was religion because he could not get permission to import some books he wanted. To provide some of the information he was looking for, Samuel explained his views on Unitarianism and Transcendentalism; Grimm was in agreement with the ideas that Samuel presented.

> With Mr. Grimm, I talked in English, as I think he understood it better than my German, & I could very well comprehend his. I did not visit him as much as I should have done, partly because he lived a good way off, and the weather was generally bad, & partly because his wife was a good deal sick. I had a very pleasant talk with her (or *from* her, for she does not understand English) the evening before I left. She told me about her mother's (Bettina's) statue of Goethe, & showed me a bas-relief of hers, full of the sweetest classic spirit; two figures representing classic song & the Volkslied. Mr. Grimm was always pleasant and refined & kind, sending me tickets to concerts & he told me his second volume would be out at Easter.[14]

In Berlin Samuel became acquainted with a young American named John Lindsley, who was studying in Europe. Samuel describes the young man and their activities in Berlin to Samuel Johnson, who knew John's father, also named John, from his congregation.

> By the way, do you remember a Mr. Lindsley, who used to be one of your congregation? A son of his, a youth of seventeen, was my chief ally and companion in Berlin. We happened to meet every evening where I went to get my cup of cocoa and read the papers, and we became fast friends. I found him frank

and intelligent, with his head full of the new ideas as was indeed natural, his father being a hearer of Parker, and his mother, now in the spirit-land, one of the early abolitionists, a friend of Garrison and Phillips.[15]

John also knew Samuel's friend Higginson, who also visited Berlin after Samuel had left. Samuel and John maintained a correspondence between Berlin and wherever Samuel was on his travels. After his trip to Spain, Samuel sent a letter inviting John to meet in Eisenach, but he was unable to go, and when Samuel arrived in England on the last stage of his trip he invited John to meet him in Salisbury, to which he responded.

> I received your kind letter a few days ago asking me to join you at Salisbury, and directly after that one from father saying "I have not said anything about your London voyage. I think a change would benefit you. Be as economical and careful as convenient." So as far as that is concerned, I think I might go, although he doesn't know.[16]

Samuel also received a letter from John's father. He was grateful for Samuel's taking an interest in his son and his being available to provide any necessary assistance to his son personally and in his studies.

> I thank you for your letter and am grateful for the interest you take in John. Your letter was most welcome at this time as I have of late questioned myself if I was doing my duty in permitting one of his age to be absent with none to report his conduct or give a friendly word of advice and counsel.
>
> Your kind letter has assured me and nothing would afford more satisfaction than for him to be with you and the idea that John in some degree appreciates the opportunity is truly gratifying to me and all his friends.[17]

From Germany, Samuel went to Paris then once again headed south to Marseilles and then took "a five-days sea voyage from Marseilles to Malaga" [*letter to Samuel Johnson*, February 20, 1862] to Spain where he planned to visit Granada, Gibraltar, Cadiz, Seville, Cordoba and Madrid "and what lies between there and Bayonne and Bordeaux." [*letter to Samuel Johnson*, February 20, 1862] However, he was almost not allowed to visit Spain because of his personal convictions. He describes this situation to Samuel Johnson.

> And by the way, at the last moment I came near losing Spain, after all, "for conscience's sake" Sam. For on the morning of the day when I am finishing this, going to the American Consulate for needed visa of passport, I am told I must take the oath of allegiance to the United States, and on reading the words of the oath, I find it includes a pledge to support "the Constitution, without any mental reservation." Of course I could not do that; and I said so, explaining my position about the Fugitive Slave clause. Finally the Consul (Mr. Bigelow of the N.Y. Post), respecting my scruple, & seeing that the object of the regulation would be obtained by a declaration of allegiance to the govt. waived the rest, and so I saved my conscience & did not lose the Alhambra.[18]

Having finished his trip to Spain, Samuel traveled north and stopped off in Paris once again. From there he went up the Rhine to Heidelberg and Nuremberg, "which unfortunately, I omitted when I was on my way to Munich, but cannot think of losing." [*letter to Samuel Johnson*, February 20, 1862] On the final stretch of his trip Samuel sailed down the Rhine stopping in Cologne and then he "sped through Brussels, Antwerp, Ghent, Bruges (charming Bruges, I spent two days there) to Ostend & England." [*letter to Henry*, July 26, 1862]

In England he received a letter from Henry who indicated he might be interested in coming over and Samuel encouraged him because a change in location might help his grief. If he did come, Samuel offered to stay longer and travel with him if he wanted, but in the end Henry did not come. Henry also suggested that he travel with his son Charley, a very independent young man, who had his own ideas of what he wanted to do. Samuel's responded to Henry and said,

Your suggestion of my traveling with Charley strikes me less favorably. I have not seen him indeed for two years; but I think he would need a person of more authority than I should have over him, & perhaps our tastes are not enough alike to make us good companions.[19]

Samuel traveled a little around England and then, after two years abroad, he sailed home where he arrived in August 1862 to a divided nation.

Notes:

[1] Longfellow, Samuel, Ed. *Lectures, Essays, and Sermons by Samuel Johnson.* Boston: The Riverside Press, 1883. p. 62.

[2] Ibid., p. 60-62.

[3] Ibid., p. 63.

[4] Letter, Samuel Johnson to his sister K, February 20, 1861. *Lectures, Essays, and Sermons by Samuel Johnson.*

[5] Longfellow, Samuel, Ed. *Henry Wadsworth Longfellow, Vol. II.* Boston: Ticknor and Company, 1886. p. 369.

[6] Letter, Samuel Longfellow to Henry W. Longfellow, August 2, 1861. SLP, LNHS.

[7] Ibid.

[8] Letter, Samuel Longfellow to Henry W. Longfellow, October 20, 1861. LP.

[9] Longfellow, Henry Wadsworth. *Hyperion.* New York: Samuel Colman, 1839. Book IV, Chapter VIII.

[10] Letter, Samuel Longfellow to Henry W. Longfellow, October 20, 1861. LP.

[11] Letter, Marshall Oliver to Samuel Longfellow, January 28, 1862. SLP, LNHS.

[12] Letter, Samuel Longfellow to Samuel Johnson, February 20, 1862. SLP, LNHS.

[13] Letter, Samuel Longfellow to Samuel Johnson, June 19, 1874. SLP, LNHS.

[14] *Letter to Samuel Johnson,* February 20, 1862.

[15] *Letter to Samuel Johnson,* February 20, 1862.

[16] *Letter from John Lindsley, Jr. to Samuel,* July 3, 1862.

[17] *Letter from John Lindsley, Sr. to Samuel,* July 15, 1862.

[18] *Letter to Samuel Johnson,* February 20, 1862.

[19] *Letter to Henry,* July 26, 1862.

CHAPTER 16 – INCIVILITY

During the time that Samuel Longfellow was traveling around Europe, America moved from arguments and threats to a war between the states without legal slavery and those that believed they had the legal right to have slaves. The content of some of the letters Samuel wrote while he was on his trip state his opinions about what he learned was going on in America from newspapers and letters from family and friends.

Below are some extracts from these letters without much comment. They clearly provide Samuel's viewpoints, and emphasize his strong belief that peace should not be broken by war for any reason. In February 1861, Samuel wrote a letter to Fanny after Lincoln's election and two weeks after the formation of the Confederate States of America.

> You wrote me on the day of the Election. How little you dreamed of what had followed. For my part I had not believed in anything but a little bluster & then a quiet acceptance on the part of the slave states. I begin to be afraid, now, that it will be the story, only a little intensified and prolonged; until the Free States shall have been alarmed or weaned into conceding everything & demanding nothing, which is called a compromise. For my part I long to have the Slave States go: I would give them forts, arsenals, custom houses & mints, if they would really & positively go. I long to see the Free States accept this providentially offered opportunity of emancipating themselves from their long & irksome bondage to such arrogant masters, & still more from their moral complicity in the guile of slavery. Indeed, as a simple matter of self respect I do not see how a northern man can remain in a union with states where he is liable merely as a northern man & a suspect to such insult & outrages as have been continually inflicted on travelers in the Slave States.[1]

Three months after Fort Sumter was attacked, Samuel wrote his last letter to Fanny, which arrived after her death.

> Your two letters reflecting across the water patriotic fires greatly kindled my enthusiasm, already stirred by the newspapers, and I felt as if it were a great loss to be absent when our country was so aflame with generous spirit. There is something grand even at this distance in this self-devotion & pouring out of money like water among a people who, there was reason to fear had grown too loving of money to care much for ideas & the nobler sentiments. What a pity that only the war trumpet seems to be able to kindle such enthusiasm. Had half this devotion, this sacrifice of money been thrown in behalf of principles & human rights – the war need never have come to pass. For I firmly believe that, while there is no justification of the course pursued by the seceding states, yet that course has been brought about to a great extent by the perpetual concessions which have been the perpetual encouragement to that domineering spirit which culminates at last in violent rebellion.[2]

Writing to Mr. R.H. Manning, Samuel talks about the justification of the American Civil War.

> I wonder if you are still a disunionist, or like Wendall Phillips now a union-with-emancipation-ist? I am one or the other, I am not perfectly clear which. I suppose that to be a disunionist is counted rank treason now in the United States. I can't help it. I am not a secessionist. I count the Southern States to have acted in a manner utterly unjustifiable, politically and morally; both in their method of declaring themselves independent without political cause, and without consent asked of their confederates, and also in their seizure of federal property and outrage upon the federal flag, thus compelling the government of the United States to resort to arms, and so, by their rash unreasonableness and violence driving the country into war. The government, on the contrary acted with the greatest forbearance and moderation, which could not have been carried farther except upon the extreme peace principle that war is never justifiable. This

of course, the government did not believe, and, believing in war, I don't see how it could do other wise than it has done. I don't believe in war yet; that is, I don't believe it to be otherwise than a very barbarous, cruel, and unjust way of settling a difference, or even of establishing a just cause. And what I have read of this war in America does not change my feeling.[3]

Samuel also tells his brother Henry about his feelings concerning the war, which the brothers virtually shared.

With the rest, I want for decisiveness from America. All this bloodshed without results is terrible to me. I can be reconciled to the war only if it shall bring an end the Nation's Wrongdoing & Freedom & clear assurance of Freedom to the Slave. I cannot feel much more interest for a slave-restoring union than for a slave holding Confederacy. I see that Sumner has advocated emancipation by the government. I am very glad that he has done it: though I don't doubt there will be plenty to call him "injudicious" if nothing worse. I should prefer certainly that the slaveholders should of their own will emancipate. If they will not, whoever holds the rightful power should use it, in wise methods of course.[4]

A letter to his sister Anne reiterates his feelings about peace.

And now I am earnestly hoping to see before long the end of the war at home. I am as much a peace man as you; and war looks to me a very barbarous way of getting even the Right. But I see that the world must still employ it, because it is not yet imbued with the principles of Peace & does not possess those moral forces which might take the place of the physical.[5]

On September 22, 1862, shortly after Samuel's return from Europe, President Lincoln issued the Preliminary Emancipation Proclamation. He comments on it to Samuel Johnson.

This morning I heard Emerson at the Music Hall. It was good; not especially powerful. With all drawbacks, I think we can't but rejoice greatly at the President's proclamation. That little paragraph, that stands so simple, plain, direct, after the shambling introduction, – it is the death-warrant of slavery. Blessed are our ears that they hear! I should have liked that little paragraph all by itself. I should have liked the 1ˢᵗ of October instead of the 1ˢᵗ of January. But surely we can wait a little, and meanwhile, as Sumner said, immediate emancipation follows every advance of our army to every man who will come within its lines. Of course we should have been glad if freedom had come to the slave by the virtue of the North rather than by the madness of the South; by the free gift rather than the compulsion of his master; if it had been proclaimed as an act of national justice rather than a military necessity. But we know, too, that behind it all as a divine law is working, so is a moral sentiment. Think of it, Sam, slavery abolished in one day! Could we have dreamed it, when we went over the ocean two years ago! John Brown just hung for attempting by arms that liberation which the President of the United States by arms now proclaims! Two years before, the army and navy of the United States joining to take back Anthony Burns to slavery; now army and navy pledged to protect the liberty of every escaping black man![6]

Samuel returned to Cambridge and had news of the war arriving daily rather than in the periodic letter. He lived in the Craigie house where Henry and his children were still feeling the sorrow of Fanny's death. However, Samuel felt he had to get back to work and told Samuel Johnson that he didn't "want to be pulpitless." As a result, during the period of the Civil War he went back to "candidating" and substituting in a number of churches. Many of these he had been to before and he went to the pulpit in Brooklyn several times.

Henry did not want to lose more members of his family, but he knew that his oldest son Charley was interested in signing up for the Army. Charley was always restless and looking for excitement and adventure. In order to distract Charley's interest in the war, which many expected not to last long, Henry sent him on a supply ship going to an island off the Gulf Coast, something he enjoyed greatly. When Charley returned Henry sent him on a trip to Europe with a friend, hoping the war would be over before they returned. Unfortunately it wasn't and in March 1863, in order to get extra time, 18-year old Charley had a friend mail a letter from Portland, Maine to Henry saying that he was going to enlist.

Once Charley was in the army, Henry did what he could to get him back home, but without success. An officer recognized Charley and had him transferred into his artillery troops. He also notified Henry about this and told him he was on his way to Rappahannock. One of the Appletons helped Charley get a commission, which was more in keeping with his social status, and he was transferred to the First Massachusetts Cavalry. In April 1863 Samuel went to Washington, D.C., accompanied by Charley's younger brother Erny.

> We reached Washington Saturday evening & after tea called on Mr. Sumner. He at once said that it would not be possible for us to get a pass to visit Charley: that the department was very strict & would give passes only to persons who had relatives sick in the army.
>
> Sumner thinks our relations with England are critical, & is using his utmost efforts to ward off a war, by warning his English correspondents of the consequences of their government continuing to allow the fitting out of *Alabamas.*
>
> ***
>
> My letter did not get mailed this morning & I open it to say that I have just seen Mr. Higginson who came up today from the Rappahannock. He says he saw Charley this morning in good health & spirits. The cavalry left camp this morning in light marching order: Charley with them – but whither bound no one knew.
>
> Erny sends his love.[7]

The *Alabama* referred to was a Confederate warship built in Liverpool and equipped in the Azores. It created problems for the

Dabney family on the island of Faial, where Samuel had spent a year tutoring the Dabney children.

At the end of November 1863, Charley was wounded in action. On December 1 a telegram arrived at Craigie house informing the Longfellows of the incident. Henry and Erny rushed to Washington and on December 8 they were able to take Charley back to Cambridge, where he recuperated and never returned to the military. Samuel wrote to his sister Mary telling her what was going on; the letter indicates how poor the flow of information could be.

> Charley was wounded in the fighting on Tuesday. Henry & Erny immediately went on to Washington. To-day comes word that Charley is doing well & will be in Washington to-day. The wound was reported in the face & was said to be severe. But the report in today's newspaper, says it was slightly. Probably a saber cut, but we have not heard any particulars. [*letter to Mary*, December 4, 1863.]

> I find Charley at home sitting in the study, dining at table & in short looking well & comfortable. But one sleeve loose shows that something is lost. He was wounded not in the face but, as he was stooping to tire was hit by a ball under one shoulder, which passed along outside the spine, just touching the vertebra & out at the other side. He says his first thought was of Libby Bison & he took to his heels, but before long fell & was soon in the surgeon's hands in a log-hut close by. Then he was taken in the ambulance to the rear & finally to Alexandria. His father & Erny waited in Washington from Tuesday night till Saturday before seeing him. They left Washington, accompanied by Capt. Bowditch (son of Ingersoll) who had a flesh wound in the arm.
>
> Charley is in good spirits & glad to be at home. 'Tis possible that the wound may be some months in perfectly healing.[8]

Incredibly, Samuel almost found himself in the army. One day someone came to Craigie house to inform Samuel he was being drafted into the army. However, he was not at home and Erny talked to them, He let them know that Samuel was 44 years old and they left without their "old soldier."

Others in the family affected by the Civil War were Samuel's sister Mary and her husband James Greenleaf. They had left their business in New Orleans and were living not far from the Craigie House. Samuel felt that James was "coppery", referring to his Copperhead leanings – the term applied to Democrats who opposed the war and wanted peace with the Confederates. Samuel alleged that James believed "Nothing is so unpardonable as abolition. To give a black man his freedom, even incidentally, would appear to be the greatest of calamities, the worst of crimes. [*letter to Henry*, 1863 (month and day unknown).] James died on August 22, 1865.

In April 1863, not long after Charley enlisted, Samuel wrote to Mary, the daughter of Mr. Murray who ran the school where Samuel had taught over 20 years earlier. Mr. Murray had died and his daughter told him what was going on with the other members of her family and the students she knew about. They were an example of a family torn by the war with brother fighting brother. Two of her brothers were in Virginia in the Confederate states and two were in the north. Her letter also indicates Mr. Murray was anti-slavery and answers the question why Samuel never mentioned the issue of slavery in his letters from Rockburn.

> Thank you for why you say of my precious father. I am sure you are right & feel truly thankful that he is not here to be pained, as he would be by, this wicked rebellion.[9]

Mary also mentioned that she visited Samuel's nephew and took him "books & flowers and any little thing that I thought might contribute to his comfort." This nephew was Steve, son of Samuel's brother Stephen. Steve had been wounded in the foot and was in the hospital when Samuel and Erny visited him while they were in Washington trying to see Charley.

As active support for his anti-slavery beliefs, Samuel wrote the hymn below for the 31st anniversary of the American Anti-Slavery

Society. This abolitionist organization was founded by William Lloyd Garrison and Arthur Tappan and was in disagreement with other abolitionist groups over several issues not related to their joint belief in the abolition of slavery.

> Out of the dark the circling sphere
>   Is rounding onward to the light;
> We see not yet the full day here,
>   But we do see the paling night;
>
> And Hope, that lights her fadeless fires,
>   And Faith, that shines, a heavenly will,
> And Love, that courage re-inspires –
>   These stars have been above us still.
>
> Look backward, how much has been won;
>   Look round, how much is yet to win!
> The watches of the night are done;
>   The watches of the day begin.
>
> O Thou, whose mighty patience holds
>   The night and day alike in view,
> Thy will our dearest hopes enfolds,
>   O keep us steadfast, patient, true![10]

This was not the only hymn that Samuel published in 1864. All the hard work that the two Sams had done in Nice came to fruition when *Hymns of the Spirit* was published and made available to the Unitarian community. This was the last hymnbook that the two friends produced together.

When Samuel went to Washington he talked with his nephew Steve, and also seems to have talked with other recuperating soldiers. There are no letters at the time of the war referring to this, but it seems likely that he continued this in other locations. However, later in his life he received letters from some men who thanked him for the kindness he showed them. He was always willing to help young men whom he met, whether in the military hospital or other places. To some he was a supportive friend and to a few he provided financial assistance for their studies. In New York once he visited

> A picture gallery & the Soldiers' Home. Tell Edie to keep her German papers for me. I promised to lend some to a little German bugler in the Army.[11]

In this same letter Samuel asks Anne, "Isn't it a grand thing to have the Act of Emancipations passed by Congress?" [*letter to Anne*, February 4, 1865.] The Act of Emancipation he refers to was the 13th Amendment to the Constitution, which was passed by Congress and forwarded to the States for their approval.

Toward the end of the war, Samuel began to feel ill again. It is not clear what the problem was, but it was something he had had before. This time the treatment was different than other times.

> It was not "sponge-cake" my dear, but an old trouble which the doctor thought he might cure. I cannot say that he has, yet; but I do not think I shall stay much longer under his hands at present. I say "under his hands" literally, for he cures by magnetism & the laying on of hands, as in the old New Testament times and many persons have been greatly benefited by him.[12]

The Civil War ended on April 9, 1865 when General Lee surrendered his Confederate troops to General Grant at Appomattox Court House in Virginia. In October, while Samuel was living with his sister Mary who was grieving over the death of her husband, the suggestion of a trip to Europe arose. This time he would be the companion of his nephew Erny who wanted to study art. Samuel wrote to Samuel Johnson and told him about the upcoming trip.

> The die is cast. I have taken passage with Ernest in the *Cuba* which steams October 11th. A week from Wednesday Charles T. Brooks goes at the same time. Our programme is to spend the winter in Paris, early in the Spring to by Nice & the

Cornice to Italy, then northward to Switzerland, Germany, Belgium, England (in September). Ernest has made a plan by which we shall go over all the passes of the Alps. It will be much the old thing – pardon the expression – but I shall try to see some things unseen before.[13]

Notes:

[1] Letter, Samuel Longfellow to Frances (Fanny) Appleton Longfellow, February 27, 1861. SLP, LNHS.

[2] Ibid., July 12, 1861.

[3] Letter, Samuel Longfellow to R.H. Manning, October 1861. SLP, LNHS.

[4] Letter, Samuel Longfellow to Henry W. Longfellow, October 20, 1861. LP.

[5] Letter, Samuel Longfellow to Anne Longfellow Pierce, February 2, 1862. SLP, LNHS.

[6] Letter, Samuel Longfellow to Samuel Johnson, September 11, 1862. SLP, LNHS.

[7] Letter, Samuel Longfellow to Henry W. Longfellow, April 13, 1863. LP.

[8] Letter, Samuel Longfellow to Mary Longfellow Greenleaf, December 12, 1863. SLP, LNHS.

[9] Letter, Samuel Longfellow to Mary Murray H., April 21, 1863. SLP, LNHS.

[10] "America Singing: Nineteenth-Century Song Sheets." Thirty-first anniversary of the American Anti-Slavery Society, at the Church of the Puritans, Tuesday, May 10th. 1864. Anti-Slavery Printing Office, 21 Spruce St., 2d. floor. [n. d.]. http://memory.loc.gov/ammem/index.html.

[11] Letter, Samuel Longfellow to Anne Longfellow Pierce, February 4, 1865. SLP, LNHS.

[12] Ibid.

[13] Letter, Samuel Longfellow to Samuel Johnson, October 2, 1865. SLP, LNHS.

CHAPTER 17-ARTFUL VOYAGERS

Samuel Longfellow had enjoyed his earlier trips to Europe and now had the chance to show it to his nephew Erny. Family was important to Samuel and enjoyed educating young men about things he considered important. Not only would he have the opportunity to teach Erny about art, but they would also be able to visit places that Erny's father Henry had written about in some of his works.

Ernest Longfellow, known as Erny, was the younger of Henry's two sons. He grew up in the large, beautiful Craigie House, surrounded by gardens and trees, with a widely renowned poet as father and a mother who was from one of the richest families in New England. Many years later Erny wrote a book, *Random Memories*, which he said was "not meant for a serious autobiography." The book tells about some of his experiences, and a comment he makes indicates that his life in such a privileged home may not have been as easy as outsiders might have assumed.

> Any one who has had the misfortune to be the son of an illustrious parent knows how hard it is to be taken seriously by people. He remains, with them, always the son of his father. They generally try to make matters better by reminding him that it is a well-known fact that genius skips one generation.[1]

In describing his home, he said, "we had some good pictures in our house," among which he highlights a Tintoretto, a Copley, although he thought it might have been by Sir William Beechey, and two paintings by Stuart. Despite being surrounded by such art treasures, he said he did "not think they made much impression on my childish mind."[2] Nevertheless, his interest in art finally began to develop through contact with his uncle Thomas Gold

Appleton and progressed to the point he developed an interest in becoming an artist himself.

> I, of course, drew pictures, as all children do, but it was not till a summer at Newport, when I was ten or eleven, and we were living in the same house with Kensett, the artist, that I really became interested in painting. I remember I used to watch him paint, and when he lent me some of his paints and brushes I painted my first picture in oils, I think of a sailboat in a rough sea, on a piece of tobacco-box. My uncle, Mr. Appleton, was an amateur painter of some talent, who might have become a real artist if he had been willing to devote himself to art and had not been too indolent to take lessons and work hard.[3]

Kensett was one of the most renowned artists of the Civil War period and was one of the early members of the Hudson River School. It also seems that Appleton may not have been the best role model for an art student. He seems to have expected artists to meet the same work standards as other people he paid for a "product." Once he ordered a painting from Millet for $200, but the artist took too long for him and he canceled the order; the painting was the "Angelus," which around 40 years later sold for $100,000 and is now in the Musée d'Orsay.[4]

Nevertheless, Erny's uncles Samuel and Thomas did know a lot of artists. *Random Memories* was written many years after Erny had met these artists and had become familiar with their work. This mature Erny gives his opinion about them.

> John Kensett – "a charming man, and had as an artist a delightful touch; but his pictures lack what artists call quality."
>
> Frederick Church – "was well known for his large ambitious compositions …which appeal to the uneducated."
>
> Jasper Cropsey – "was devoted to autumn foliage of the most brilliant description, which you might say was a trifle gaudy.
>
> Jervis McEntee – "was perhaps the best of the [Hudson River] school with his quiet, brown autumn scenes."[5]

Among the other artists he knew, or knew of, were Stillman, Hill, Burstatt, William Gay and William Morris Hunt.

> The pictures of the Barbison school that these artists brought home, and others that began to appear in the dealer's galleries, inspired me with such enthusiasm for the French school that I determined to go to Paris to study when I had finished my studies at the Lawrence Scientific School.[6]

In order to learn more about art, Erny went to Europe to learn more, not only about artists and the art they had produced, but also to have practical experience in producing art. Samuel, with his extensive knowledge about art and music was asked to be Erny's companion.

> Accordingly, accompanied by my uncle, the Reverend Samuel Longfellow, as bear leader, and to keep me out of mischief, I suppose, I sailed in October of 1865 for the great adventure. And it was a great adventure, for I was not yet quite twenty; I had never taken any lessons in drawing or painting, except such as one has at school, which practically amounted to nothing; I had never drawn from the life, and not even from casts. There were no good art schools in Boston then that I could have gone to; but I had a natural gift for drawing and a correct eye.[7]

As Samuel discovered on his first sea voyage when he went to the Azores, his body didn't fully agree with sea life. Erny also found problems with the sea and "was deadly seasick" his first three days. They had a room on the lower level that the "awful" smells of the ship filled. As they got their sea legs, they enjoyed the trip more and met a man about Erny's age traveling with his wife and one of her friends. When they got to Paris, they met up again, and "saw a good deal of them."

They arrived in London and saw the galleries, sights and some of Samuel's friends. One of the highlights was having Moncure Conway, a Unitarian minister Samuel knew from Cambridge, take them to see the Scottish historian and writer Thomas Carlyle.

He received us in a dingy old grey dressing-gown and sat humped up in front of the fire, and railed at almost everything, especially America, where he had never been and never wished to go. He was a fine, vigorous old Scotchman, and not at all the rather sick-looking individual painted by Whistler.[8]

The visited the National Gallery, which interested Erny "very much." He saw paintings by famous artists he had only heard about, such as Sir Joshua Reynolds, Romney and Turner. However, in general they really didn't appreciate London and ran into some unhappy supporters of the Confederate States during the Civil War.

London in late October is not a very cheerful place, and all the people we met had sympathized with the South, and were vexed at having put their money on the wrong horse. One gentleman, who had invested largely in Confederate bonds, declared roundly that it was an outrage that the North would not pay him for them. So after a week we crossed to Havre.[9]

The two travelers arrived in Paris and took a room in a hotel. However, they needed something more affordable since they were going to be staying there through the winter. They wandered through the streets of the Latin Quarter and then to a pension that had been recommended, but they didn't like it and decided against pensions in general. On their way back they saw a place with furnished rooms on Quai de la Messagerie near Place du Châtelet. After looking them over they took them and "came over bag and baggage" that afternoon. The small apartment had a salon, two bedrooms and a dressing room for Samuel. In a letter to Erny's sister Alice, Samuel said that an apartment was "very nice when you are up with a fine wide outlook up & down the river & across."[10] Erny provides some insight into the way Samuel looked for places to stay, which he sometimes did not appreciate.

Arrived in Paris, the first question was where to establish ourselves for the winter. My uncle thought the large hotels much

too expensive, so we started out apartment-hunting. My uncle
had an obsession for having a view, which is not always easy
in a city. I have known him, if only passing a night in a place,
to chase all over a hotel to get a room with a view, even if we
arrived after dark and were leaving early the next morning;
much to my disgust when I was tired with a long journey and
wished only to get to bed.[11]

Their daily routine began with coffee and bread followed by
Samuel taking a short walk and "then there is reading, writing,
studying till noon, when we go out for our lunch." In the afternoon
they went sightseeing and Samuel felt that "The city itself is for
some time a sufficient 'sight'." They visited the École des Beaux
Arts, the Louvre, the Luxembourg and the Tuilerie Gardens. On one
of their walks Erny bought a "bust of Venus de Milo to draw from."
Erny felt himself fortunate to have Samuel show him around
and explain the music and art that he was not familiar with.[12]

With my uncle as guide, I was able to get acquainted with
all the best music, and have always been glad that my taste was
cultivated so early, so that music has always been a great pleasure to me.

Of course, we spent many hours at the Louvre studying the
old masters, and here again I owe a great deal to my uncle for
his guidance and knowledge in art; also at the Luxembourg,
where the pictures of the modern French school were shown
in the large gallery at the eastern end of the place, not as now,
in the Orangerie. However, the great question was, How was
I to begin my studies? I had not the least idea; neither had my
uncle. I did not think of entering the Beaux-Arts, because I did
not think I knew enough, and I spoke so little French.[13]

As Erny indicated, the biggest problem they had was to find
a place for Erny to study. Since he felt the Ecole des Beaux-Arts
was not a possibility, they looked for private ateliers. They finally
made contact with Mr. May, who was an American artist living in
Paris. He was very helpful and took Erny to the Atelier of the artist
Antoine-August-Ernest Hébert, who had studied under David

Augurs and Paul Delaroche and won the Grand Prix de Rome at the age of 22. May also introduced Erny to the head painter in the atelier which was in Montmartre "in rue de Leval around the corner from rue Pigalle." He also took him to meet Hébert in his studio.

All the members of the atelier paid for its operation and models and Hébert donated his time twice a week to critique the work of those learning in the atelier. He didn't really say much to the artists and Erny said "he paid little attention to me."

As the new member, Erny had to learn the rules of the atelier, such as the early arrivals on Mondays got the choice of places. He also notes that "there was always more or less of a hubbub going on,"[14] [*Random Memories*, p. 106-107.] which he couldn't participate in because of his lack of ability in the French language. He could not understand all they said and spoke only a little, while only one spoke fair English. As the newest member of the atelier, he was asked to provide a treat one day, which he did, and he "became popular at once at the expense of a few francs."[15]

On his first day at the atelier, they were using a female model. This was something completely new to him and he describes his reaction.

> The model that morning happened to be a woman, and I must confess that to my Puritan mind, and reverencing woman as I had been taught to do, it seemed to me a dreadful dese-cration to put this poor naked girl up for all those ribald youths to stare at. You must remember that I had never drawn from the nude before; but I soon learned, what few people under-stand, that artists regard their models, at least when they are drawing or painting from them, as so much furniture. The ques-tion of sex does not come in.[16]

Despite the unstructured teaching situation, the extensive practice Erny got and his observation of the variety of techniques used in the atelier helped him improve his skills. Sometimes he and a few others hired models for the afternoon or he went to the Louvre to copy pictures, his "favorite painters were Titian and Rembrandt.

At the beginning of 1866, the young couple and their traveling companion that they had met on the boat arrived in Paris. Erny and the young man took a studio together and Erny worked there full time. His companion was in the unusual situation of divorcing his wife to marry her companion and best friend, this with the wife's support.

Another American, Henry Marker, showed up in the atelier. He had been with *Harpers Weekly* during the Civil War, had studied in Munich and then went to Paris to work in oils. Several years after this sojourn in Paris, Erny met him on "a Mediterranean steamer and we recalled with pleasure our former comradeship."[17]

After a few months in Paris, Erny began to find life in the atelier, as well as the Paris weather, tiresome. Samuel suggested that they go to Italy in March, which Erny gladly accepted.

In later years, Erny returned to Paris to study art, and one of his teachers was Léon Bonnat, who was known as a portraitist. Bonnat, who had taken over Erny's old atelier, had won the Medal of Honor in Paris in 1869 and was one of the leading artists of the day. Another teacher Erny had was Thomas Couture, who was known for his historical paintings and portrait work. His most famous student was Manet.

While Erny was studying in the Atelier, Samuel wrote an article for *The Radical Magazine* before the formal founding of the Radical Club. It printed texts for the Radical Club, which was founded in the Spring of 1867 and ceased to exist in 1880.

> The Radical Club may be said to have its origin, in the spring of 1867, in the growing desire of certain ministers and laymen for larger liberty of faith, fellowship, and communion. In this respect it was akin to the Transcendental movement of earlier date. It was designed to meet a demand for the freest investigation of all forms of religious thought and inquiry.[18]

In his communication, Samuel wanted to express his interest in the publication of *The Radical Magazine,* and its ideas, tone and spirit and, in general to encourage its publication of new ideas. He goes on to disagree with an article in an earlier edition and describes some of the religious currents in Paris and the denouncing of some of these the Catholic Church found too radical. In his article, Samuel presents some of his theological beliefs.

> I protest against every theology founded on the Fall of Man. I protest against this merely *pathological* view of Religion. Religion is *Health*; but it is not necessarily *Cure*. I believe in the falls of men; but I believe it better to be saved from falling, than to be saved from the consequences of having fallen. We should do well to carry the modern therapeutics into the spiritual sphere, and substitute, as much as possible, Regimen for Medicine. I have no doubt that we inherit some bad tendencies from our ancestor, the Past, but many good ones, too, and among them the power to do better than he. Some men, it has been said, are so well born that they do not need to be born again; and this is true of most men, in some particular. Our aim should be to make it true of all men in all respects. Thankful we needs must be for the Divine Physician, the Healing Spirit beyond whose restorative power no soul can ever sink.[19]

In March 1866, Samuel and Erny departed by train to Nice, stayed there a few days and then took the three-day carriage trip along the Cornice Road to Genoa. From Genoa they went by "diligence" and train to Pisa, continuing further south by train and then "diligence", but now along a route "infested" with brigands to Rome. Fortunately they were not accosted.

They were glad to finally get off the road from their long, uncomfortable journey, sometimes crammed in coaches with Italians smelling of garlic, and into the interesting city of Rome. Erny gives a description of a Rome that is very different from today's city or the one he was familiar with when he wrote this in 1921.

> Rome in those days was a medieval city. The Pope still drove in state through the streets, while all the people fell on their knees in the mud as he passed. Cardinals were as thick as blackberries, and in their scarlet robes gave a welcome bit of

color as they walked in the villas or on the Pincio. The streets were ill-paved and ill-lighted, and it was not considered safe to walk alone at night in any but the most frequented thoroughfares.

The Coliseum was still draped in its mantle of moss and hanging vines, before the hand of archæologists had scraped and repaired its crumbling walls, in what they call preservation – Heaven save the mark!

The Forum was a resting-place for those magnificent white oxen attached to the red-wheeled carts of the Campagna, not as now a perfect rabbit warren, with so many holes dug in it that it no longer resembles a Forum – all to make a Roman holiday for the antiquaries! There were no new streets and brand-new apartments, but crumbling walls, ruins, and decay, much more picturesque and interesting than at present.[20]

They stayed at the Hôtel d'Angleterre, where they were shocked to see the proprietor's wife carrying their trunks on her head while her husband walked around with his hands in his pockets. They visited the Vatican and its museum and a number of other galleries in Rome, and Erny "learned a great deal from studying the pictures and scuptures."[21]

They met two American artists who were living in Rome. One was the classical sculptor William Wetmore Story, who was at the highpoint of his career. He was from Boston and had graduated from Harvard the year before Samuel. He was a lawyer and his father was a U.S. Supreme Court Justice. Erny says that "Mr. Story was a most charming man, but as a sculptor perhaps the less said the better."[22]

The other artist they met was the painter John Rollin Tilton. He was from Portland and Erny says he "had been helped by my father when beginning his career... He was very conceited and people made much fun of him on that account."[23] Tilton painted an oil for Henry named "Building of a Ship" based on one of Henry's poems; it shows the shipyards of Cape Elizabeth and the Portland skyline.[24]

They remained in Rome over the Easter period and saw the religious ceremonies in the Vatican and the blessing by the Pope.

They decided to go further south, but Italy was divided into separate states, as it had been during Samuel's earlier visit. To get to Naples they had to get a visa in their passports from the Rome police.

In Naples, they visited both Pompeii and Herculaneum. With some acquaintances, Erny climbed Vesuvius and looked "down into that devil's cauldron of the crater, with steam and poisonous vapors arising all around us."[25] They also went to Sorrento, Amalfi and the island of Capri.

They returned northward because of the threat of war and barely stopped in Rome, and continued on to Perugia on their way to Florence. The Austro-Prussian War, or the Third Italian Independence War, was a war between the Austrian Empire and its German allies against Prussia with its German allies and Italy, and lasted about seven weeks. Prussia won the conflict and attained control over the German states and, among other things, Mantua and Venice were returned to Italian control.

They arrived in Florence, which held fond memories for Samuel from his previous trip with Samuel Johnson. Erny found Florence "lovely" after "the gloom of Rome." In a letter to Samuel Johnson, Samuel describes the city from his hotel room – with a view, of course.

> Ah, how good it is to be here again – now for a fortnight. But how strange to be here without you & Marshall. Our windows at the Hotel look down from the fourth story upon the well-remembered river, every ripple of it lighted up by the afternoon sun except where the bridges throw their broad shadows across. The picturesque house-backs with their supporting arches & over them the whole line of the encircling hills from Miniato, by Boboli cypresses & Bellosquaids tower to Oliveto with its belfry & its little circle of crowning trees, where Ernest & I climbed the other evening to see the sun set upon Arno vale. Now the gold floods & melts all the western hills into glory beyond the Cascine.[26]

Samuel and Erny spent their time looking at pictures and churches and visited the Uffizi gallery and Pitti palace. Samuel also made sure to visit Theodore Parker's grave and recalls his visit there with Samuel Johnson not long after Parker died.

> This morning of Sunday I went out to Theodore Parker's grave. The earth had not been kind to our vines. At first I could see nothing of them. At last I discovered two small sprays at the foot of the grave. Did we set any there? The Massachusetts pine tree is growing in the ground above the head-stone. How much he had of its sinew & its sap & its wholesomeness in him! There is another grave now that one seeks: that of Mrs. Browning. It is on the central path with a monument of the best taste & fitness: of white marble with delicate inlaid bordering of black.[27]

They finished their sightseeing in Florence quickly, again because of the impending war, and went to Bologna and Ravenna and "Dante's tomb and arrived in Venice, controlled by the Austrians at the time, with Austrian soldiers everywhere. There were few tourists so they had the galleries and churches almost to themselves, and Erny said that he should "not forget my first impression of those glowing canvases, and the Venetian school has ever since been my favorite." They cut their sightseeing short and left because they were warned that the borders of Venice might be closed at any time. Their decision was justified since "the following day nobody was given permission to leave."

The two travelers went up to Lake Como, "which was full of Garibaldians in their red shirts, and we had the good fortune to see Garibaldi himself."[28] They steamed up the lake and stopped at Cadenabbia, where there were friends "from home." One day a group went up to the head of the lake and Samuel stayed in town "poking about" and talking to the local peasants, "as was his wont."

> He was suddenly arrested as an Austrian spy. He certainly had a German look with his reddish beard. He was marched off to the guard-house, where fortunately he was able to produce his letter of credit on Barings and to prove that he was an American.[29]

After Lake Como they went into Switzerland. Erny had arranged to meet Frederic Crowninshield, a Harvard friend there. He later became an artist and Erny thought "it is possible that my example may have influenced him."[30] He became an instructor of drawing and painting at the Museum of Fine arts. Crowninshield returned to Italy and later became Director of the American Academy in Rome.

Erny and Frederic started in Chamonix with some preliminary hikes to get in shape. They then began to walk and climb in earnest until Frederic sprained his ankle slightly. Samuel went with them by carriage to a starting point where they could walk to Zermatt and the area of the Matterhorn. From a hotel not far from Zermatt they made a number of day trips into the mountains.

Returning to meet Samuel, as well as Crowninshield's mother and friends, the two young men passed the Rhone Glacier. Many years earlier Henry Longfellow saw the glacier at a time when it reached almost to their hotel. When Erny saw it, the glacier had withdrawn, "and like other glaciers in Switzerland, it had shrunk to half its size."[31] – perhaps due to 19th century global warming. The two young men arrived in Interlaken, "two rather disreputable-looking youngsters,"[32] and rejoined those waiting for them.

Samuel and Erny walked around the town hunting up places in Interlaken mentioned in 'Hyperion'."[33] Erny had a theory about why his father wrote "Hyperion", since he had first met Fanny in the Alps not long after his first wife's death.

> As is well known, the heroine of "Hyperion," the romance written by my father before his second marriage, was supposed to be his future wife, and he may have written the book hoping thereby to forward his courtship.[34]

Samuel and Erny stayed in the alps several weeks enjoying "the beauty of Switzerland" in its lakes and valleys, its luxurious vegetation and its snow-covered mountains. They then decided to travel by carriage back into Italy since the war had ended and Germany and Italy the victors. Their idea was to go over the Stelvio Pass into Austria, however, when they arrived at the Italian-

-Austrian border, sentinels from both countries would not let them pass. An Italian officer told them to go back down a little and they could follow a path into Switzerland and then cross into Austria and on through Innsbruck, Munich and Salzburg to Vienna.

Erny "was somewhat disappointed in the galleries in Vienna; there were few pictures of the first class," in his opinion.[35] The next stop on their trip was Prague and then Dresden, "where we reveled in that wonderful gallery, certainly one of the finest in Europe."[36] In Dresden they saw the Grenadiers of the German Guard in their impressive uniforms returning from the recent war. They continued on "to Holland to study the Dutch school, and the wonderful Rembrandts confirmed the admiration for that painter which I had formed in Paris."[37] The only other Dutch painter that interested Erny was Vermeer.

Their trip was winding down and Samuel was going to return to America. However, Erny was not sure whether to go back or stay on for a year or two and study in Rome or Paris. He still felt that he needed "a great deal more work in the technique of my profession and that [he] had hardly begun to paint at all."[38] He finally decided to return home with Samuel, but in retrospect he thought it was "a great mistake" that he didn't stay.

> But I was rather homesick at the idea of being deserted by my traveling companion. My father was writing for me to come home, and most potent of all was the desire to see again a certain person of the opposite sex.[39]

The traveling duo went back to Paris for a short while and sailed home in a French steamer from Brest in October. They arrived back in America in time for Erny's twenty-first birthday in November 1866.

In 1862 Henry Wadsworth Longfellow decided to focus his efforts on the translation of Dante's *Divine Comedy*, a project he had been interested in and working on periodically since he had visited Italy in 1828. He worked with a group of friends knowledgeable in literature, known as the Dante Club, who read the cantos as they were translated and critiqued them in gatherings at the Craigie House. Henry's translation of the *Divine Comedy* was published in 1867. A dinner was held to celebrate the publication of Henry's translation, and Samuel describes the festivities to Samuel Johnson.

> Yesterday I went to a very pleasant & very elegant six o'clock dinner given by Mr. Fields to celebrate the completion of the Dante Translation (why delayed till now I know not). Richard Dana (Senior), Emerson, Dr. Holmes, Lowell, Norton & twenty others were present including all the firm. Coming out to Cambridge Lowell expressed to me his interest in the Radical religious movement.[40]

Back in Cambridge after his trip, Samuel went back to preaching in several different churches. However, he took the opportunity provided to stay in the Twenty-eighth Congregational Society for over a year in 1867-1868. This Boston church was organized by Theodore Parker and supported a "strictly free platform, wholly unembarrassed by creed or covenant."[41] Samuel enjoyed the freedom to preach as he wished, and in February 1868 tells Samuel Wyllys Dabney, one of his students in the Azores 25 years earlier, about preaching at Parker's church.

> I have been preaching for the past year in Boston to the "28th Congregational Society," founded by Theodore Parker, but my engagement will cease in the Spring. They have no church preferring to hold their meetings in a Hall, the seats in which are free to all comers.[42]

Also in February 1868, Samuel had the chance to hear Charles Dickens give a reading in Boston during his 1867-1868 tour of America. Samuel went to hear him three times and gives us a picture of Dickens as a person who seemed to enjoy presenting his works.

> I went in last evening to hear Mr. Dickens read for the third time. It is very entertaining. He acts, rather than reads, scarcely

looking on his book, and using a great deal of descriptive gesture, sometimes very expressive. His face, too, he throws into a great variety of expression, often irresistibly comic. He enjoys his own humor, too, and the appreciation of his audience, and his eye fairly shines with fun. I have heard him in David Copperfield, Bob Sawyer's party (from Pickwick), the " Christmas Carol" and "Boots at the Holly Tree Inn." The Hall is always crowded.[43]

There were two political events during 1867-1868 which interested Samuel. In Massachusetts over the years there had been a number of licensing and prohibition laws for alcohol that had been pushed by temperance groups. In 1852, Massachusetts passed a prohibitory law. During the Civil War, sanitary inspectors of Union camps reported that malt liquors were healthful, and a similar report was issued in Massachusetts, resulting in less support of prohibitory laws. In 1867, Massachusetts voted to repeal the prohibitory law effective in 1868. Samuel provides Samuel Johnson with his views on these laws.

> You see the people of Massachusetts have decided against the Prohibitory Law. I am not sorry for that I do not think it quite right in principle and I am confident it could never be persistently, but only spasmodically carried out, & even that by methods from which good men instinctively shrink.[44]

The other event was the impeachment proceedings against President Andrew Johnson. Johnson had been selected as Vice President to run with Lincoln because he had been the only Senator from a seceding state to remain in office and to argue for black suffrage. After Lincoln's assassination, he started on reconstruction in the south, but conflicted with the Radical Republicans, who did not agree with some of his actions. They eventually found a basis to proceed with articles of impeachment of Johnson, which did not pass. Samuel Longfellow tells Samuel Dabney about the failings of the President.

> Johnson, after putting every obstruction in the way of Congress and its reconstruction measures, and thereby exciting and

keeping alive the hopes of the rebels at the South, and their allies, the old Democratic party at the North, has at last, openly and directly violated the law regularly passed by a two thirds vote of the Congress, that no Executive officer shall be removed during the term for which he was appointed without the consent of the Senate. He has removed Mr. Stanton, who was appointed by Mr. Lincoln for his term of four years, the remainder of which is filled by Johnson as acting President. Of course there was nothing left but to impeach Johnson, which the House have done, and the trial will soon take place. This conflict between the Congress and the Executive has been most unfortunate in hindering the reconstruction, but I do not think the demands of the Congress have been anything but just and liberal. I do not think any other conditions would have given us any guaranty for the future peace of the country.[45]

Samuel was to be in America for just over a year and a half before traveling again. He returned from his trip with Erny in the fall of 1866 and was preparing for another trip in the summer of 1868. This time it would be with Henry Longfellow's family and Samuel would be taking care of the arrangements as they traveled.

Notes:

[1] Longfellow, Ernest Wadsworth. *Random Memories*. Cambridge: The Riverside Press, 1922. preface.

[2] Ibid., p. 96.

[3] Ibid., p. 96-97.

[4] Ibid., p. 101.

[5] Ibid., p. 97.

[6] Ibid., p. 101.

[7] Ibid., p. 101-102.

[8] Ibid., p. 103.

[9] Ibid., p. 103-104.

[10] Letter Samuel Longfellow to Alice Longfellow Pierce, November 14, 1865. SLP, LNHS.

[11] Longfellow, Ernest Wadsworth. *Random Memories*. p. 104-105.

[12] Letter, Samuel Longfellow to Alice Longfellow Pierce, November 14, 1865. SLP, LNHS.

[13] Longfellow, Ernest Wadsworth. *Random Memories*. p. 106-107.

[14] Ibid.

[15] Ibid., p. 110.

[16] Ibid., p. 109.

[17] Ibid., p. 118.

[18] Sargent, Mrs. John T. *Sketches And Reminiscences of the Radical Club of Chestnut Street, Boston.* Boston: James R. Osgood and Company, 1880.

[19] Longfellow, Samuel. "Letter from Paris." *The Radical.* January 1866. p. 304-310. Boston. Sidney H. Morse, Editor.

[20] Longfellow, Ernest Wadsworth. *Random Memories.* p. 120-121.

[21] Ibid., p. 122.

[22] Ibid., p. 121.

[23] Ibid., p. 120-121.

[24] "Building of a Ship" by John Rollin Tilton, ca. 1851, *Maine Memory Network, Maine's Online Museum http://www.mainememory.net/bin/Detail?ln=18699.* Maine Historical Society, 489 Congress Street, Portland, ME.

[25] Longfellow, Ernest Wadsworth. *Random Memories.* p. 125.

[26] Letter, Samuel Longfellow to Samuel Johnson, May 20, 1866. SLP, LNHS.

[27] Ibid.

[28] Longfellow, Ernest Wadsworth. *Random Memories.* p. 128.

[29] Ibid.

[30] Ibid., p. 142.

[31] Ibid., p. 151.

[32] Ibid., p. 152.

[33] Ibid.

[34] Ibid.

[35] Ibid., p. 155.

[36] Ibid.

[37] Ibid., p. 156.

[38] Ibid.

[39] Ibid., p. 156-157.

[40] Letter, Samuel Longfellow to Samuel Johnson, November 7, 1867. SLP, LNHS.

[41] May, Joseph, Ed.. *Samuel Longfellow.* Cambridge: The Riverside Press, 1894. p. 243-244.

[42] Letter, Samuel Longfellow to Samuel Wyllys Dabney, February 26, 1868. ADF.

[43] Ibid.

[44] Letter, Samuel Longfellow to Samuel Johnson, November 7, 1867. SLP, LNHS.

[45] Letter, Samuel Longfellow to Samuel Wyllys Dabney, February 26, 1868. ADF.

CHAPTER 18 – THE TOUR GUIDE

In June 1868, Samuel and several other members of the Long-fellow family sailed for Europe on a "Grand Tour." The traveling party consisted of Henry Wadsworth Longfellow; Erny Longfellow and his new wife Harriet (Hattie) Spelman Longfellow (this was their wedding trip); Henry's daughters Alice, Edith and Anne Allegra; Thomas Gold Appleton, Fanny's oldest sibling; Henry and Samuel's sisters Anne Longfellow Pierce and Mary Longfellow Greenleaf; and, of course Samuel Longfellow. Henry's oldest child Charles Longfellow had sailed over with the group, but then left to travel on his own.

Samuel ended up with the unenviable task of taking care of the organizational aspects of the trip. He was responsible for taking care of the transportation, lodging, sightseeing and other practical details, but this time he wouldn't have a revolution or war to contend with.

> The duty of directing the movements of the party and managing its business was confided to his somewhat unpractical, although experienced hands. His absent-mindedness and absorption in the beautiful or interesting scenes through which they passed led to some amusing misadventures. The number of umbrellas left resting against the trees of Switzerland, after he had concluded hasty sketches of its scenery, became a standing jest among his companions. But his enthusiasms surrounded all their way with a romantic charm, and to the younger travelers their journey became an education in history, art, and literature. The associations of each place visited were made vivid by his own eager interest and his familiarity with them, and the pains and skill with which he arranged the details of the tour to give them full and even dramatic effect.[1]

With a group this large, it was difficult to accomplish some things. There were days when Henry and a couple of others went one way and Samuel another, and days when Erny and his new bride decided they wanted some privacy, but there were times when they were all together in search of a place to stay. This could be difficult and created problems for Samuel. Erny mentions one place they stayed where they "so completely filled the little place that nobody else could get in, much to the disgust of some English people, who loudly proclaimed their contempt for American tourists."[2]

They landed in Liverpool and began their travels to several places that Samuel thought of interest. They went through the Lake Country and visited the home of Wordsworth, as he had done with Charles Appleton in 1851, but this time they arrived at the front door.

> His interest was not only in the romantic and picturesque, but still more in present human concerns. Everywhere he had friendly chats with the peasant people, with the old vergers in cathedrals, and with innumerable young men and boys.[3]

Conversely, Henry had specific interests and did not enjoy the typical tourist fare. In addition, his time was limited by the various invitations he received and the people he had meetings with. Samuel mentions Henry's tourism preferences in the biography of his brother. Henry's fame as a poet preceded him and he found himself meeting some of the most important people in England. Erny said that his father "received much attention and hospitality in different parts of England and often went with my two sisters to visit where the rest of us were naturally not expected.[4] Frank Preston Stearns in *Cambridge Sketches* summed up Henry's visit to England in one sentence: "In fact their tour was like a triumphal procession."[5]

Stearns also described how Henry was received and his avoidance of publicity, a characteristic shared by Samuel.

> Longfellow was everywhere treated with the distinction of a famous poet and his fine appearance and dignified bearing increased the reputation which had already preceded.

***

Longfellow, however, hated lionizing in all its forms, and he avoided ceremonious receptions as much as possible. He enjoyed the entertainment of meeting distinguished people, but he evidently preferred to meet them in an unconventional manner, and to have them as much to himself as possible. Princes and savants called on him, but he declined every invitation that might tend to give him publicity.[6]

Henry Longfellow met a lot of Britain's most famous, but almost all in circumstances that minimized the publicity he would receive. Two places where he did receive public acclaim, however, were at Cambridge and Oxford where he received honorary degrees. Samuel records some of the people Henry met with after they arrived in London, where they stayed in the Langham Hotel.

Immediately a flood of hospitality flowed in upon him, – calls, cards, invitations, letters of welcome. He breakfasted with Mr. Gladstone, Sir Henry Holland, The Duke of Argyll; lunched with Lord John Russell at Richmond, dined with various hosts, received midnight calls from Bulwer and Aubrey de Vere.[7]

Henry also met with Dean Stanley at Westminster Abbey and the Archbishop of Canterbury and spent a weekend with Dickens at Gads' Hill. The most important person whom he met with was Queen Victoria. Both Samuel and Erny describe this event.

Through Lady Augusta Stanley came an intimation that the Queen would be sorry to have Mr. Longfellow pass through England without her meeting him, and a day was named for his visit to Windsor. The Queen received him cordially and without ceremony in one of the galleries of the Castle. He also called by request, upon the Prince of Wales.[8]

***

Queen Victoria sent for my father, and he went with Lady Stanley, the wife of Dean Stanley to the Palace. They waited in a hall till the Queen came in; my father was presented and they had a pleasant chat, then the queen withdrew. It was not like some of the weird tales imaginative writers have conjured up.[9]

After two weeks in London, the whole family went to the Isle of Wight and had a "pleasant visit" with Alfred, Lord Tennyson, Poet Laureate of England. Frank Stearns in *Cambridge Sketches* mentions how this meeting between the two great poets was viewed.

His meeting with Tennyson was considered as important as the visit of the King of Prussia to Napoleon III, and much less dangerous to the peace of Europe. It was talked of from Edinburgh to Rome.[10]

In a letter to Samuel Johnson, Samuel Longfellow gives a long description of the meeting between his brother Henry and Tennyson. It is worthwhile including it almost in its entirety.

The house is so ugly, architecturally, that I have not been able to make up my mind to buy a photograph of it. Indoors it is roomy, homely, old fashioned & as "careless-ordered" as the garden. We passed through a vestibule, a hall with casts of Elgin marbles and a relief by Michael Angelo on the walls and boxes of minerals lying round; through a staircase-entry with a bust of Dante; a medallion head of Carlyle, & numerous framed photographic portraits through a sitting room with books & pictures into a large drawing-room lighted by a great bay--window outside of which on the lawn stands an ivy-clambered elm. There were tables covered with books & on the walls engravings, among them Michael Angelo's Prophets & Sybils from the Sistine Chapel. Mrs. Tennyson received us quietly & cordially: a woman about fifty with a delicate invalid look, a tranquil face & manner & great sweetness of expression &

voice; dressed in black with something white on the back of her head. We fell into conversation & to my surprise she express-ed some timidities as to the result of the enlargement of the franchise here (the new elections are soon to take place). "We should have preferred," she said, "that education should have preceded." It made me think of the old proslavery argument. Here no mere anticipation ever would have done. Education will go hand in hand with enfranchisement. Then she asked me to go out in the garden where Tennyson was smoking with the gentlemen (H.W.L. having preceded us). She showed me through a study (filled up with books where the boys get their lessons) & out of its open window upon the lawn where sat T. with a short pipe in his mouth & a long wooden bowl of tobacco at his side, under the shadow of a large clump of trees & shrubbery. He wore spectacles & a high-crowned, broad-brimmed felt hat, looking just as when we saw him & speaking in the same deep voice. There is something a little brusque not to say rough about his manner, yet kindly enough under it all. They were talking about spiritism, of which he seemed quite incredulous yet interested in hearing about it from Mr. Appleton (a believer) when some one said " I see you are bitten by it," he replied, "No, I wish I could be bitten by something; but I always stay in suspense neither believing nor unbelieving." We went in to lunch speaking of our going to the Rhine he said "I hate the Rhine. It is overrun with Cock-neys. We went to the Rhine; & there came on board two Life--Guardsmen; they fairly stunk of Windsor soap (Alfred said that, he was wrote Break, break, break!) and they washed their lily white hands in the drinking water, so that we had nothing to drink. I hate the Rhine!" After lunch, he showed us all round the garden and grounds, & out into the fields under "the brink of the noble down" – he said he used to walk on the down, but didn't much now; then up on the roof of the house to see the view, which is very lovely. Then he took part of us to drive upon the down to see the "needles." I went again at 7 in the evening to dine. His two boys were there, about 17 & 15. The oldest is named Hallam. I asked him if his name was also Arthur. He said no, & thought he was named from the father. The younger is Lionel, named from the Constellation Leo. Two very nice boys. During dinner the door bell rang; & T. exclaimed "who's that ringing the bell? Some wretched Cockney I'm sure it is." He seems to have perfect mania on the subject of Cockneys. He is building a house in Suffolk to get out of their way. After dinner we went into the drawing room where the fruit was served, with wines & coffee. T. said some pleasant things about waterfalls, describing beautifully some that he had seen. Then he asked us to go up into his den, which is at the top of the house under the roof, with dormer windows, full of books. On the table I noticed a large volume of Lucretius & a new translation of the Psalms. I told him that I tried in London to hear his friend Maurice. He said he had never heard him preach; but one Sunday when he was staying with them he had read the service with great feeling –"the only time," he added, "that he had ever heard it read with any." "And think," said he, "of their turning that man out of his college because he didn't believe in eternal hell! That's putting the Devil on the throne of the universe! The clergyman here preaches it. I never go to church. I used to go sometimes in the afternoon; but hearing that the clergyman said I never went, I left off going. I couldn't tolerate it. They gabble off the prayers & the sermons are such nonsense." He went on to say that there was a great shaking of the church & of Christianity in these days. My brother remarking that the essentials of Christianity would remain unshaken; he said, "I don't know – the great central idea of Christianity seems to be that a God descended on earth to redeem man – that's what all the churches teach, except the Unitarians." "And yet," he added, "I can't quite take Renan, with his talk about 'ce charmant philosophe'." The conversation turning to verse, I spoke of his "Daisy" & its peculiar and exquisite metre. He seemed pleased & said he had prided himself on the invention of a new metre, but none of the critics had ever noticed it, except to say that he had written a poem called the "Daisy" much inferior to one by Burns on the same subject (!!). Then he said, "Can you read Boadicea?" and got the book; we declining, he began to read it through in the most astonishing sort of high-pitched chant, half guttural, half nasal. It was almost ludicrous, yet brought out the metre of the poem well. His boys then came up to say good night, & kissed their father. And after a time we took our leave, T. himself lighting us out over the lawn & through the shrubbery to the land, with a candle in his hand like a glow-worm.[11]

From the Isle of Wight, the travelers went to Dover and then across the channel to continental Europe. They then went to the Rhine and traveled up it to Switzerland where they spent the summer. The honeymooners Erny and his wife had left London early and gone to Paris, Brussels and Antwerp and joined the others on the Rhine at Cologne. In the mountains and valleys, both Samuel and Henry relived memories from their earlier trips. They also were able to take the others to places that were referred to in Henry's poetry. As summer moved to fall, the traveling party turned north to Paris.

Samuel showed his charges around Paris, visiting galleries, museums and sights of interest that he remembered with pleasure from his earlier trips. Henry "was most interested in hearing Molière at the Théâtre Français, in explaining what remained of the old localities of literary history, or in haunting the booksellers and the stalls of the *quais*."[12] Erny spent the time in Paris practicing drawing at his old atelier, now run by the artist Bonnat, as well as copying in the Louvre. Erny returned to Paris once again in 1876 and studied with Couture.

Fall came to an end and the travelers headed south to Arles and then east by carriage along the Cornice road to Italy. They stopped off in Genoa and then went on to Florence. They stayed there a few weeks, saw the galleries and churches and the Arno. After enjoying the sights of Florence, they went on to Rome where they stayed for the winter in the Hotel Castanzi. Samuel must have worked his magic in finding hotels with a view because the Castanzi had a view over the whole city with the dome of St. Peter's in the background. Samuel says that in Rome,

> Mr. Longfellow became for the season the centre of the group of American visitors and resident artists, whose well-
> -known names need not be recounted. Here he made, also

acquaintances among the Italians, – especially the Duke of Sermoneta, the Dantean scholar, and Monsignore Nardi, of the papal court.[13]

Samuel took the group around to the museums, galleries and historical sites. This was something that Samuel enjoyed doing, but Henry did not have quite the same interest. In his biography of Henry, Samuel talks about his brother's style of tourism.

> To "see Rome," as all travelers know, is a work for many months; and it was pursued with tolerable diligence. But Mr. Longfellow was never a good sight-seer. He was impatient of lingering in picture-galleries, churches, or ruins. He saw quickly the essential points, and soon tired of any minuter examination.[14] [*Henry Wadsworth Longfellow, v. II,* p. 447.]

The group also got involved with the American and English expatriate communities. At Christmas they enjoyed all the ceremonies and services of the season and attended other festivities of the communities during their stay. Someone who became involved with the group in an interesting manner was George P.A. Healy, the internationally famous portraitist who produced portraits of American Presidents and other important figures in the U. S. and abroad.

One night Henry and Healy went to visit Franz Liszt, who was staying in an abandoned convent in the Forum. Liszt opened the door of his apartment holding only a candle and Henry was so taken by the appearance of the illuminated figure that he asked Healy to put it on canvas. The painting now hangs in the library of the Craigie House. A few days later Liszt invited a number of the family during a morning visit[15] and he "delighted the party with a performance upon his Chickering piano-forte."[16] Liszt later set the introduction of the "Golden Legend" to music. Healy also painted a life-size portrait of Henry and his daughter Edith, as well as "a small picture with them both standing beneath the Arch of Titus."[17]

From Rome the family traveled south to Naples and the surrounding area, Monte Cassino, Amalfi and Sorrento. They then headed north again to Venice, the last stop in Italy. They went over the Brenner Pass to Innsbruck, Munich, Nuremberg and Dresden, followed by Switzerland and a return to Paris. The final stage of their trip was back to London and after a few days there they went north to Scotland. There they went to Edinburgh and the Scottish lakes and they visited the areas identified in *Rob Roy* and *The Lady of the Lake.*

The European tour of the Longfellow family and Thomas Gold Appleton came to an end. They sailed back to America where they arrived in September 1869 and Samuel was not to return to Europe for another twenty years.

Notes:

[1] May, Joseph, Ed.. *Samuel Longfellow.* Cambridge: The Riverside Press, 1894. p. 230-231.

[2] Longfellow, Ernest Wadsworth. *Random Memories.* Cambridge: The Riverside Press, 1922. p. 165.

[3] May, Joseph, Ed.. *Samuel Longfellow.* p. 232.

[4] Longfellow, Ernest Wadsworth. *Random Memories.* p. 165.

[5] Stearns, Frank Preston. *Cambridge Sketches.* Philadelphia: J.B. Lippincott Company, 1905. p. 34.

[6] Ibid.

[7] Longfellow, Samuel, Ed. *Henry Wadsworth Longfellow, Vol. II.* Boston: Ticknor and Company, 1886. p. 443.

[8] Ibid., p. 443-444.

[9] Longfellow, Ernest Wadsworth. *Random Memories.* p. 166.

[10] Stearns, Frank Preston. *Cambridge Sketches.* p. 34.

[11] Letter, Samuel Longfellow to Samuel Johnson, July 23, 1868. SLP, LNHS.

[12] Longfellow, Samuel. *Henry Wadsworth Longfellow, Vol. II.* p. 447.

[13] Ibid.

[14] Ibid., p. 447.

[15] Longfellow, Ernest Wadsworth. *Random Memories.* p. 173.

[16] Longfellow, Samuel. *Henry Wadsworth Longfellow, Vol. II.* p. 447.

[17] Longfellow, Ernest Wadsworth. *Random Memories.* p. 173.

CHAPTER 19 – CAMBRIDGE YEARS

When Samuel gave up his position at the Second Unitarian Church of Brooklyn in 1860, it was as if he retired from ever being a preacher in a Unitarian Society again. His first activity after leaving Brooklyn was a European trip with Samuel Johnson. Samuel Longfellow hoped to improve his health, and during the trip the two friends wrote a new hymnal. However, when he returned he still was not in very good health, and the "not infrequent suffering to which he was now liable constituted a practical condition which was nearly insuperable."[1] During this period he established a permanent base in the Craigie House with his brother Henry and his family, although he sometimes he had a room elsewhere in the Cambridge area.

Samuel also had trouble finding a Unitarian society that would accept him on a full-time basis. His religious philosophy had progressed beyond the point that these churches had reached and it was important to him to be able to stick with his theological principles. On the other hand, he was welcomed for temporary preaching in the very few very liberal Unitarian churches. However, these were generally weak and hardly able to keep going.

> His convictions and sympathies were deeply with those who believed that, in the interest of religious feeling not less than of mental independence, organized religious should be released from all theological restrictions and implications; that no doctrinal restrictions and implications; that no doctrinal test, even the slightest and most remote, should be suggested by the relation of church-membership.[2]

As a result, of his very liberal beliefs, he was essentially limited to temporary assignments or periodic requests for a substitute preacher, maybe for only a single Sunday. One church where he was more welcome than others was the church in Newburyport, where his friend Higginson, as well as other "progressive" ministers had preached. As mentioned previously, in between his trip to Europe with Erny and that with the family, Samuel preached in the 28th Congregational Society of Boston, which Theodore Parker had organized. Samuel enjoyed the freedom he had in that pulpit to preach what he wanted and in 1873 returned there to speak at the dedication of their new home, the Parker Fraternity Hall.[3]

His life took this direction for several years. However, his preaching was not limited to pulpits in the Boston area, but extended to "many Unitarian churches of New England and of the West and South,"[4]

Once Samuel was invited to a new liberal church in Montclair, New Jersey, and after he finished there, he took the opportunity to visit some of his old friends in Brooklyn.[5] After New Jersey, he said, "I had so much vacation from preaching during the winter that I felt I ought to avail myself of the opposite duty."[6] As a result he accepted an offer to go to Milwaukee, Wisconsin, where he stayed almost two months. He found it an attractive place with trees and nice houses where he could relax next to Lake Superior, "as good as the sea to look at and gives as cool breezes only there is no salt in them.[7]

One of the more interesting places Samuel went to preach was Baraboo, Wisconsin, about 100 miles northwest of Milwaukee. The radical preacher, who was not feeling well, Frederick May Holland (who wrote a biography of Frederick Douglass), invited him. Holland said that the society had always been radical and had nearly 100 families and that Samuel "would be free here too. We have no church, organization ceremonies or traditions & but a nominal connection with the A[merican] U[nitarian] A[ssociation]."[8] It is an area of hills and rocky bluffs on the Baraboo River and near Devils Lake, the type of area Samuel enjoyed.

> The evening of my arrival walking thro' the village it looked rather forlorn & I "doubted the wisdom" of having come. But soon I began to feel at home & have liked being here very

much. The charm of Baraboo is the woods & hills close in to which it is built. There are pleasant walks in plenty; and the "trees of ages" do "Nod" – or do something better. There is a Lake only three miles off, reached by train, where I have twice been, & found very fine cliffs & pine trees high overhanging the water.[9]

During his stay he was able to take some time off for "excursions." Once he went to "St. Paul to see the Mississippi and Minnehaha rivers," a 24-hour trip "in the steamboat."

Samuel liked the people in his society and they were "accustomed to pretty radical preaching." Samuel spent about three months there, and left around the end of July, 1874 with pleasant memories.

The weeks have slipped by very pleasantly, and the preaching has been to appreciative people accustomed from the first to liberal gospel.[11]

He also had some experiences in the pulpit he had not had before. One was during an invitation to speak at the Presbyterian Church in a series of talks by different ministers. His topic was on Temperance.

Some people liked it & some people didn't, as you will understand, when I say that I took this ground: Abstinence not a duty though often an expedience. Temperance a duty always & in all things.

Do you know that I never gave A Temperance lecture before! And had to write this. Well, I hope it did some good.[12]

After his western trip, Samuel returned to Cambridge and continued taking pulpits temporarily for varying periods. This went on until 1878 when he accepted his final permanent pulpit in Germantown, Pennsylvania.

Throughout his career, Samuel was greatly concerned with the radical movements of the period. Among the organizations he was involved with was the Radical Club, which was formed in the spring of 1867. It focused on greater freedom in religious thought and fellowship and was somewhat like the Transcendentalist movement that had been strong earlier in the century. The Radical Club accepted people from all religious denominations and had very little strict organization. The first meeting had thirty persons and its future meetings were dedicated to "theological and religious questions". The Club's journal was *The Radical*, edited by second generation Transcendentalist Sidney H. Morse. Samuel contributed articles containing "some of his maturest thoughts."[13] Samuel Longfellow also attended some of their meetings and was often a speaker at the group's meetings.[14] One of his papers in *The Radical* was "The Idea of Law" and was included in the history of the club, one that talked about religion and theology in the French capital was called "Letter from Paris" (January, 1866), and another written in 1868 on Europe entitled "Liberal Religion in Europe."[15]

> The fullest utterances of Mr. Longfellow on religious thought may be found in his various contributions to "The Radical" in the days when that free-spoken magazine was in existence.[16]

Those ministers who did not find that the American Unitarian Association (AUA) reflected their views provided support for the free religion movement in the Unitarian Churches. This movement began to grow over the years, however, most society members were not in favor of this radical concept and the liberal and conservative groups tried to reach a compromise. Even though Samuel supported the philosophy advocated by the more liberal ministers, he had some problems with their saying that what they were doing was not religion – it was the more conservative ministers who were doing something else.

> By the way, I don't like the phrases "Free Religionist," "Free Religion." Isn't religious and religion enough – or universal religion?[17]

Many "progressives" were not happy with some of the concessions that were being made and decided to form their own

Association, and on May 30, 1867, the Free Religious Association (FRA) was created with Octavius Brooks Frothingham as president. Their publication was *The Index*, edited by Francis E. Abbott, a Unitarian minister and one of the FRA's founders. Among the members were Ralph Waldo Emerson, Cyrus Bartol, Louisa May Alcott, Thomas Wentworth Higginson, James Freeman Clarke, Julia Ward Howe, John Weiss and Ednah D. Cheney.

As mentioned in other sections of this book, Samuel did not like belonging to groups. This is best signified by his lack of active participation, other than speaking and writing, with two groups whose religious philosophy was very close to his own – The Radical Club and The Free Religious Association. Although he was a member of the AUA, Samuel was not active in it. He primarily used it to arrange for pulpits where he could preach, either in churches with no permanent minister or as a substitute for permanent ministers. Nevertheless, he eventually tired of its stances and submitted his resignation.

> When I read the report of the AUA meeting in Boston, I wrote to have my name taken off the "list." I hope many others have done the same.[18]

As a result, he may not have been as effective as he could have been in making his theological thoughts known, and could have had greater influence in the direction the FRA and radical theology progressed. Oscar Fay Adams points this out.

> I cannot help feeling that this aversion to organized methods, to all species of formalism, resulted in loss to him in some sense, however little he may have realized it. He May not have needed the help which such things can sometimes afford; he seems to have been quite able to do without such help; but many of us are not thus gifted, and this he may not have fully apprehended. Standing where he did, so far removed from religious formalism, he failed, I think, to see the beauty of any form.[19]

The FRA gradually lost membership and, as the American Unitarian Conference puts it, the "Free Religious Association eventually fizzled out."[20]

However, the FRA and Samuel both had their effect on societies and the way the Unitarian Church developed. At their 1869 meeting in Boston, there were presentations by an orthodox Christian, a non-Christian, an anti-Christian and a Jew. This demonstrates that the FRA had "no creed to propagate, differing very much in their belief, but all seeking after the truth."[21] A few years later Samuel Johnson was working on his series of books on oriental religions, his contribution to knowledge about the basis of religions, for which Samuel Longfellow provided moral support and encouragement. One time Johnson told Longfellow, a Theist, that he had met with Felix Adler, a Jewish Radical who was working on essays on Hebrew Theism,[22] Adler's father Samuel Adler was important in establishing Reform Judaism in the United States.

Samuel Longfellow's writings from the Radical Club and the Free Radical Association continued to have effects into the 20th century. An example is a woman who became a Theosophist after a religious search that began in her childhood.

> Then came, long afterwards of course, when I was about fourteen, the teachings of the Rev. Samuel Longfellow, a brother of the poet. Of him it was said that while Henry Longfellow was made a poet, Samuel was born one, and also it was said that he was good enough to be a saint and interesting enough to be a sinner. He was certainly a mystic, and his teachings were like those of all the mystics, – but another term for Theology.[23]

Simultaneously with the development of radical religious ideas in the 19th century, radical social ideas and ideals also developed. Again, Samuel was not one of the prime movers, but he was a highly respected supporter of new or modified ideas who had influence on the direction things moved.

The principles of the Universal Peace Union (UPU) was in keeping with Samuel's beliefs about peace he advocated at the beginning of the Civil War: war should not break peace for any reason.[24] The UPU was formed just after the Civil War as a reaction against the American Peace Society's compromises during the War.

> The UPU labored to remove the causes of war, to discountenance all resorts to deadly force... They tolerated no compromise with the principles of love and nonviolence... The UPU denounced imperialism, compulsory, military training, memorials and war demonstrations, war taxes, capital punishment, the spread of white imperialism in Africa, the exclusion of Asian immigration and the continued denial of rights to native Americans.[25]

The UPU was in advance of its time in that it accepted women to participate in the organization on an equal basis with men. In 1887-1888, Samuel Longfellow was one of the many vice--presidents of the UPU.

Other reforms during this period addressed the economic aspect of living in America. Most of the socio-economic reform movements in America had their origin in Socialism, Communism and Fourierism that originated in Europe. In New England the Transcendentalists were involved with the development of the utopian Brook Farm community. It was in existence from 1841-1847 and based on the socialistic system of Frenchman Charles Fourier, which advocated the development of small communal groups.

Another utopian community was Fruitlands, which Samuel's friend A. Bronson Alcott helped found because Brook Farm was not pure enough in the way it functioned. Fruitlands was located about 15 miles west of Concord and composed of a spiritual elite and was a place for people to realize their potential. Because of their philosophy regarding capital, work and not using animals, many chose spiritual living over the practical needs of the community. As a result, it was unable to support itself and gradually fell apart after about six months. Members began to leave, but their basic beliefs remained for most of them, including Alcott.

Samuel knew several of the people involved with Brook Farm and Fruitlands and they, as well as Samuel, continued to agree with the position of Fourierism, even after the two communities closed. In a profile of Walt Whitman, The Religious Archives Network states that "Brooklyn was at various times home to Fourierist reformers such as [William Henry] Channing, [Samuel] Longfellow, Isaac Hopper's dear friend Lydia Maria Child, and the Quaker philanthropist Marcus Spring."[26] Almost two decades later, Samuel Longfellow sent a letter to Samuel Johnson supporting the same ideas he published in an article.

> I have read your article in the *Radical* with the greatest satisfaction. It is most timely and valuable and I wish it might be taken to heart. You protest against the narrow & exclusive definition of labor, against the idea of class, against the assumed antagonism of capital against revolutionary & loose notions of property, against the perils of politician & party management of their questions. Your suggestions of the higher & truer aims & methods all seem to be admirable.[27]

Samuel's interests were not limited to just religious organizations, but extended to what was going on in the Cambridge community. After the Civil War, communities around the country started to establish social unions. Their purpose was to provide a space where the underprivileged local youth could enjoy a variety of activities and receive support for their moral and intellectual improvement.

The Cambridge Social Union was created in January 1871 and Samuel Longfellow was one of its founders. He also participated as a member regardless of his feelings about working with groups. In 1889, the Social Union had raised enough money to build a multipurpose space to be known as Brattle Hall, just down the street from the Craigie House. The architect was Samuel's nephew Alexander Wadsworth Longfellow, Jr. and his niece Alice Mary Longfellow later performed on the Brattle Hall stage.[28]

Samuel actively worked with the youth at the Social Union, but he also spent time with the University students, providing assistance and friendship as requested. Joseph May provides a description of Samuel's work with the youth in Cambridge.

> The interest which Mr. Longfellow felt for whatever concerned his young relatives extended to all other youth whom he could reach. In Cambridge he always had a large acquaintance among the students of the college, visiting them in their rooms, bringing them about him in his own, and, with an attraction which seemed magnetic, enlisting their affection and opening avenues of kindly and helpful influence over them. He attended many courses of lectures in the University and it was felt that much of his pleasure in them was derived from the society of the young men whom he thus met. Among the less fortunate youth of the town he was also widely known and trusted. He actively interested himself in the Cambridge "Social Union," an organization for the benefit of young men and boys, and was its vice-president and president, until obliged by increasing age to retire. The "Boys' Aid Club" made him an honorary member, and he went to their meetings, helping them with advice and practical assistance in their plans. "He could pass no boy in the street without some token of kindness, If it was only a touch of the hand as he went by." Once, on a certain field, which was his property, a group of boys had gathered for a game of ball. Seeing him coming they began to run away. But he beckoned to them, and succeeded in inducing them to come to him, when he explained that he was glad to see them in his field, and was willing they should play there as much as they pleased, an announcement which was received with hearty gratitude. At one time, when he lived near a boys' school, he was approached by neighbors for his signature to a petition that the noise they made should be suppressed. "But I *like* their noise," he replied.[29]

When the Cambridge Hospital was dedicated in 1886, Samuel considered it a noteworthy event and wrote a hymn for the dedication.

HYMN

Written for the dedication of the Cambridge Hospital.

Thou Lord of life, our saving Health
    Who mak'st Thy suffering once our care
Our gifts are still our truest wealth,
    To serve Thee our sincerest prayer

As on the river's rising tide
    Flow strength and coolness from the sea,
So, through the ways our hands provide,
    May quickening life flow in from thee, –

To heal the wound, to still the pain,
    And strength to failing pulses bring,
Till the lame feet shall leap again
    And the parched lips with gladness sing.

Bless Thou the gifts our hands have brought!
    Bless Thou the work our hearts have planned!
Ours is the hope, the will, the thought;
    The rest, O God, is in Thy hand!

This was not the only hymn that Samuel wrote during this period of his life. In 1876, he was preparing a new hymnal by himself. This one was meant for the smaller, radical Unitarian societies that did not have funds to purchase expensive books. In a letter to Samuel Johnson, Sam Longfellow describes the preparation of his new book.

I hope you will like the new *Hymns & Tunes* of which I sent you some copies, one with your name in it. And I hope you (and Osgood) will not think I have drawn too largely from the *Hymns of the Spirit*, which I by no means desire that this should supersede. I had in view the small radical societies who want an inexpensive book (those in "1/2 cloth" are put, in quantities, at 50 cents) & congregational singing. I am sure you will like many of the new hymns, & wish they could be put into a new edition of H.S. This new book, however, will not enable me to buy the old, at least at present. The first edition of 500 will not quite pay its own cost. I had not idea how expensive it was to alter old plates. On that account I left in, some of the old hymns which are not choice, tho' not objectionable.

And you have no idea how transferring the tunes are, both to the selection & arrangement of the hymns. Consider only, the necessity of having at least two, & perhaps three or four consecutive hymns of the same metre. This will account for some incoherences.[30]

While Samuel was preaching in various pulpits, preparing articles or speeches and working with the Cambridge community, he still had sufficient time to get involved in other activities.

Although he was unmethodical in his habits, [he] had the art of filling his days with intellectual activities and refined amusements, with quiet philanthropies and kindly services of many sorts.[31]

Samuel's lighter interests included music, literature and art. His favorite pastime was music, which was basically limited to listening and studying since he had "mastered no instruments."[32] He took every opportunity to go to Symphony concerts and was exceptionally well-informed about the works. His favorite composer was Beethoven and, naturally, his knowledge about the maestro's works was greater than that of other composers.

Literature was unquestionably Samuel's most constant companion, whether it was his own or other persons. In addition to Literature in English, he also read books in modern European Languages. Poetry was of special interest to Samuel, "and whatever it was beautiful in many literatures was familiar to him."[33] Through his reading, he kept himself well-informed about the arts and sciences.

Samuel was very much involved with Henry's work, and even provided assistance in preparing the works for publication.

The relation of these brothers was one of the closest affection; a union of kindred spirits bound by happiest family ties, and by a perfect community of tastes and sentiments. It was the blessing of the group of children who had filled the rooms of the ancient dwelling in Portland that their mutual love was to persist unsevered, and to grow deeper throughout their lives.[34]

In two letters that Samuel wrote to Henry, he provides some suggestions and corrections to poems in progress that Henry sent him. From the casual character of Samuel's responses, it appears that this was a customary occurrence and comments are contained in a few future letters.

I think the added verse will be an improvement making a less abrupt close & 'linking together' the beginning & the end by the echoing line; not giving I think too much moralizing of your theme.

But the last line does not convey a clear thought to me. It may be my dullness. Whose soul with whose? What should you think of

Link together day and day?

or . . today and yesterday

. . tomorrow with today

But I should want to keep the "self-control".

In a recent number of the Fortnightly Review you will find an article on the pavement of the Cathedral of Siena, with some reference to Dante.[35]

I send some verses which may serve your purpose – if you have found nothing better – for the page which you wish to cancel. Do with them as you will

I find some errata on pages 12 & 13 Yungfrau, Tête Noir_ & Ghewmi.

I enclose a slip which may amuse you with its rather irreverent use of a line of yours.[36]

Samuel Longfellow's relationship with his brother Henry extended to the Craigie House children and to the children of his siblings. He had strong feelings toward his nieces and nephews and they happily returned it in kind. "He was adopted with equal warmth and trust by their companions, and to all, indiscriminately, became Uncle Sam."[37] He was a regular visitor to their schoolroom in the house, "sometimes aiding the discipline, quite as often disturbing it; and his own room was always a refuge for sad or rebellious scholars."[38]

During their summer holidays, groups of the young people took trips to the White Mountains or other vacation spots. Of course Samuel was always welcome to join them.

> He was completely one of us on our walks and drives and climbs, only occasionally moderating our exuberance when we went too far, and then making up for it by songs and poems full of fun, and jokes suited to the occasion. Perhaps we did not always quite remember the respect due him for the ministerial side was, at such times, far less prominent than the playful one.[39]

Samuel enjoyed art and was considered quite knowledgeable about it. Stearns in *Cambridge Sketches* says that Samuel "knew almost every picture in the galleries of Europe". On his trips to Europe he wrote letters that mentioned artists he met, mainly Americans, in Paris, Florence and Rome. In America, he also knew several artists, some of whom became well known. Among these were Stephen Van Schaik and Wyatt Eaton, who were both around twenty-years old when Samuel returned from the family trip to Europe. Although there are no letters in the archives from Samuel, it is very likely he communicated with both of them and provided his usual supportive remarks and advice.

Stephen Van Schaik studied at the National Academy of Design in New York City, as well as in Europe. In the Craigie House there is a copy of a renaissance painting with the dedication on the back, "copied by S.W. Van Schaik for S. Longfellow Florence 1875."

Wyatt Eaton also studied at the National Academy of Design and was friends with Van Schaik. He was a disciple of Millet and studied with other Barbizon artists. In 1878 Samuel wrote a Letter to Henry about a letter he had received from Eaton. Apparently Henry had not met Eaton, who was planning to paint his portrait.

> I received a letter today from a young friend of mine – Mr. Wyatt Eaton – who tells me that he has been commissioned by Messrs. Scribner & Co to paint for them the portraits of Whittier, Emerson & yourself. Whether the consent of these gentlemen is taken for granted I do not know. Or whether you will be willing to give your. But I write to say that I think you will like Mr. Eaton & find him simple, sincere & earnest. And if you can overcome your objections to sitting, it will be a great satisfaction to him, who quite has his heart in this plan. He sent me a photograph of his drawing of Bryant's head, which is striking & poetic.[40]

William Morris Hunt was an artist acquaintance of Samuel's who was a generation older than the two just mentioned. He studied with Millet, who became his friend, and brought his Barbizon style back to Boston with him. He was friends with the Longfellows and other friend of Samuel. He painted portraits of some of them including Charles Sumner and Louis Agassiz. In November 1872, the Great Boston fire was a disaster for Hunt when his studio was one of the 776 buildings that the fire destroyed. He lost all his own paintings plus his collection of works by other artists, including Millet.

Not all the art Samuel enjoyed was by individuals he knew. On July 4, 1876, the Boston Museum of Fine Arts opened its doors. It was one of the largest in the world, although it was in a different building than the current museum. It was a few months before Samuel went to see the new collection. While it did not overwhelm him, he did enjoy his walk through the collection.

The presidential election of 1876 was the most hotly contested up till that time. It also interested Samuel more than he previously had been. The Republican Party was associated with reconstruction of the south, which supported the Democratic Party. However, in the 1876 campaign, both parties looked to ending reconstruction. The Democratic candidate was Samuel J. Tilden who beat the Republican candidate Rutherford B. Hayes in the popular vote, but lost the presidency by one electoral vote. An exchange of letters between Samuel Longfellow and Samuel Johnson shows the opinions of two liberal New Englanders.

> I have been in the midst of the Political Campaign, witnessing torch-light processions & attending Republican meetings. There has been some good speaking. Blaine, Ingersoll, Pratt, Woodford, etc.; mainly given to arraignment of the Democratic party. For myself, you will readily believe, that I am not prepared to half put the Country into the hands of the Democrats for them to put it into the hands of ex-rebels & ex-slaveholders.[41]

> I confess nothing has so disgusted me as the conduct of the so-called Independents, and the persistent abuse of the President [Grant], who, in my judgment, would at this moment make a better man for the coming struggles than Hayes. I find that, on every point where he has been assailed, waiting for a fair verdict has convinced me that he was nearer right than his adversaries.[42]

Samuel also spent time visiting friends. In September 1874, he received an invitation from A. Bronson Alcott to come to visit him for dinner in Concord. Since Emerson, who also lived in Concord, was available, Alcott invited him too. Samuel and Alcott must have dined together other times since Samuel wrote a letter to Samuel Johnson describing a dinner he had with Alcott in early May 1875. He also mentions how Emerson had quietly helped Alcott financially because he was in debt and without a job.

> I remember you once expressed the will to visit us at Concord. Also that you missed L. Bartol's reading here in June last.
> And now that you have returned from the west, will you not oblige us on some day of this week.
> I am free from engagements after Tuesday till Saturday. Please name the day that you will come.
> Mr. Emerson tells me that he is to be at home all this week and will be most happy to meet you at dinner.[43]

Alcott, with whom I spent a day last week, told me that when he first went to Concord Emerson used to come to see him & on leaving would be seen to put his hand on the mantelpiece, where afterwards would be discovered a twenty-dollar bill! I had a pleasant visit, staying all night. Emerson came to tea & spent the evening; but we did not get on any very interior themes. I spoke to him of Alcott's "New Academy" at Concord; he said "our friends build castles in the air. However, if any thing should come of it, I shall be like a lamb in his hands & do whatever he commands of service."[44]

On a vacation to the Adirondacks in 1872 Samuel went to the residence of someone he had never met, but who had affected his life. He went to John Brown's farm and grave. He also went to the large rock with Brown's name carved on it and saw where John Brown had sat and read the Bible. Samuel left quietly and returned to where he was staying.[45]

In 1876, the United States celebrated its first centennial in Philadelphia. The Philadelphia Exhibition was organized to celebrate the event and was a great attraction. Samuel and other family members went to visit it in May 1876. He wrote a letter to Samuel Johnson about going to the Philadelphia Exhibition and indicates that he was still active with the Free Religious Association.

> I depart tomorrow, with a family party, to visit the Philadelphia Exhibition. Shall return to read something at the F.R.A. meeting June 2nd on the "Relation of Free Religion to the Churches," of which something I only know that it will be short.[46]

In September of 1876, Samuel returned to Philadelphia and indicated in a letter to Samuel Johnson that he was going to Bryn Mawr (Welsh for "big hill") and Germantown, where Dr. Furness preached. Samuel met people from the Germantown Unitarian Society and this may have led to his return the following year that ended up in his last permanent pastorship.

At Germantown you will see Ames. If I go, I expect to be in a place named Bryn-Mawr (Welsh I suppose) about half an hour's ride by steam from the Exhibition.[47]

Notes:

[1] May, Joseph, Ed. *Samuel Longfellow, Essays and Sermons.* Boston: The Riverside Press, 1894. p. 242.

[2] Ibid.

[3] Ibid., p. 243-244.

[4] Ibid., p. 243.

[5] Letter, Samuel Longfellow to Samuel Johnson, December 9, 1869.SLP, LNHS.

[6] Letter, Samuel Longfellow to Samuel Johnson, June 20, 1870. SLP, LNHS.

[7] Ibid.

[8] Letter, Frederick Holland to Samuel Longfellow, April 30, 1874. SLP, LNHS.

[9] Letter, Samuel Longfellow to Samuel Johnson, June 19, 1874. SLP, LNHS.

[10] Ibid.

[11] Letter, Samuel Longfellow to Samuel Johnson, July 27, 1874. SLP, LNHS.

[12] Letter, Samuel Longfellow to Samuel Johnson, June 19, 1874. SLP, LNHS.

[13] May, Joseph, Ed.. *Samuel Longfellow: Memoir and Letters.* p. 244.

[14] Ibid.

[15] *The Radical.* Boston. Sidney H. Morse, Editor.

[16] Adams, Oscar Fay. "Samuel Longfellow." *The New England Magazine*, October 1894, v. 17, n.° 2, p. 205-213. Boston. p. 212.

[17] Letter, Samuel Longfellow to Samuel Johnson, December 9, 1869. SLP, LNHS.

[18] Letter, Samuel Longfellow to Samuel Johnson, June 19, 1874. SLP, LNHS.

[19] Adams, Oscar Fay. "Samuel Longfellow." Boston. p. 212.

[20] "The Free Religion Movement in Unitariansim: Opening the way for Non-Christians." American Unitarian Conference. www.americanunitarian.org/.

[21] "Boston Religious Anniversaries." *The New-York Herald.* May 28, 1869. New York.

[22] Letter, Samuel Johnson to Samuel Longfellow, March 1, 1876. Samuel Longfellow, *Lectures, Essays, and Sermons by Samuel Johnson.*

[23] Hilliard, Katherine. "Why I Became a Thesophist." *The Theosophical Quarterly.* July 1909, p. 59-61. New York. Blavatsky Archives.

[24] Letter, Samuel Longfellow to R.H. Manning, October 1861. SLP, LNHS.

[25] Swarthmore College Peace Collection. "Universal Peace Union." Swarthmore, PA: Swarthmore College, nd.

[26] Religious Archives Network. "Review of *Walt Whitman* by Mitchell Santine Gould." Chicago: Chicago Theological Seminary, available at www.lgbtran.org/index.aspx, www.lgbtran.org//index.aspx 2005.

[27] Letter, Samuel Longfellow to Samuel Johnson, October 27, 1871.SLP, LNHS.

[28] Engstrom, John. "100 Years of the Brattle" *Brattle Film Foundation.* 2001. Cambridge. Brattle Film Foundation (find at www.brattlefilm.org/brattlefilm/first100.htmlwww.brattlefilm. .org/brattlefilm/first100.html).

[29] May, Joseph, Ed.. *Samuel Longfellow.* p. 249-250.

[30] Letter, Samuel Longfellow to Samuel Johnson, May 15, 1876. SLP, LNHS.

[31] May, Joseph, Ed.. *Samuel Longfellow.* p. 244.

[32] Ibid., p. 245.

[33] Ibid., p. 246.

[34] Ibid.

[35] Letter, Samuel Longfellow to Henry W. Longfellow, September 30, 1875. LP.

[36] Letter, Samuel Longfellow to Henry W. Longfellow, September 27, 1877. LP.

[37] May, Joseph, Ed.. *Samuel Longfellow.* p. 247.

[38] Ibid.

[39] Ibid.

[40] Letter, Samuel Longfellow to Henry W. Longfellow, June 28, 1878. LP.

[41] Letter, Samuel Longfellow to Samuel Johnson, September 12, 1876. SLP, LNHS.

[42] Letter, Samuel Johnson to Samuel Longfellow, September 17, 1876. Samuel Longfellow, *Lectures, Essays, and Sermons by Samuel Johnson.*

[43] Letter, A. Bronson Alcott to Samuel Longfellow, September 7, 1874. SLP, LNHS.

[44] Letter, Samuel Longfellow to Samuel Johnson, May 16, 1875. SLP, LNHS.

[45] Letter, Samuel Longfellow to Mary Longfellow Greenleaf, July 19, 1872. SLP, LNHS.

[46] Letter, Samuel Longfellow to Samuel Johnson, May 15, 1876. SLP, LNHS.

[47] Letter to Samuel Johnson, September 28, 1876. SLP, LNHS.

CHAPTER 20 – GERMANTOWN

A year after Samuel first preached at the Unitarian church in Germantown, he returned there to visit his friend Dr. Furness. In September 1877, the Society's former minister, Dr. Ames, had resigned his pulpit and went to become the editor of the Christian Register in Boston. The Society then began using temporary pastors, one of whom was seventy-five-year old Dr. Furness. Furness was a Harvard Divinity School graduate and in the front line of the liberal revolt by the Transcendentalists in the Unitarian Church. When Samuel arrived for the visit, he found that Furness was ill so he substituted for him in the pulpit and then agreed to preach another week and then for a month. To his surprise, the Society did not even wait until he left to hold a meeting to invite him to become their permanent pastor.[1]

In a letter to Samuel Johnson, Samuel describes how he started out by preaching one Sunday to being called to a full-time position. After so many years of short-term obligations, "his decision to accept the call was a surprise even to himself."[2]

> I forget whether I wrote you that I was coming to this place after Newburgh. ...I came for two Sundays, but have been asked to stay thro' the month which I shall gladly do. The question has even been put to me whether I would be a candidate – and you will perhaps be surprised that I feel a little inclined to entertain the question. It would take me far from my family, & would impose the routine travails again – but it would give me constant occupation for a few years & the opportunity to lay by something for the "declining years" which are not far off. Please say nothing of this matter, however, as it lies only as a possibility in my mind as yet.[3]

One month later, Samuel had accepted the offer from the Germantown Society to take their pulpit on a permanent basis. Their letter to him was friendly and expressed their wishes to accommodate to his style.

> I am instructed by them to express thanks to you and also to inquire of your pleasure in regard to an Installation – They wish you to indicate in what manner and form you desire to be introduced to our field of labor.
>
> We care nothing for a flourish of trumpets, but wish to emphasize the beginning of the new relation in a manner which shall be entirely in accordance with your wishes.[4]

The installation was held on January 6, 1878. In keeping with Samuel's custom, the service was short and informal. The Society president welcomed the new pastor and Dr. Furness offered the prayer and Samuel took most of the rest of the service. The sermon that he preached was entitled "The Continuity of Life." In it he set forth that he intended to preach to them "as a teacher of a pure and simple theism, in absolute mental independence."[5] The book *Five Prophets of To-day*, enlarges on Samuel's mission to Germantown.

> It was said of Longfellow that his mission was "to put religious sentiment into free thought," – a task in which many have failed. At the opening of his ministry in Germantown (1878) he told the people that he had come to be simply a minister of religion, – not of Unitarianism nor of Christianity, but of religion alone. He could bear the name of no sect. But he felt himself in accord with the most developed form of Unitarianism and with all that he found true and serviceable to man in Christianity. The religion he must preach was natural to man, and was made up of piety and righteousness, in contradistinction from a religion which was ecclesiastical or miraculous.[6]

Despite the freedom in Germantown, Samuel wished something even more liberal, which was the elimination of an affiliation with any organized church. This was something he had supported over the years and constantly moved farther in this direction.

> I should prefer, of course, a society not called a Unitarian Society. But none such affirms. And I have for some time thought that I ought on several accounts to take up some such charge.[7]

Samuel liked the Germantown area and the people of his congregation. For a relatively small area, it is rich in history. It was founded in 1682 as the first German settlement in America with the population being Mennonite and Quaker. The area followed a liberal path with many abolitionists and supported the "Underground Railroad." This continued into the 20ᵗʰ century with Germantown being the first Philadelphia neighborhood to eliminate segregation in housing. In letters to his friend Samuel Johnson, Samuel describes the area and people with whom he had contact.

> The place is attractive. The old street of the town quaint & old-fashioned as you know, & reminding me pleasantly of the English Country towns, as the surrounding scenery does of the English landscape. The people whom I have met are very cordial & hospitable, & intelligent, I think. The little Gothic church is simple, open & pleasant to speak in. The presumably mild winters have an attraction also.[8]

As usual Samuel was happiest when he was with young people. He enjoyed their company and they his. Joseph May in his *Memoir* reports that Samuel also sometimes carried candy in his pockets or had apples in his home for the youth. He was also careful of their religious beliefs and showed Quaker children picture books of animals rather than the illustrated fairy tales that he had in order not to offend their parents. In the second of the two excerpts below, one child raises an interesting question.

> Among the guests in Mr. Longfellow's home, it was natural that the young should be especially welcome. Living near the

large Germantown Academy (the picturesque old building of which peculiarly interested him), he became familiarly acquainted with the pupils, whose sports he loved to watch, and who learned to confide frankly in him. He went frequently among them, and they came often in groups or singly to his house. For their freer access, he had a gateway opened in his fence. It was, perhaps, one of these boys who afterwards said, "I used to be very much ashamed to have anybody caress me in the presence of others; but when Mr. Longfellow did so, I felt proud and happy." But with boys in all parts of the town Mr. Longfellow established an acquaintance. Many were familiar with him who did not know his name. "That kind gentleman" was a title which, as in another town, was applied to him by one of these.[9]

But fond as he was of all children, some of the little girls had a feeling that his preference was for the boys. One of them taxed him with this and commissioned a friend to demand why it should be so. He seemed to admit the partiality when, after a moment, he replied, "Tell her it is, perhaps, because I never *was* a little girl."[10] [*Memoir*, p. 281.]

In addition to children, Samuel took great interest, as in his other parishes, in the poor and suffering, and especially "those burthened by the distresses of the mind and heart." He quietly observed what was happening in the town and discovered many families in need. He proceeded to help them through public agencies or through his own means. "The poor knew and loved him as the children did."[11]

During Samuel's stay in Germantown, he had a new experience. Until moving there, he had lived in his family's homes, in boarding houses and with families. In Germantown, he arranged for a place to stay that he would have to take care of himself. He wrote to Samuel Johnson and described his bachelor pad.

And now be prepared to open your eyes in astonishment – on the first of February I am going to housekeeping. Do not imagine that there is any fair widow or other lady in the case.

But, the best boarding house here not being very attractive & board in a private family not being exactly desirable – I am going to try the experiment of a bachelor household. A lady is leaving a very attractive house & offers it to me, all furnished & with a cook, till next May, at a moderate rent, with permission to give it up as much sooner as I choose should the experiment not be satisfactory. You must come & make me a visit & see me in the entirely new role of housekeeper. Some day I hope to persuade my sister Mrs. [Anne] Pierce to come & keep house for me.[12]

Samuel liked his parsonage in Germantown and his congregation liked him. He did not have problems like those that beset him in Fall River or Brooklyn. Perhaps the liberal movement in the Unitarian Church had reached to some of the congregations, such as Germantown, and they were more willing to accept ideas that congregations were not a generation earlier. A comment from one of his Germantown parishioners demonstrates how the presence of Samuel Longfellow among them affected them.

I hardly know how to convey my impressions of Mr. Longfellow's influence in Germantown, for his whole personality was so essentially spiritual that it eludes one's effort to portray it in words. When, later, he died, I felt that the transition from this world to the world of spirit would be to him a very natural change, – a much shorter step than it could be in most lives, – for there seemed to be in his nature so little that tied him to earthly things.

He was not an active worker in the days when we knew him; largely because of his delicate health, but also from temperament. He thought, truly, that the weight of one's best assistance to it. What he *was*, was always much more important than what he did. He strongly disliked *argument*, and had a quiet way of letting a subject drop and introducing a new topic if there seemed to be danger of increasing warmth in a conversation. He had no desire to convince others that they were in the wrong, except by standing himself quietly and firmly on the other side.

In this way there sometimes seemed in him a lack of warmth, which made him more especially the preacher to the older and maturer minds of his congregation, rather than to the glowing enthusiasts of our younger circle.

Yet many of his quiet bits of philosophy sank deeply into our young hearts, and were a real balm for us in that time of stress and strain which comes to those who while feeling that they must struggle for something higher, are not quite sure of their aim.[13]

This all ended in 1882. Samuel Johnson, Samuel Longfellow's best friend throughout his life from the time they met at Harvard, died on February 19, 1882. Just over a month later his brother Henry, perhaps the only person closer to him than Johnson, died on March 24, 1882. The grief from these two deaths would be almost impossible to bear for someone who was not as strong in their beliefs as Samuel Longfellow. After the two funerals, Samuel returned to Germantown

to his people full of tender feeling, but oppressed by no gloom of sorrow. On the following Sunday he preached to them an uplifting sermon, into which the spiritual experiences of the time were gathered, full of faith and thankfulness.[14]

Nevertheless, Samuel was struggling with feelings that those around him were not aware of.

I wonder sometimes if this feeling will last that he is not dead, not gone. Yet truly he is not "As one who is dead but not absent" he lays in one of his poems – Evangeline I think. And it seems to me as if in the thought of him this sense of life & presence will always remain uppermost. I never before had felt it so strongly.

I shall want to hear how Aunt Anne is – & all of your. I think you will find much comfort from the church services this week.[15]

In the year before their deaths, Samuel Johnson and Henry Longfellow both had physical problems. Johnson wrote to Samuel Longfellow and gave a short description of the problem

As for health, I hope for better things, but last winter's troubles have so taken hold of my lower limbs that I cannot use them for any length of time. I think I am gaining. I am certainly taking my best care to that end. How lovely the world is up here under the great elms and the green hills I need not say; it only waits for you.[16]

Relative to Henry, his health problems were more serious and his sister Anne went to Cambridge from Portland. Samuel wrote to Anne about what his sister Mary had told him and also gave some words of encouragement.

I was about writing you when I heard from Mary that you were expected in Cambridge, on account of Henry's illness, I suppose. I have not heard since, but I trust he is ere this entirely well. Such an attack is of course alarming, at his years. Yet, why should we fear? We know that for any of us the event cannot be many years off. The thought for myself has been very familiar to see for years: and come when it may, it can bring us no harm. It is only by looking above & beyond that we can be superior to all earthly events, which do not reach the spiritual life.[17]

About a month after Henry's death, his daughter Alice wrote to Samuel about the possibility of his returning to Cambridge and moving in with them in the Craigie House. However, Samuel had been at Germantown around four years and had originally planned to stay five or possibly seven years. He also regretted leaving them without giving much notice. Nevertheless, if he were asked to write Henry's biography, his need to move to Cambridge would be stronger.

Nothing would be more pleasant to me than to come & live with you & Annie. If I have not said so before, if I have any hesitation, you will understand that it came from the difficulty of leaving & giving up my work here. Of course it all turns upon my undertaking the Biography & upon your need of some one with you, which my people here would have to see the ground of my going away from them. Seven years however has always been the utmost limit of my thought of staying here: that would be two years longer: and the getting away would hardly be any easier.[18]

Samuel decided to prepare a written memorial for his friend Samuel Johnson. He also was willing to write a biography of his brother, but this situation was not as straight forward as his memorial for Johnson.

> During the year following Mr. Johnson's death, Mr. Long-fellow (as has already been mentioned) gathered up some of his lectures, essays, and sermons into a volume, prefixing a memorial sketch through which the love he bore his friend, and the admiration he felt for his character, talents, and scholarship, and for his services to morals and to literature, are brightly conspicuous.[19]

After Henry's death, his good friend George Washington Greene wrote to Henry's son Erny to say he was willing to write Henry's biography as Henry wished him to do. Some of the children agreed to accept Mr. Greene's offer. However, Alice was not convinced that this was the best choice or that her father really meant for Mr. Greene to write the biography of her father. Samuel wrote to Alice saying he was willing to write the biography if they wished, but he did not want to get involved in the disagreement about Greene. He also wrote to his sister Anne explaining the situation to her.

> I should at once have accepted the proposal to prepare the biography, but for Mr. Greene. His last letter to Ernest touches me both by its generosity & the keen disappointment it shows. Are you quite sure that your father's wishes in this matter might not to be carried out? They seem to have been very clearly expressed to Mr. G. & justified by their long intimacy.
> It seems to me at least that I ought either to write to Mr. G. or to see him. Yet I am afraid I should give in to his feelings, if I did. And therefore I would rather that you should decide.

If you think Mr. G's infirmities & any other reasons are sufficient to set aside your father's wishes.

I am afraid that in any matter requiring decision I am apt at first to see all the difficulties in the way, more than the reasons in favor of a course.

I need not say that it is pleasant to me that you should all wish me to do this work of love.[20]

I should like much to be able to talk with you about Mr. Greene's letter to Ernest. It seems to have made the way very clear to the children. Tho' Alice thought it "very touching" she did not think it need change her position. For she holds that he is really incapacitated – and that private papers would have to pass under too many eyes. Then she thinks that her father did not very seriously believe that Mr. G. would write his biography. Indeed, there was little reason to suppose that he would outlive H.[21]

In the end, the family asked Samuel to write Henry's biography. In any event, Mr. Greene unexpectedly died a few months after Henry did and never would have been able to complete the biography. Since writing the biography would be a full-time project and he needed to do the work in Cambridge, Samuel submitted his resignation to the Germantown Society.

At the urgent request of my brother's family, I have taken upon myself the duty of writing his Biography. It will, as I judge, fully occupy the time I am able to give to work for the greater part of the coming year. It can be best done by my residence at Cambridge where are the materials I shall have to use and the persons I shall need to consult in the work. My brother's daughters, also remaining in his house, are desirous that I should come to live with them.

Under these circumstances, I have to ask you to accept my resignation of the office of minister to the Unitarian Society.[22]

The Society tried to talk Samuel out of his decision, but his reasons were too compelling. Samuel's resignation was accepted on June 11 and he returned to Cambridge, finally retiring from actively seeking places to preach. However, his congregation in Germantown remembered him warmly. The Women's Work Society, founded in 1877, worked to raise funds for the Society through various activities. Samuel often gave readings at their meetings and after he left they changed the name of the group to "The Samuel Longfellow Guild."

Notes:

[1] Letter, Samuel Longfellow to Samuel Johnson, November 8, 1877. SLP, LNHS.

[2] May, Joseph, Ed. *Samuel Longfellow, Essays and Sermons*. Boston: The Riverside Press, 1894. p. 269.

[3] Letter, Samuel Longfellow to Samuel Johnson, November 8, 1877. SLP, LNHS.

[4] Letter, E.H. Clark to Samuel Longfellow, December 10, 1877. SLP, LNHS.

[5] May, Joseph, Ed. *Samuel Longfellow, Essays and Sermons*. p. 270.

[6] Hale, E. E., Curtis, Whittier and Longfellow. *Five Prophets of Today*. Boston: 1892. p. 52.

[7] Letter, Samuel Longfellow to Samuel Johnson, November 23, 1877. SLP, LNHS.

[8] Letter; Samuel Longfellow to Samuel Johnson, November 8, 1877. SLP, LNHS.

[9] May, Joseph, Ed. *Samuel Longfellow, Essays and Sermons*. p. 278-279.

[10] Ibid., p. 281.

[11] Ibid.

[12] Letter, Samuel Longfellow to Samuel Johnson, January 28, 1878. SLP, LNHS.

[13] May, Joseph, Ed. *Samuel Longfellow, Essays and Sermons*. p. 282-283.

[14] Ibid., p. 288.

[15] Letter, Samuel Longfellow to Mary Longfellow Greenleaf, April 1882. SLP, LNHS.

[16] Letter, Samuel Johnson to Samuel Longfellow, June 5, 1881. Samuel Longfellow, *Lectures, Essays, and Sermons by Samuel Johnson.*

[17] Letter, Samuel Longfellow to Anne Longfellow Pierce, November 1, 1881. SLP, LNHS.

[18] Letter, Samuel Longfellow to Alice Longfellow, April 18, 1882. SLP, LNHS.

[19] May, Joseph, Ed. *Samuel Longfellow, Essays and Sermons*. p. 288.

[20] Letter, Samuel Longfellow to Alice Longfellow, April 18, 1882. SLP, LNHS.

[21] Letter, Samuel Longfellow to Anne Longfellow Pierce, April 25, 1882. SLP, LNHS.

[22] Letter, Samuel Longfellow to Germantown Unitarian Society, June 4, 1882. SLP, LNHS.

CHAPTER 21 – THE NEXT STEP

Back in Cambridge, Samuel was once again a resident of the Craigie house. He lived there with his nieces and began work on Henry's biography, *Life of Henry Wadsworth Longfellow*. In the resignation letter that he had written to the Germantown Society, Samuel mentioned that the *Life* would keep him busy "for the greater part of the coming year." In fact, the preparation of Henry's biography took Samuel over three years working full time.

The undertaking must have been enormous. He had to collect the journals and all the many letters that Henry had left in the Craigie House. In addition, Samuel wrote letters to the people he knew of that had communicated with Henry. He asked them if they still had copies of the letters from Henry and, if so, if they would be willing to send them to him for use in the *Life*.

Samuel then had to read all the material and next to decide what was too private and what could be included in the book, what was worth using and what he thought would not be interesting to others. Furthermore, Samuel said "that [he] was obliged to leave out some genealogical & other matters which [he] had intended to put into an appendix.[1]

Samuel's objective was to write a comprehensive biography so people would be able to know his brother. In addition, it was a source of information from which others could select what they wanted for their own purposes.

> He felt that of one whose worked had made him so widely known and loved, there should exist an exhaustive account; while he wished and trusted that, from it, memoirs, briefer and adapted to wider circulation, might be composed. He even urged upon Mr. James Russell Lowell, who had lately completed such a biography of Hawthorne, to write a one-volume memoir of his neighbor and friend and brother-poet. Mr. Long-

fellow's own work was one of devoted love and reverence for the man, as well as admiration for the poet, and he spared no pains to give it accuracy and completeness.[2]

However, Samuel has been criticized for leaving out material to protect Henry's character and biasing the way he is perceived. This is discussed more completely in academic studies of Henry and Samuel's biography. Regardless of more recent opinions about Samuel's biography of Henry, it was not uncommon for biographers at this time to edit out material in order to protect their subject. For example, in the *Memoir of Samuel Longfellow,* Joseph May changed some of the letters from their original wording, often used initials instead of names included in letters and left out some relevant events mentioned in other documents; his editing marks can be seen in some of the original letters.

The two-volume *Life* of Henry Wadsworth Longfellow was finally finished in 1886. Samuel wanted it to come out on February 27, Henry's birth date, but the publishers did not think it was possible because there was still work to be done on the book. Nevertheless, he wanted to get at least a few copies for his family.

> And so, my long work is finished. I can hardly tell how it has lasted so long. But a large part of it makes no appearance in the book – The reading, sifting, glossing, deciding, rejecting – yet on the whole I am well satisfied. Do you know that letters do not read as well, in print as in manuscript?

> I was very anxious to have the book appear on the birthday – a week from Saturday. But there have lately been some delays about one little thing & another, which I fear will postpone the publication a few days. However, I hope to get some copies to the family & intimate friends by the 27th.[3]

However, there was much more work to do than Samuel had thought. Throughout 1886 and into 1887, there was a large amount of correspondence between Samuel and the publishers. Samuel wanted to make sure that the engravings and woodcuts were of high quality and accurately portrayed their subjects. He also wanted to make changes in the content, which he felt were minor but the printers thought significant.

> I was very much surprised at the printers' charge for cancelled matter. I occasionally marked out in the proofs an entry in the Journals or even a letter which seemed less interesting in print than it had in MS. I should have thought not more than a dozen pages in all.[4]

In early 1887, as the result of comments and requests for more information about Henry, Samuel prepared a third volume, even though the editor was reluctant to prepare the new volume. The third volume contains journals and letters from the last 15 years of Henry's life, which did not have "the same fullness of detail as the earlier portions." It also had letters, "for which room was not found in the Life," plus material that arrived after the completion of the first two volumes along with tributes and reminiscences from others. Thus, Samuel finished the biography of his beloved brother.

> I think the volume will be of nearly three hundred pages.
> I do not want it called the third volume of the Life. For I want it understood that the Life is complete in the two volumes, as it is; only the latter part is given in less detail than the earlier. I still think that <u>Final Memorials</u> will be a good name. And it will be understood that nobody need buy it, except those who wish for more journal and letters than were given in the Life. Man I do not doubt thought there was too much in that.[5]

During the first couple of months that he was working on Henry's *Life*, Samuel also spent time on *Lectures, Essays and Sermons by Samuel Johnson*. It included a Memoir by Samuel Longfellow, who so fondly remembered his friend. In June 1883, the *Atlantic Monthly* published a review of *Lectures, Essays and Sermons*, and gave a synopsis of the book.

Mr. Longfellow's volume, made up of a biography of some one hundred and fifty pages, and a series of lectures, sermons, essays, and addresses, selected with excellent judgment from the mass of Mr. Johnson's manuscripts and printed writings, should not only be a very precious one to those who have heretofore been well acquainted with this thinker and his thoughts, but it should attract to him a host of fresh readers.[6]

Now Samuel was free to do what he wanted, but at this time in his life, Samuel was less active with the various groups he had generally participated with. In part, this was also due to a decrease in activity of the groups themselves, or even to their no longer functioning. Additionally, his friends were participating less, partly because of age, but also because the issues that concerned them had changed. Some of what Samuel had supported actively had been achieved, or there had been a move back to the situation prior to attempts to achieve change. A letter from the Massachusetts Woman Suffrage Association inviting him to participate showed that people still remembered him for his liberal beliefs and willingness to support them publicly. With this group there was a difference from when Samuel spoke three decades earlier when suffrage was considered too controversial to be included on the agenda.

Three young men were important in Samuel's life through the decade of the 1880s. These were Harry Wilson Barnitz, William Allan Klapp and Willam Morton Fullerton. These three had only one similarity among them: they were of university age. They came from different backgrounds and they were heading along different life paths and a glance at these relationships with Samuel provides a more complete picture of Samuel's relationship with the young.

Harry Wilson Barnitz was a high school student when Samuel arrived at his position as pastor in Germantown. His father was a Methodist minister and an artist and Harry inherited his father's skills in this area. Harry's parents lived in York, Pennsylvania and probably knew Samuel Longfellow.[7]

In 1880, Harry graduated from high school and in 1881 went to Philadelphia to attend the Pennsylvania Academy of Fine Arts.

While he was in Philadelphia, he stayed in Germantown with Samuel until Samuel returned to Cambridge after Henry's death.

Samuel provided encouragement for Harry and helped him financially while he was in school. Harry studied at the Academy from 1881-1886 and after he left the Academy Samuel provided funds over the years when Harry needed them, but then he sometimes received artwork in return, some Samuel ordered, some as unexpected presents.

> You will now very soon be again in Philadelphia. I was glad to hear that you had laid up enough to meet your expenses there this winter, very nearly. I do not think you will have any difficulty in making up the rest. I wish to give you an order for a picture to the amount of 25 dollars. I expect to be in Germantown in April or May & will pay you for it then.[8]

In 1890, Samuel wrote Harry and told him that two years before he had "lent $150 to a young man here [Cambridge] to help him through college,"[9] and if the young man paid him back he would give this money to Harry.

In 1887, Harry went to Atlanta, Georgia where he and Walter Downing had a studio. He got engaged there, but did not stay in Atlanta long and returned to Philadelphia without marrying the young woman. He returned to the Academy and met fellow student Myrtle Townsend, whom he did later marry. They both continued working in art after they left the Academy, Harry specializing in portraits and stained glass and Myrtle becoming a sculptor. They both became recognized in their areas and Harry became good enough with stained glass to be asked to design the stained glass windows for the National Cathedral in Washington, DC, and for the Chapel at the U.S. Military Academy at West Point.

Many of Samuel's letters to Harry were about religion. Harry was curious about Unitarianism and Samuel explained what it was to him. However, Samuel was hesitant to explain at first because he had some concerns about Harry's Methodist minister father finding out and being upset with what he would consider as Samuel's interference. Harry eventually converted to Unitarianism and Samuel sent a letter congratulating him.

I wish you a happy New Year. This is indeed spiritually a new year to you, is it not? Of new thoughts & new faith & new hope in respect to the highest subjects which can occupy the human minds & heart. To have found God infinitely near, with nothing between your soul & him, when you wish to approach him; no false ideas or unworthy theologies – no belief that you are unable or unworthy to appeal to him.[10]

In 1891, Harry and Myrtle got married and he opened a studio where he taught art and painted portraits. Unhappily for Samuel, Harry decided to convert away from Unitarianism, and Samuel expressed his sadness about this. Later, Harry moved to several locations in Ohio and Illinois to work and went to Paris to study. He became recognized for his stained glass work and the portraits he painted.

William Allan Klapp, who Samuel called Allan, was a young man just entering university when Samuel met him in the early 1880s. William "was adopted by him into an affection and watchful interest which were truly parental."[11] They carried on a regular correspondence which Joseph May says, "show Samuel's power of reaching the hearts of the young, and how elevating was the influence which he exerted upon them."[12] Excerpts from two letters give an idea of the type of advice he provided the young throughout his life.

I am glad you have been enjoying your holidays. By another week I suppose you will be at your books again. I rejoice that you are doing well in your studies and hope you have done with "cutting up." Try to stand as high in character as in your lessons. It is a great thing for a man to be *high-toned* morally: to have a high sense of what is manly and worthy in motives and aims and principles; to have a high standard of action that hates everything low.[13]

I am glad that you are not satisfied with a standing which is merely good by comparison with "the other fellows," and that you have a higher standard of your own, namely, what is really good and high. And I hope you will carry this out in other things besides your studies.[14]

At one point, he suggested that Allan write an article for the youth sporting activities magazine, *The Outing Magazine*, about a summer trip he took to Brandt Lake in the Adirondacks – "Do it! I shall send you the September number in a day or two." The article, "A Day's Trout-Fishing in Maine," was published in 1887 and Samuel congratulated him and provided more advice for his next article.

Allan wanted to buy an island in Brandt Lake and build a house on it, which he would call "Longfellow Lodge." Samuel encouraged him to buy the island along with the adjacent island and wanted to "make the island (or islands) my entire gift."[15] Allan eventually did buy one island and still planned to build on it.

In June of 1886, Allan entered Columbia University in 1886, although Samuel would have preferred he go to Harvard, "because I want to have you nearer me."[16] Six months later, Allan went to Paris, and Samuel stressed to him the importance of taking advantage of learning French while in Paris and gave him advice on how best to learn it.

Just over a year later, Allan died of an illness and was notified by a telegram from Allan's father. Samuel wrote to Allan's mother and father. His mother sent him portraits of Allan and a "paper-knife" that Allan had used. Samuel expressed his feelings about Allan to his father.

> You know how warmly and strongly attached I had become to him and how much I prized his affection. How hard it is to believe and feel that I shall not look upon his face again! But I shall always cherish his bright memory, and be glad that I have known him. With no son of my own, I had taken him to my heart.[17]

William Morton Fullerton entered Harvard in 1882 and his "university course Mr. Longfellow had watched with the warmest interest."[18] One of William's classmates was Richard Longfellow, who was the youngest son of Samuel's brother Alexander. In 1888, William was 22-years old and working on the Boston *Record-Advertiser*. At times, he was Samuel's companion in the Craigie

House, which he enjoyed: "It is most delightful to be here in the Craigie House study writing to you, my Marian. Mr. Longfellow sits near by reading."[19]

Fullerton became a writer who went into journalism and was regularly published in the *Record-Advertiser.* He also wrote articles and poetry for a number of other publications; in addition, he tried his hand at books later in life. As with other young men, Samuel provided advice and support.

> Of what inestimable benefit his influence was to this brilliant young journalist at the outset of his career, the latter has more than once gratefully spoken; while to Mr. Longfellow himself the association with this bright and winsome personality was a very real joy and satisfaction.[20]

William knew many noteworthy people throughout his life in America and later in Europe. Some of these individuals provided information for articles, or were themselves subjects of articles. Furthermore, they were valuable for making additional introductions and increasing his network of contacts.

> Will Fullerton knew everyone who was anyone in New England letters: John Greenleaf Whittier, Oliver Wendell Holmes, Francis Parkman, and writers more obscure, *oscurissimi,*. He invited them to participate in a supplement honoring Whittier's eightieth birthday.
>
> He published verse in the *Travelers' Insurance Company Record* and elsewhere, alongside Adeline Treadwell Parsons, Francesca's mother, and Constance Fenimore Woolson, whose death in Venice was to harrow Henry James.[21]

Besides his work for publications, William wrote poetry for friends such as Samuel Longfellow and Oscar Fay Adams. In 1885, William wrote a letter in verse to Samuel and at the end asked,

> These are the verses. Now again I am tempted to give up my plan of sending them to you. I have been reading Keats today. For some hours now I have been delighting and will continue

to delight my mind with his ethereal thoughts – It may be that this is why I spurn the Earth, paw up against the clouds, and find no merit in these lines. Please tell me sincerely what you think about them.[22]

Samuel also wrote poetry to William. In a small book published in 1887 and entitled *A Few Verses of Many Years*, Samuel dedicated a poem he had written in 1866 to William.

THE CASCADE
To W. M. F.
To Whom I Owe Half of the Lines

Adown the jagged rock I spring,
   All life and sparkling gladness;
For very joy I leap and sing,
   Unknowing yet of sadness.

I pause within a crystal well,
   Then tumble o'er its edges,
And hasten down the shadows dell
   Hemmed in by granite ledges

Above me arch the calm blue skies,
   Serene beyond my hurry;
Beside me solemn cedars rise,
   Unshaken by my worry.

The sumac leans its sprays across
   To drink from my cool chalice,
Where maiden-hair and starry moss
   Weave hangings for my palace.

The rustic bridge its shadow throws
   Across the cool, deep dingle;
And where my water darkling flows
   The sunbeams intermingle

Their golden threads with my brown tints,
    Their gloaming with my gloaming,
And touch with bright mosaic glints
    The stones o'er which I'm roaming.

Two rhymers on my rocky stairs
    Their little verses ponder;
My rhymes are better far than theirs,
    So, swift away I wander.

They cannot catch me in their lines;
    I laugh as I evade them;
My words are Nature's artless signs,
    But theirs – with toil they've made them!

                    Crawford, White Mountains, 1866[23]

Samuel and William sailed for Europe on May 5, 1888 on the ship *Elbe*. They landed in Bremen and were going to travel for several months. Samuel wanted to go to Venice and then wend their way north to Switzerland, Germany and England and return to the U.S. in October. He wrote a letter to his sister Mary describing the trip and their free time, which bears a resemblance to an afternoon at Craigie House described above.

> F. is writing by my side for the Advertiser. He lends his regards & tells me to say that he appreciates your approval of his enthusiastic letters. We have not seen any of them in print.[24]

Although Samuel returned as planned, William had met some people along the way and decided to live in Europe at the beginning of 1889. Thus, William

> passed out of the daily life of his friend, though not out of that friend's constant thought and care. The separation was keenly felt by Mr. Longfellow, though he said but little

on the subject, and he was always hoping that circumstances would some time allow him to see his young friend again.[25]

William led a life in Paris that attracted attention for years. His mother wrote him and said she was going to give a talk to the Women's Alliance about Samuel Longfellow and said to her son, "What a friend you had in him. ...I wonder what he would say to you now if he knew your Paris life."[26] As he grew older his fame and then knowledge of him dwindled and he was virtually unknown when he died in 1952.

In the 1920s and 1930s many French readers, oblivious of Gertrude Stein, Fitzgerald, Hemingway, Henry Miller, regarded him as a spokesman for "Anglo-Saxon" culture.[27]

Nevertheless, William continued to have affection for Samuel. In a letter to Samuel in 1891, William told him, "know of my profound and unalterable attachment."[28] After Samuel's death William published "Three Sonnets" that were considered an elegy for Samuel.

THREE SONNETS
By William Morton Fullerton

I
With melody of soft accented word
   He spoke as speak whose lips the Muse have kissed,
   Whom She enamoured summons to a tryst,
To whisper secrets by no others hears;
And then with shyness of a mountain bird,
   Flying from valleys of the evening mist,
   He vanished far, nor knew his song was missed
By us whom rarely others voices stirred

We spoke not when he left us, but did sigh,
   And knit our brows the tighter for the fray;

But with the Joy of Dionysos I
　　Poured sad libation to our yesterday.
His empty glass before me clinked to mine
Rang hollow, void of sympathizing wine.

II
Oh, sweet communion of the vanished days
　　When his large eyes looked calmly into mine!
　　Oh, moments buried in the purple wine
When Gods stood by, submissive to out gaze!
　　Oh, Hours irresolute that gave no sign
Our dreams would melt as into autumn haze,
But half-convinced us Time itself delays
　　If men but drug it with an anodyne!

Yet gone he is, and I am left alone,
　　And pleasant places knowing him of yore
Seem strange without him for their charm is flown,
　　And yet they speak of him as not before.
Ah, this were better than the vague regret:
To know, to love, then loving to forget.

III
To know, to love, then loving to forget!
　　We speak half-wisdom when we wisest seem.
　　Men are as pebbles in a rushing stream
That huddled lie, amid the foam and fret,
All that we are is ours but as a debt
　　The polish and the beauty and the gleam;
　　Through sunlit medium so fair we beam
Contented are we – but as stones; and yet

Here in the current of the Things-that-Are,
　　Of Things-that-have-Been, and of Things-to-Be,
We press the tighter lest the waters jar,
　　Kenning but hearsay of the distant sea.
Ay, prisoners we, and vanity is all-
Save only love, and loving to recall.[29]

While Samuel was working on Henry's *Life*, his own life "was of quietude and sunny cheerfulness which were characteristic of him." [*Memoir*, p. 296.] However, just as he was beginning his new activities, the special event of his 70th birthday had to be celebrated. He describes the three-day long celebration in a letter to Anne.

The affair opened by the arrival of the first guest on Monday Afternoon. Mrs. Fields came up from Manchester, to attend Alice's afternoon reception to the working women from some of the Boston stores (it being a holiday; Bunker Hill Day, 17th). About 30 of these wandered through the rooms & walked in the garden, & sat on the piazza. I read to them the account of the Craigie House from the Life & Mrs. Fields read some of the poems. Mrs. F. brought me a box of lovely delicate & fragrant sweet briar roses, which looked charmingly in a round flat dish. The next morning (18th) she presented me with a fine etched portrait of James Martineau, a strong & earnest face. At breakfast came a great bunch of carnations from one of my boy friends, then a box of fine red roses from Mrs. Spelman; then Cora came with her smallest boy bringing a bouquet. Flowers poured in during the day. Dear Mrs. Nichols sent a pretty basket of roses set in a glass of water so that they did not have to be removed; Wentworth Higginson a large basket "70 roses". Mary a bouquet with white roses from the old Portland bush, Charley a box of true florist roses – & so on. Charley himself came in the forenoon "to see the good uncle" but could not stay, & Dick. Mary came to early dinner. There were notes from Edward Hale & Sam Eliot both of whom had engagements elsewhere. About 5, came William & Harriet Preble bringing a large book & a small one: the latter a tiny scrap-book in which at the age of 11 I had copied some verses as we used to do. Then Mary Haskins & her husband who gave me some good advice such as that I must now begin to grow young again. Nelly from Avondale brought a bowl of very artistically arranged white & scarlet flowers; Miss Palfrey, a pretty paper-knife from her mother & a bunch of maiden's blush roses which she gave to Alice; & so in thickening numbers – about fifty in all, nearly all who were invited. Presently

Alice came to me & said "It can be kept secret no longer; go into the front parlor & see your surprise." I went & found Mr. Kneisel, Mr. Löffler & Mr. Foote with piano, violin and 'cello, who said they would play me some trios of Beethoven. Others came in & the music was delicate & charming. Wasn't it very nice in Alice to think of this & take all the trouble to arrange it? Ices & strawberries were served in the dining room, and all was very pleasant & cordial & I was not at all tired. After the most had gone, some invited ones stayed to tea, sitting round the great table & a smaller one. Anne Wells, the Danas & Thorps who had come up from Manchester & returned at 9; Will & Emily had brought a fine book, etc. etc. Last of all came Wad. Who had been to New Bedford to a wedding, & whom we had missed at tea.

One of my gifts was a package that came by mail & which on opening proved to contain a tin rattle stamped "For a good child." The address was in a feigned hand & no clue has yet been found to the perpetrator; tho' the detectives have some suspicions. Wad was arrested on the charges, but denied the impeachment.

I must not forget to say that James Croswell sent me some pretty & characteristic verses; and John Holmes also. I said that everybody could have birth-day verses from Dr. Holmes, but few from his brother John.

The occasion only wanted your presence, dear Anne, & that of the South Streeters; but you were here in our thoughts & in your kind gifts & words.[30]

As the 1880s moved into the 1890s, Samuel's lifelong health problems began to take their toll. In the fall of 1891, he went to Portland because of the death of his brother Alex's youngest daughter, Elizabeth Porter Longfellow, known as Bessie, at the age of 35. Samuel joined the family there and "A more lovely, calming influence in a home was never known." However, his family did notice Samuel's loss of strength. In keeping with his character, Samuel never complained, but "he sometimes seemed languid and even depressed."[31]

In July 1892, Samuel returned to Portland and lived for several weeks in the family home. The illness he had suffered from for so many years was rapidly getting worse. Nevertheless, in August he went with some of the family to the seaside at Cape Elizabeth not far from Portland.

While at the shore he suffered from "a sudden and violent attack, which the physicians at once pronounced the beginning of the end."[32] He improved somewhat and it seemed like he would recover. Edward Everett Hale came to see him and they had an enjoyable visit. In addition, much of the family was always around. Regardless of his illness, Samuel was not upset and only once did he refer to what he knew would not be long in coming.

On October 3, just as the sun was rising into the sky, Samuel Longfellow died. A few days later, the family held simple services "of devotion and commemoration" in the home. A public service followed in the First Parish Church, in which Samuel worshipped as a child. One of the participants was Rev. John T.G. Nichols, whose father had been pastor when Samuel was young. He was then buried in the family tomb in the Western Cemetery in Portland. The pallbearers were members of the family: Henry's son Ernest Longfellow; Mr. Thorp, husband of Henry's daughter Anna Allegra; his brother Stephen's son William Pitt Preble Longfellow; his brother Alexander's son Richard; and, Richard Henry Dana III, the husband of Henry's daughter Edith.

Samuel's death certificate indicates he died of Bright's disease. This included a variety of inflammatory kidney diseases, including nephritis. If the diagnosis is right, Samuel probably suffered from chronic nephritis, but it is not possible to determine with certainty how long. However, his periodic feelings of weakness and tiredness along with his stomach complaints may have been symptoms of the disease from which he died. It was untreatable with the methods available at the time, but now there a number of treatment possibilities.

After Samuel's death, newspapers and magazines published obituary notices and articles, some of the latter years later. Excerpts from a sermon given the week after Samuel's death by Charles G. Ames of the Church of the Disciples in Dorchester provides an overview of the contents of the obituaries.

> He was a doer, as well as a teacher – his life as good as his
> word. Indeed, this beauty of his speech and song lay largely in

the quality of the man behind. Many have lived more conspicuously and eventfully, there have been many broader and more exact scholars; but none have lived more simply and sweetly, more truly and usefully, or with so small a percentage of alloy in character, – pure gold, seven times refined!

A Portland gentleman tells me that his children used to speak of Mr. Longfellow as "the kind man;" and in other towns where he has lived they still speak of his fondness for children, as if he were one of their angels, always beholding the face of their heavenly Father. So child-like himself was he in his very manliness!

Ten years ago he left the pulpit in Germantown; thirty-two years ago he left that of Brooklyn. Surviving parishioners will surely speak of him as one of the few mortals who made it seem worthwhile to be immortal, and as one of the few who walk in the unseen companionship of the Spirit of Truth, the Holy Ghost, the Comforter.

***

He was no play-actor; he meant what he said, and said what he meant, without fear or mental reservation. As for "popular noises," he seemed not to heed or hear them, so attentive was he to the still, small Voice, which out-thundered them all. Nor did he come into the field of controversy, or appear as the assailant of error and evil, with weapons drawn from the armory of the old Adam. He was a champion of truth in the spirit of truth, and of goodness in the spirit of goodness; never hostile or antagonistic in temper. He acted on the principle that the best way to get rid of darkness is by bringing in the light. If any custom, opinion, or phrase ceased to serve or satisfy him, he simply dropped it and forgot it, or went along without it, leaving the dead to bury their dead.

***

Samuel Longfellow was a prophet of the new time, mightily believing that the best things are possible, if we will but live for the best. The past with all its treasures of good is ours; but it is our servant, not our master. We do highest honor to all great souls, "not by following them, but by following what they followed."

***

His power lay not in his personality, but in his imperson-
ality. He was the most secluded of spirits, always kneeling
at the shrine of the heart, silent, quiet, peaceful, patient; going
about mingling freely with people, always having a cheerful
word, never a morose one; always in an attitude of belief,
always in an attitude of hope; brave as a lion, but never boasting, never saying what he meant to do or what he wished
he could do, but keeping his own counsel and going a straight
path; ploughing a very straight furrow through a very crooked world. He was immovable as adamant, yet playful as a
sunbeam.[33]

Samuel's will, of which Richard H. Dana was executor, was
simple. He left sums of money to some of his nieces and nephews and to four other people, "In token of affectionate remembrance," as well as house furnishings to his nieces Edith
and Anna Allegra. In addition he left funds to the Cambridge
Social Union, homes for aged people in Cambridge, the Avon
Home for children in Cambridge, the Longfellow Memorial
Association in Cambridge and the Temporary Home for Women
and Children in the Portland area. He left his niece Alice "the
furniture, books, pictures and other contents of my study in
Craigie House." The remainder of his estate he left to his brother
Alexander's children.

On the back of his will he told Alice that she could do what
she wanted with the contents of his study except for the "books
in the glass-book-case to be given to William Fullerton when he
comes home." William spent so many years in Europe, it is un-
likely he claimed his inheritance.

To the rest of us he left his example of what it means to live,
what is important in life. He showed that it is not necessary to
be an active voice at the front of a group of advocates to get
one's point across. "Always he heard a voice saying: 'Serve the
present age; deal with the existing situation; live among men
as one of them, and not as a solitary monk or hermit. Share the
common life, and help to lift it up to higher levels.'"

Notes:

[1] Letter, Samuel LLetter, Samuel Longfellow to Anne Longfellow Pierce, February 17, 1886. SLP, LNHS.

[2] May, Joseph, Ed. *Samuel Longfellow, Essays and Sermons.* Boston: The Riverside Press, 1894. p. 294.

[3] Letter, Samuel Longfellow to Anne Longfellow Pierce, February 17, 1886. SLP, LNHS.

[4] Letter, Samuel Longfellow to William Davis Ticknor, March 9, 1886. LC.

[5] Ibid., January 21, 1887. LC.

[6] "Samuel Johnson." *Atlantic Monthly.* June 1883. v. 51. n.° 308. p. 848-852. Boston Atlantic Monthly Co.

[7] Catron, Particia D'Arcy. The Barnitz triad: Paintings, drawings and sculpture: August 25 September 20, 1978, [catalogue of] a loan exhibit at the Springfield Art Center. Springfield Art Center. Springfield, Ohio. 1978. p. 8.

[8] Letter, Samuel Longfellow to Harry Barnitz, January 1, 1883. SLP, LNHS.

[9] Ibid., February 20, 1890.

[10] Ibid., January 2, 1882.

[11] May, Joseph, Ed. *Samuel Longfellow, Essays and Sermons.* p. 294.

[12] Ibid., p. 251.

[13] Letter, Samuel Longfellow to Allan Klapp, December 31, 1885. SLP, LNHS.

[14] Ibid., February 20, 1886.

[15] Ibid., August 24, 1885.

[16] Ibid., June 30, 1886.

[17] Letter, Samuel Longfellow to Mr. Klapp, February 26, 1887. SLP, LNHS.

[18] Adams, Oscar Fay. "Samuel Longfellow." *The New England Magazine*, October 1894, v. 17, n.° 2, p. 205-213. Boston. p. 212.

[19] Mainwaring, Marion. *Mysteries of Paris, The Quest for Morton Fullerton.* Hanover, NH: University Press of New England, 2001. p. 42.

[20] Adams, Oscar Fay. "Samuel Longfellow." p. 212.

[21] Mainwaring, Marion. *Mysteries of Paris, The Quest for Morton Fullerton.* Hanover, NH: University Press of New England, 2001. p. 75.

[22] Letter, William Morton Fullerton to Samuel Longfellow, 1885. SLP, LNHS.

[23] Longfellow, Samuel. *A Few Verses of Many Years.* Cambridge University Press: John Williams and Son, 1887. p. 6-7.

[24] Letter, Samuel Longfellow to Mary Greenleaf Longfellow, summer 1888. SLP, LNHS.

[25] Adams, Oscar Fay. "Samuel Longfellow." p. 212. Mainwaring, Marion. *Mysteries of Paris*

[26] Letter, Julia Fullerton to William Morton Fullerton, January 24, 1898. Mainwaring, Marion. *Mysteries of Paris, The Quest for Morton Fullerton.*

[27] Ibid., p. 4.

[28] Letter, William Morton Fullerton to Samuel Longfellow, 1891. SLP, LNHS.

[29] Fullerton, William Morton. "Three Sonnets." *Scribner's Magazine*. March 1895, v. 17, issue 3, p. 304. New York. Charles Scribner and Sons.

[30] Letter, Samuel Longfellow to Anne Longfellow Pierce, June 20, 1889. SLP, LNHS.

[31] May, Joseph, Ed. *Samuel Longfellow, Essays and Sermons*. p. 304.

[32] Ibid., p. 305.

[33] Ames, Charles G. "A sermon preached in the Church of the Disciples, Oct. 10, 1892." *Boston Gazette, Sunday Morning edition*. October 15, 1898.

[34] Ibid.

ACRONYMS

ADF: Annals of the Dabney Family in Fayal

HDS: Harvard Divinity School

HHL: Harvard Houghton Library

HL: Huntington Library

LC: Library of Congress

LNHS: Longfellow Family Papers, Longfellow National Historic Site, Cambridge, MA.

LP: Longfellow Papers, Houghton Library, Harvard University.

MHS: Maine Historical Society.

SLP: Samuel Longfellow Papers, Longfellow National Historic Site, Cambridge, MA.

ZLP: Zilpah Longfellow Papers, Longfellow National Historic Site, Cambridge, MA.

BIBLIOGRAPHY

[About hymnbook]. *The Christian Register*, v. 11, April 18, 1907. p. 435.

"America Singing: Nineteenth-Century Song Sheets." Thirty-first anniversary of the American Anti-Slavery Society, at the Church of the Puritans, Tuesday, May 10th. 1864. Anti-Slavery Printing Office, 21 Spruce St., 2nd. floor. [n. d.]. http://memory.loc.gov/ammem/index.html.

"Boston Religious Anniversaries." *The New-York Herald.* May 28, 1869. New York.

"Building of a Ship" by John Rollin Tilton, ca. 1851, *Maine Memory Network, Maine's Online Museum http://www.mainememory.net/bin/Detail?ln=18699.* Maine Historical Society, 489 Congress Street, Portland, ME.

"Editor's Table." *New England Magazine, New Series.* September 1899, v. 21. Issue 6. p.762-764. Boston.

"The Free Religion Movement in Unitariansim: Opening the way for Non-Christians." American Unitarian Conference. www.americanunitarian.org/.

"Frothingham, Octavius Brooks" American Unitarian Conference. www.americanunitarian.orgwww.americanunitarian.org/.

"Greenleaf and Hubbard, Business Records 1850-1860. Mss: 761, 1850-1860, G814. Cambridge Baker Library, Harvard Business School. www.library.hbs.edu/hc/sfa/greenleaf&h.htm

"The Harvard Divinity School." *The New England Magazine*, February 1895, v.17, n.° 6, pp 740-756. Boston.

"Jenny Lind." *Wikipedia, The Free Encyclopedia.* 17 Nov 2007, 07:38 UTC. Wikimedia Foundation, Inc. 17 Nov 2007 <http://en.wikipedia.org/w/index.php?title=Jenny_Lind&oldid= =172051727>.

"Rough Draft of the Declaration of Independence" Boston Public Broadcasting System – WGBH Educational Foundation www.pbs.org/wgbh/aia/part2/2h33.html. 1999.

"Samuel Johnson." *Atlantic Monthly.* June 1883. v. 51. n.° 308. p. 848-852. Boston Atlantic Monthly Co.

"The Seneca Falls Convention." Washington, DC. National Portrait Gallery Collection Description, www.npg.si.edu/col/seneca/senfalls1.htm.www.npt.si.edu/col/seneca/senfalls1.htm

A. F. "Mr. Emerson in the Lecture Room." *Atlantic Monthly*. June 1883, v. 51. n.° 308, p. 818-832. Boston Atlantic Monthly Co.

Adams, Oscar Fay. "Samuel Longfellow." *The New England Magazine*, October 1894, v. 17, n.° 2, p. 205-213. Boston.

Ames, Charles G. "A sermon preached in the Church of the Disciples, Oct. 10, 1892." *Boston Gazette, Sunday Morning edition*. October 15, 1898.

Betinck-Smith, William, Ed. *The Harvard Book, Selections from Three Centuries, Revised Edition*. Cambridge: Harvard University Press, 1982.

Bosco, Carla "Harvard University and the Fugitive Slave Act." *The New England Quarterly,* June 2006. p. 227-247. Boston. The New England Quarterly, Inc.

Calhoun, Charles C. *Longfellow, A Rediscovered Life*. Boston: Beacon Press, 2004.

Carpenter, Frank. "William Ellery Channing." Unitarian Universalist Historical Society, www.uua.org/uuhs/duub/articles/williamellerychanning.html.

Catron, Particia D'Arcy. The Barnitz triad: Paintings, drawings and sculpture: August 25 September 20, 1978, [catalogue of] a loan exhibit at the Springfield Art Center. Springfield Art Center. Springfield, Ohio. 1978.

Chadwick, Annie Horton Hathaway. *Second Unitarian Society of Brooklyn*. Brooklyn: Private (handwritten), nd.

Chadwick, John White. "The Harvard Divinity School." *The New England Magazine*, February 1895, v. 17, n.° 6, p 740-756. Boston.

_____. *Historical Discourse*. Brooklyn: Private, 1901.

Chapman, Mary and Glenn Hendler, Eds. *Sentimental Men: Masculinity and the Politics of Affect in American Culture*. Berkeley and Los Angeles: University of California Press, 1999.

Chaney, Karen Elizabeth. *The Cambridge Tragedy: The George Parkman Murder Case and a Community in Crisis in Mid-Nineteenth Century*. Boston, Personal Communication.

Clarke, Edward H. *Sex in education, or, A fair chance for the girls*. James R. Osgood and Company. Boston.1875.

Commager, Henry Steele. *Theodore Parker*. Boston: The Beacon Press, 1947.

Committee of The Free Religious Association, Ed. *Freedom and Fellowship in Religion: A Collection of Essays and Addresses*. Boston: Roberts Brothers, 1875.

Conway, John Joseph. *Footprints of Famous Americans in Paris*. London: John Lane The Bodley Head, 1912.

Cott, Nancy F. *The Bonds of Womanhood*. New Haven: Yale University Press, 1977.

Crain, Caleb. *American Sympathy.* New Haven: Yale University Press, 2001.

Cunliffe, Marcus Ed. *Penguin History of Literature: Vol. 8, American Literature to 1900.* London: Penguin Books, Ltd., 1973.

Dabney, Roxana Lewis, *Annals of the Dabney Family in Fayal.* n.p., 1912. p. 455-6.

Emerson, Ralph Waldo. *Nature* in *Nature/Walking.* Boston: Beacon Press, 1991.

Engstrom, John. "100 Years of the Brattle" *Brattle Film Foundation.* 2001. Cambridge. Brattle Film Foundation (find at www.brattlefilm.org/brattlefilm/first100.htmlwww.brattle-film.org/brattlefilm/first100.html).

Frothingham, Octavius Brooks. *Transcendentalism in New England: A History.* New York: Harper & Brothers, 1959 (original 1876).

Fullerton, William Morton. "Three Sonnets." *Scribner's Magazine.* March 1895, v. 17, issue 3, p. 304. New York. Charles Scribner and Sons.

Hale, E. E., Curtis, Whittier and Longfellow. *Five Prophets of Today.* Boston: 1892.

Hale, Edward Everett. *Philip Nolan's Friends: A Story of the Change of Western Empire.* New York: Scribner, Armstrong and Company, 1877.

_____. Ed. *James Freeman Clarke, Autobiography, Diary and Correspondence.* Boston: The Riverside Press, 1891.

_____ "Samuel Longfellow." *Commonwealth Weekly.* October 8, 1892. Boston.

Hale, Edward E., Jr. *The Life and Letters of Edward Everett Hale, Vol. I.* Boston: Little, Brown, and Company, 1917.

_____. *The Life and Letters of Edward Everett Hale, Vol. II.* Boston: Little, Brown, and Company, 1917.

Halttunen, Karen. "Divine Providence and Dr. Parkman's Jawbone: The Cultural Construction of Murder as Mystery." *Ideas, vol.4, N.° 1.* National Humanities Center. Research Triangle Park, North Carolina. 1996.

Higginson, Thomas Wentworth. "The sympathy of religions." An address delivered at Horticultural Hall. Boston: February 6, 1870.

_____. *Cheerful Yesterdays.* Boston: Houghton, Mifflin and Company, 1898.

_____. *Olde Cambridge.* Boston: Houghton, Mifflin and Company, 1899.

Hilliard, Katherine. "Why I Became a Thesophist." *The Theosophical Quarterly.* July 1909, p. 59-61. New York. Blavatsky Archives.

Hoogenboom, Olive. *The First Unitarian Church of Brooklyn, One Hundred Fifty Years.* New York: The First Unitarian Church of Brooklyn, 1987.

Howe, Julia WardJulia Ward. "Reminiscences of Julia Ward Howe." *The Atlantic monthly.* May 1899, v. 83, Issue 499, pp. 701-712. Boston. Atlantic Monthly Co.

Howell, Charles D. "An Unforgettable Scientist: the Life of Louis Agassiz." Redlands, CA. The Fortnightly Club of Redlands, Meeting #1407.www.redlandsfortnightly.org March 13, 1986.

Kaplan, Justin. *Walt Whitman: A Life.* New York: A Bantam Book, 1982.

Klapp, William Allan. "A Day's Trout-Fishing in Maine." *The Outing Magazine.* 1887, v. 10, p. 415-416.

Longfellow, Ernest Wadsworth. *Random Memories.* Cambridge: The Riverside Press, 1922.

Longfellow, Henry Wadsworth. *Hyperion.* New York: Samuel Colman, 1839.

Longfellow, Samuel. *A Few Verses of Many Years.* Cambridge University Press: John Williams and Son, 1887.

_____. *Hymns and Verses.* Cambridge: The Riverside Press, 1894.

_____. *Journal, January 1, 1833 – March 26, 1833.*

_____. *Journal, September 24, 1836 – May 30, 1839.*

_____. *Journal, October 13, 1839 – April 26, 1843.*

_____. *Journal, January 1, 1845 – March 24, 1847.*

_____. *Journal, 1851 – 1852*

_____. "Letter from Paris." *The Radical.* January 1866. p. 304-310. Boston. Sidney H. Morse, Editor.

_____. "Liberal Religion in Europe." *The Radical.* Boston. Sidney H. Morse, Editor.

_____. "Longfellow's Boyhood." *Wide Awake, vol. 24, n.º 1.* Boston Dec. 1884

_____. "The Old Portland Academy: Longfellow's 'Fitting School'." *The New England Quarterly.* June 1945, v. 18, n.º 2. p 247-251. Boston. The New England Quarterly, Inc.

_____. Ed. *Henry Wadsworth Longfellow, Vol. I.* Boston: Ticknor and Company, 1886.

_____. Ed. *Henry Wadsworth Longfellow, Vol. II.* Boston: Ticknor and Company, 1886.

_____. Ed. *Final Memorials of Henry Wadsworth Longfellow.* Boston: Ticknor and Company, 1887.

_____. Ed. *Lectures, Essays, and Sermons by Samuel Johnson.* Boston: The Riverside Press, 1883.

Mainwaring, Marion. *Mysteries of Paris, The Quest for Morton Fullerton*. Hanover, NH: University Press of New England, 2001.

May, Joseph, Ed. *Samuel Longfellow, Essays and Sermons*. Boston: The Riverside Press, 1894.

____, Ed.. *Samuel Longfellow: Memoir and Letters*. Cambridge: The Riverside Press, 1894.

Oates, Stephen B. *To Purge this Land with Blood, A Biography of John Brown*. New York: Harper & Row, 1972.

Parini., Jay, Ed. *The Columbia History of American Poetry*. New York: Columbia University Press, 1993.

Pascoe, Judith. "'The House Encore Me So': Emily Dickinson and Jenny Lind." *The Emily Dickinson Journal*. 1992, 1.1, p. 1-18. Baltimore. Emily Dickinson International Society. John Hopkins University Press.

Pearl, Matthew. *The Dante Club*. London: Vintage, 2004.

Peterson, Gayle. "On being the youngest child."www.parentsplace.com/expert/family/ /qas/0..166966_105889.00.html?arrivalSA=1&cobrandRef=0&arrival_freqCap=1&pba=adid =13013112, www.parentsplace.com/expert/family/qas/ 0..166966_105889.00.html?arrivalSA= =1&cobrandRef=0?arrival_freqCap=1&pba=adid=13013112, nd.

Religious Archives Network. "Review of *Walt Whitman* by Mitchell Santine Gould." Chicago: Chicago Theological Seminary, available at www.lgbtran.org/index.aspx,www. .lgbtran.org/index.aspx 2005.

Reynolds, Larry J., Ed. *Margaret Fuller: Woman in the Nineteenth Century*. New York: W.W. North & Company, 1998.

Richardson, Robert D., Jr. *Emerson, The Mind on Fire*. Berkeley: University of California Press, 1995.

Robinson, William F. *A Certain Slant of Light: The first hundred years of New England photography*. Boston: New York Graphic Society, 1980.

Ruchames, Louis. *The Abolitionists*. New York: Capricorn Books, 1964.

Sargent, Mrs. John T. *Sketches And Reminiscences of the Radical Club of Chestnut Street, Boston*. Boston: James R. Osgood and Company, 1880.

Schneir, Miriam, Ed. *Feminism, The Essential Historical Writings*. New York: Vintage Books, 1994.

Stanton, Elizabeth Cady. *Eighty Years and More: Reminiscences 1815-1897*. New York: European Publishing Co., 1898.

____, Susan B. Anthony, Matilda Joslyn Gage and Ida Husted Harper, Eds. *History of Woman Suffrage, 6 vols*. New York: Fowler and Wells, 1881-1922.

Stearns, Frank Preston. *Cambridge Sketches*. Philadelphia: J.B. Lippincott Company, 1905:

Swarthmore College Peace Collection. "Universal Peace Union." Swarthmore, PA: Swarthmore College, nd.

The History Project. *Improper Bostonians*. Boston: Beacon Press, 1998.

Thoreau, Henry David. *Walking* in *Nature/Walking*. Boston: Beacon Press, 1991.

Tyack, David B. *George Ticknor and the Boston Brahmins*. Cambridge: Harvard University Press, 1967.

Wagenknecht, Edward, Ed. *Mrs. Longfellow: Selected Letters and Journals of Fanny Appleton Longfellow (1817-1861)*. New York: Longmans, Green and Co., 1856.

Wesley, Alice Blair, Peter Hughes and Frank Carpenter. "The Unitarian Controversy and Its Puritan Roots." Unitarian Universalist Historical Society, www.uua.org/uuhs/duub/ /articles/unitariancontroversy.html

Yerrington, I.M.W., Ed. *Proceedings of the Tenth National Woman's Rights Convention, Held at the Cooper Institute, New York City, May 10ᵗʰ and 11ᵗʰ, 1860*. Boston Yerrinton and Garrison, 1860.

INDEX